# THE KNUTSFORD LADS WHO NEVER CAME HOME

### By
**Tony Davies**

Published By - **Tony Davies 2014**

ISBN 978-09568294-6-7

Printed by
**Dolman Scott Ltd**
www.dolmanscott.com

*The author would like to say a big thank you to Tina Large
and the Manchester Airport Community Trust Fund -
without whose assistance this book might never have seen
the light of day.*

*This book is dedicated to the millions of men and women of all nations who fought and died during The Great War especially Edward Davies of the Royal Welsh Fusiliers and John Dykins of the Royal Engineers (my grand-father and great-grandfather respectively), who both, fortunately for me, came home safely.*

## PREFACE

I am certain that my fascination for The First World War all started when I was about 11 years old and I would walk the two miles to the home of my grand-parents one evening a week (I think it was a Thursday) and together with my grand-father I watched the 27 weekly part of a programme on the BBC, showing The Great War. I sat there and he would explain to me all that was happening in those very grainy pictures. It was a long time after that I truly realised that the gentle, kind and softly spoken man I sat with had been through all that carnage.

He spoke of being on the Somme and going over with the Royal Welsh Fusiliers at Mametz Woods; it was later, when reading his letters to my grand-mother, then of course, only his girlfriend, telling of how he had been knocked off his feet by a shell, and the sergeant being very pleased with him as I never spilt a drop of the tea I was carrying'. My Grand-father was born in 1900, making him just 16 years old at the time of The Somme.

In this book I am writing to celebrate the lives of the local lads who went to fight 'the war to end all wars', but never came home.

**Knutsford**
**Cheshire**
November 2013

# IN MEMORY OF THE LADS FROM KNUTSFORD WHO GAVE THEIR LIVES IN THE GREAT WAR.

**William Ainscoe** – Cheshire Regiment
**Wilfred Cecil Alcock** – Royal Flying Corp
**Herbert Aldcroft** – Cheshire Regiment
**William Peter Allen** – Duke of Wellington (West Riding Regiment)
**Albert Andrew Arthern** – Royal Irish Rifles
**Albert Atkinson** – Royal Engineers
**Daniel Bailey** – Ox & Bucks Light Infantry
**John Bailey** – Kings Shropshire Light Infantry
**John Bailey** – Inniskillings Regiment
**Lionel Bailey** – Manchester Regiment
**Vernon Bailey** – Ox & Bucks Light Infantry
**William Henry Bainbridge** – Dragoon Guards
**Harold Seymour Baird** – Kings Shropshire Light Infantry
**James Robertson Barber** – Royal Field Artillery
**James Robertson Barber** – Cheshire Regiment
**Thomas E Barber** – New Zealand Expeditionary Force
**John Barnes** – Cheshire Regiment
**Harold Baronian** – Cheshire Regiment
**Frank Barrow** – Cheshire Regiment
**Joseph Barrow** – Manchester Regiment
**Tom barrow** – Royal Sussex Regiment
**Nathaniel James Merriman Barry** – East African Transport Company
**George Edward Baskerville** – Cheshire Regiment
**John Fred Baskerville** – Lancashire Fusiliers
**George Arthur Bebbington** – Royal Field Artillery
**Harold Bebbington** – Kings Liverpool Regiment
**John Thomas Bell** – Cheshire Regiment
**Philip Oswald Bell** – Royal Field Artillery
**Tom Bell** – Cheshire Regiment
**Ernest Bentley** – Kings Own Royal Lancaster Regiment
**Arthur J Berry** – Cheshire Regiment
**Albert Beswick** – Border Regiment
**Harry Birchall** – Manchester Regiment
**George J Birkenhead** – Lancashire Fusiliers
**James Bradley** – Suffolk Regiment
**Shephin Bradley** – Suffolk Regiment
**George H Brandreth** – Manchester Regiment
**Raymond Arthur Brereton** – Northumberland Fusiliers
**Frederick Brierley** – Cheshire Regiment
**Thomas Britcliffe** – Kings Liverpool Regiment

**Joseph Booth** – Cheshire Regiment
**Harry Bowyer** – East Yorkshire Regiment
**Samuel Bowyer** – Kings Shropshire Light Infantry
**Matthew Ollier Bostock** – Cheshire Regiment
**Gilbert John Bracegirdle** – Royal Garrison Artillery
**James Bracegirdle** – Kings Shropshire Light Infantry
**William Bracegirdle** – Kings Shropshire Light Infantry
**Arthur Cuthbert Brooke-Taylor** – Manchester Regiment
**John Brooks** – Royal Field Artillery
**John Henry Brown** – Machine Gun Corp
**Leonard Brown** – Machine Gun Corp
**William Brown** – Cheshire Regiment
**John Arthur Burgess** – Cheshire Regiment
**Sidney Burgess** – Royal Field Artillery
**Sidney Burgess** – Kings Shropshire Light Infantry
**John Burns** – Cheshire Regiment
**Albert Cash** – Cheshire Regiment
**Donald Cash** – Royal Field Artillery
**George Cash** – South Wales Borderers
**Daniel Caulfield** – Cheshire Regiment
**Joseph Chapman** – Welsh Regiment
**Harry Clarke** – Leicester Regiment
**Leonard Clarke** – Kings Shropshire Light Infantry
**Robert Clarke** – Labour Corp
**William Taberer Clayton** – Rifle Brigade
**John Brook Close-Brooks** – Manchester Regiment
**James Collier** – Royal Engineers
**Edward Connor** – Royal Fusiliers
**Joseph Consterdine** – Grenadier Guards
**William Cooper** – Cheshire Regiment
**Christopher Cork** – Grenadier Guards
**Thomas Cork** – Royal Dublin Fusiliers
**Alfred Cottrell** – Cheshire Regiment
**Donald Cragg** – Loyal North Lancashire Regiment
**Harry Cragg** – East Lancashire Regiment
**Harry Cummins** – Royal Engineers
**James Cummins** – Cheshire Regiment
**Albert E Curbishley** – Cheshire Regiment
**Edward Curbishley** – Prince of Wales South Lancashire Regiment
**Oliver Curbishley** – Cheshire Regiment
**Charles Henry Daniel** – Cheshire Regiment
**Thomas Daniel** – Royal Warwickshire Regiment
**Samuel Daniel** – Cheshire Regiment

**Fred Darlington** – Cheshire Regiment
**Frederick Darlington** – Royal Flying Corp
**Harry Darlington** – Loyal North Lancashire Regiment
**Tom Darlington M.C.** – Queens Royal West Surrey Regiment
**Hugh Mercer Davies D.C.M.** – Royal Engineers
**Reginald Alexander Forbes Downie** – Cameron Highlander Regiment
**Robert Theodore Manners Downie** – Highland Light Infantry
**Arthur Lancelot Dawson** – Royal Field Artillery
**Peter Drinkwater** – Royal Army Service Corp
**William Henry Dutton** – Royal Field Artillery
**William Eden** – Cheshire Regiment
**Fred Edge Edwards** – Cheshire Regiment
**John Eyres** – Cheshire Regiment
**James Fagan** – Lancashire Fusiliers
**James Finn** – Prince of Wales Own West Yorkshire Regiment
**Benjamin Ford** – Scots Fusiliers
**James Foster** – Cheshire Regiment
**John George Fowles** – Royal Engineers
**George Walter Garft** – Manchester Regiment
**Herbert Garner** – West Yorkshire Regiment
**John Garner** – East Lancashire regiment
**Arthur Ewan Gidman** – Loyal North Lancashire Regiment
**Joseph Gidman** – Manchester Regiment
**Thomas Gillett** – South Lancashire Regiment
**George Marcus Erskine Girard** – Prince of Wales (Leinster Regiment)
**William Gott** – Royal Welsh Fusiliers
**Ernest Gough** – Royal Devon Yeomanry
**William Grear** – Australian Army
**George Gregory** – South Lancashire Regiment
**Eric Walter Greswell** – Royal Flying Corp
**Harold George Greswell** – Royal Engineers
**James Griffiths** – Royal Field Artillery
**Ernest Groves** – Kings Royal Rifle Company
**George Groves** – Royal Welsh Fusiliers
**Sidney Groves** – Tank Corp
**Alfred Hale** – Labour Corp
**George Hamman** – Cheshire Regiment
**Harry Hammond** – Ox & Bucks Light Infantry
**Jack Hammond** – Lancashire Fusiliers
**James Hammond** – Cheshire Regiment
**John James Hammond** – Cheshire Regiment
**William Hammond** – Cheshire Regiment
**Thomas Henry Harrison** – Welsh Regiment

7

**Alfred Harrop** – Cheshire Regiment
**James Harrop** – Lancashire Fusiliers
**James Harrop** – South Lancashire Regiment
**Henry Hatton** – Cheshire Regiment
**Percy Healy** – Royal Field Artillery
**Herbert Hulse** – Northumberland Fusiliers
**Thomas Holden** – Loyal North Lancashire Regiment
**Sidney Howard** – Manchester Regiment
**Samuel Starkey Howarth** – Cheshire Regiment
**Walter George Howarth** – Lancashire Fusiliers
**George Wilkinson Hulme** – Manchester Regiment
**John Hulse** – Machine Gun Corp
**Arthur Hulson** – Royal Engineers
**James Hurdsfield** – Home Defence Corp
**Harry Illidge** – Cheshire Regiment
**Peter Jackson** – South Wales Borderers
**Thomas Jackson** – Border Regiment
**Sidney Jackson** – South Wales Borderers
**Joseph Jervis** – Royal Engineers
**Arthur Johnson** – Royal Field Artillery
**Fred Johnson** – Cheshire Regiment
**Harry Johnson** – Royal Field Artillery
**William Johnson** – Manchester Regiment
**Clarence William Jones** – Lancashire Fusiliers
**Horace William Jones** – Cheshire Regiment
**George Kennerley** – Cheshire Regiment
**William Frederick Keens** – Cheshire Regiment
**Harry Kent** – South Lancashire Regiment
**Albert Kettle** – Cheshire Regiment
**Donald Currie Kingsley** – New Zealand Expeditionary Force
**Leopold Fred Kirk** – Cheshire Regiment
**Frank Knowles** – London Regiment
**Tom Lea** – Cheshire Regiment
**William Leach** – Cheshire Regiment
**Fred George Leach** – Cheshire Regiment
**Patrick Leech** – Cheshire Regiment
**William Leigh** – Manchester Regiment
**Sydney Leicester** – Manchester Regiment
**John Leonard** – Royal Welsh Fusiliers
**Harry Light** – South Wales Borderers
**Mervyn Lloyd** – Northumberland Fusiliers
**William Harrison Lomas** – South Lancashire Regiment
**Charles Asgill Lover** – North Staffordshire Regiment

**Joseph Lowe** – South Wales Borderers
**George Lucas** – Cheshire Regiment
**Rowland Francis Keith Macdonald** – London Regiment
**Francis Patrick McGowan** – Rifle Brigade
**Robert Melrose** – Cheshire Regiment
**Gordon Holland Merriman** – Royal Field Artillery
**Fred Miller** – Kings Liverpool Regiment
**William Sidney Moore** – Royal Field Artillery
**Fred Moss** – Lancashire Fusiliers
**Edward Moston** – Royal Warwickshire Regiment
**Leonard Moston** – Army Cycle Corp
**William Murphy** – Cheshire Regiment
**Peter Murphy** – Royal Field Artillery
**John Higginson Norbury** – Royal Fusiliers
**Reginald Norbury** – Royal Welsh Fusiliers
**Robert Norbury** – Royal Field Artillery
**Samuel Norbury** – Kings Shropshire Light Infantry
**William Ernest Oakes** – Northumberland Fusiliers
**Eric William Ogden** – Inniskillings Regiment
**William Ollier** – Cheshire Regiment
**Fred Padmore** – Kings Own Lancashire Regiment
**Fred Parmenter** – Durham Light Infantry
**Samuel Edward Parrot** – Gordon Highlanders
**George Peers** – Royal Army Medical Corp
**Samuel Last Peers** – Machine Gun Company
**Mason Penn** – Australian Infantry
**William Thomas Pennington** – Cheshire Regiment
**Charles Leigh Pickering** – Royal Flying Corp
**William Arthur Pierce** – Border Regiment
**Harold William Pierpoint** – Manchester Regiment
**Guy Kenyon Pierson** – Royal Fusiliers
**James Mills Preston** – Hampshire Regiment
**John Joseph Price** – Manchester Regiment
**Thomas Rayner** – Lancashire Fusiliers
**Charles Richardson** – Cheshire Regiment
**Peter Edward Richardson** – Northumberland Fusiliers
**William Richardson** – Northumberland Fusiliers
**Charles Ridgway** – East Surrey Regiment
**Donald Marshall Rigby** – Cheshire Regiment
**Charles Frederick Riley** – Cheshire Yeomanry
**George Riley** – Cheshire Regiment
**Arthur Parry Roberts** – Machine Gun Corp
**Harry Royle** – Kings Shropshire Light Infantry

**Jack Rushton** – Cheshire Regiment
**Fred Saunders** – Kings Shropshire Light Infantry
**Robert Yardley Sidebottom** – Lancashire Fusiliers
**Herbert Simcock** – Cheshire Regiment
**Heinrich Helmut Simon** – Royal Field Artillery
**John Charles Simpson** – Royal Warwickshire Regiment
**Duncan Sinclair** – South Lancashire Regiment
**James Skelhorn** – South Wales Borderers
**Fred Slade** London Regiment
**George William Slade** – London Regiment
**Edward Pierce Smith** – Kings Liverpool Regiment
**George Arthur Smith** – Manchester Regiment
**John Hubert Southern** – Manchester Regiment
**James Spilsbury** – Cheshire Regiment
**William Street** – Manchester Regiment
**Albert Sumner** – Queens Royal West Surrey Regiment
**Henry Taylor** – Cheshire Regiment
**Thomas Taylor** – Kings Royal Rifles
**Wilfred Taylor** – Grenadier Guards
**Sidney Taylor** – Cheshire Regiment
**George Thornber** – Cheshire Regiment
**George Tickle** – Welsh Regiment
**Fred Timmis** – Cheshire Regiment
**William Russell Tonge** – Manchester Regiment
**Francis Allaby Tunstall** – Canadian Infantry
**William Henry Tunstall** – London Rifles
**Henry Vernon** – Royal Field Artillery
**Percy Vernon** – Royal Engineers
**Charles Vickers** – Cheshire Regiment
**William Ward** – Cheshire Regiment
**Colin Webb** – Cheshire Regiment
**William Whiston** – Cheshire Regiment
**James Henry White** – Scots Guards
**Ernest Whittaker** – Kings Shropshire Light Infantry
**George Whittaker** – Manchester Regiment
**James Wilding** – Cheshire Regiment
**William Benjamin Wilkinson** – Canadian Infantry
**Ernest Williams** – Manchester Regiment
**Harold Wilson** – Kings Liverpool Regiment
**Walter Newton Wilson** – Royal Engineers
**Percy Ralph Winser** – Royal Horse Artillery
**Gordon Sandy Wunsch** – Canadian Infantry
**John Yarwood** – West Yorkshire Regiment

They went with songs to the battle, they were young.
Straight of limb, true of eyes, steady and aglow.
They were staunch to the end against odds uncounted,
They fell with their faces to the foe.

They shall grow not old, as we that are left grow old:
Age shall not weary them, nor the years condemn.
At the going down of the sun and in the morning,
We will remember them.

*Laurence Binyon*

# INTRODUCTION

## LIFE OF A SOLDIER DURING WORLD WAR ONE

**Britain** always had a small standing army and in 1914 it numbered around 200,000, for as an island nation we believed our strength lay in the navy.

Once the war started, in August 1914, it was soon realised that a lot more manpower would be required and when Lord Horatio Kitchener was appointed Secretary for War, he issued a call for volunteers. His finger pointing out of the posters, demanding that "Your Country Needs You". The original call was for 100,000 volunteers but by the end of September that number reached 750,000 and by January, following the defeat at the Battle of Mons, it was raised to nearly one million. The stipulation for those joining was that they would only enlist 'for the duration of the war'.

This then was the 'New Army' that was being formed, with the now famous 'Pals Battalions' coming into being, but often, once these men were trained they were sent to join other regular units to replace the losses.

The old army looked on in distain as these civilians in uniform swelled their ranks. One man wrote to this father:

*'We are distinctly queasy about this new army that they are sending us – they slouch about, salute poorly and are untidy and seem uncomfortable when in uniform and are careless with their weapons.'*

The recruit was required to have a certain physicality about him. He needed to be at least 5'3" tall and aged between 18 and 38 (He was not allowed to be sent overseas until he was 19 – but see page 108) and a chest of 331/2" but on many a recruitment form are written the words 'Will improve with drill'.

With the outbreak of the war men up to the age of 45 were accepted, provided they had previously served in the military.

As we can see, the initial response to the call 'YOUR COUNTRY NEEDS YOU' was overwhelming but soon it settled down to about 100,000 a month – but this was not enough so later conscription came into being, following the National Registration Act of July 1915 which discovered just how many men between the ages of 15 and 65 were in the UK and engaged in what trade. The result of this census was available later that year.

On the 27th January 1916 the Military Service Act was introduced, which put an end to voluntary enlistment. So all males aged between 18 and 41 were conscripted providing they met the physical criteria and were resident in Great Britain (excluding Ireland) and were un-married or a widower on the 2nd November 1915. This act was extended to Married men on the 25th May 1916. Prior to this act the recruit had a choice of the regiment he wanted to join but not any longer.

It was General Haig's view that the British army would be unable to fight an all-out war until 1917 as the country lacked the basic industrial capacity to support this massive 'New Army' but he was to become pleasantly surprised.

Britain rapidly rose to the challenge and transformed these civilians that the 'old army' had questioned into an effective fighting force, and the country, mainly thanks to its women-folk, into a highly mechanised system to feed this new ravenous beast fighting throughout the world.

So, back to our recruit – following the 'swearing in' called the attestation, the recruit 'took the kings shilling' (the recruiting sergeant getting sixpence a man), and then the recruit went home and awaited his 'call up' which could be a few days to a year to arrive.

*'Attestation'*

The British military had fought what they described as a 'limited war' against the Boers in South Africa a few years before but it was clear that the Field training manual needed to be upgraded now.

The recruit was introduced to physical training, basic drill, marching, essential field craft and later some specialised and went on to further training as a rifleman, machine gunner, signaller etc. He also received basic first aid training; instruction on 'wiring' and gas defences and most importantly, weapon safety.

**Just signed up and ready to go.**

The months of training were designed to mould the recruit into an effective fighter, part of a team, able to obey orders.

Once they arrived at the front, where-ever that front might be, training continued at a unit level – the training sergeant's favourite phrase being *"Listen well lads for what I am going to tell you, WILL save your life."*

Tactics were constantly being re-taught, and amended as the tactics and technologies changed, and of course with the vast influx of replacements coming into the Battalions. New training schools opened, specialising in certain areas of warfare.

On the Western Front training focused on the prevailing conditions of trench warfare and through this training the British Army became a highly proficient, mobile force capable of 'all arms' battles.

Training these men was one thing, but where to house them was quite another. The vast numbers joining the forces soon overwhelmed the existing training facilities, so it soon became apparent that new facilities were needed. Public buildings were forced into use, church halls, schools and warehouses were pressed into service, and even private homes were used to billet recruits.

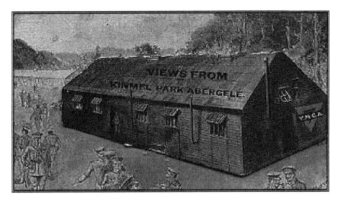

*A postcard from the new Kinmel Park camp near Abergele in North Wales.*

So new training camps were set up all over the country – some were vast, with their own canteens, hospitals and post offices (for mail was an essential part of the fighting man's life as we shall examine later).

Once on the Western Front and in the stabilised areas new camps were set up for training. One of the largest being The Bull Ring at Etaples.

One of the myths surrounding the Great War is that the armies were constantly in the trenches but as a matter of fact, only a relatively small proportion actually served there.

The trenches were of course the front line and a very dangerous place to be but behind there was a vast network of supply lines,

*WW1 postcard from author's collection.*

communication trenches, training facilities, stores, workshops and garages and of course headquarters. This is where the vast majority of the troops were employed.

The infantryman was in the trenches with the support of the machine gunners.

## The Trenches.

If you ask people to give you one words that relates to World War One they would most probably say "trenches", (the others being "slaughter" and "mud"). So what were they like?

The idea of digging a hole in the ground for the protection and movement of troops is certainly not just the province of WW1 – it has been used throughout the centuries, and used to great effect during the American Civil War some fifty years before.

But the trench system was caused by the stagnation of the armies, causing them to 'dig in' and so a trench system snaked over 450 miles from the English Channel to the Swiss border.

The basic trench varied considerably and was of course dependant on the conditions of the terrain. Some area were easier to dig than others – for in the Somme region for example, the ground was chalk and thus easier to did, but the sides crumbled easily with the rain of the vibrations of the shelling so they needed to be 'revetted' – that is reinforced with wood or sandbags. At Ypres the ground was boggy with a high water table so a breastwork type was used (the trench was built up from the ground with sandbags).

On every front trenches were cut – in Italy and Gallipoli they were hewn from rock; in the Middle East in sand.

The German trenches were dug well into the ground, their dug-outs sometimes 40 or 50 feet below, well away from the shelling – they even were equipped with furniture. The British, on the whole were not so comfortable and it has been suggested that the soldier was not to be made to feel too comfortable but to feel in a way transient, with the need to keep moving forward.

The trenches were never straight lines but as well as following the contours of the land, they had turns every so often called 'bays' or 'traverses' – this gave the defenders and easier job and also it prevented any blast from continuing along a long length of trench.

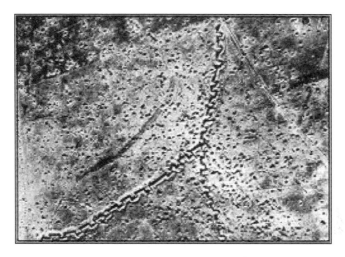

*Arial view of WW1 trench system – note the pock-marked surroundings.*

Sticking out into no-mans-land were often smaller trenches called 'saps'. These housed an artillery spotter or a listening post of perhaps a couple of infantrymen, who could give advanced warning of any enemy activity.

Firing steps were also cut into the sides of the trench, where a sentry would stand in quiet times looking out into no-mans-land, usually through a box telescope – but woe be tied if he was caught asleep at his post (see appendix six). Specialists (machine gunners or signallers) were excluded such duty. Sometime the gap between the two opposing sides was less than fifty yards.

Behind the front-line trench were the supply trenches, housing the company commanders HQ and the communication telephones. Along these trenches the vital equipment was brought to the front line.

The more static the battlefield became, the stronger the defences became. In front of the trench system vast areas of barbed wire were place, some many feet thick.

And these had to be maintained, which was one of the most dangerous of all the 'housekeeping' jobs of the trench war system.

*A German barbed wire entanglement.*

The typical trench system consisted of three main fire and support trenches connected by communication trenches, with various posts, strongpoints and saps. By 1916, the German system of defence had three or four such trench systems layered back over a couple of miles. By 1917 the system had deepened even further so that the allied assaults of 1918 faced a defensive system several miles deep.

*One of the most haunting images of the war.*

Wherever possible the floor of the trench was covered by a wooden 'duckboard' in an effort to keep the soldiers feet out of the mud. The necessary latrine was dug close-by – that being a deep hole in the ground over which a plank was place for the man to sit on. He, of course had to ask permission to use this facility.

Life in the trenches was far from comfortable and varied widely between the different theatres of war, but with so many men living in such a confined space, plus the proximity of the latrine (which was regularly targeted by the enemy), the discarded food, the lice and the rats (some the size of cats, living off the bodies of the dead), the whole place was one massive health risk. Diseases such as trench fever, trench foot, exposure and frostbite accounted for large numbers of casualties.

*Foot inspection.*

**How long did he stay in the trenches?**

Usually there was a four day rotation system in place. Four days in the 'front line', four days in what was termed 'close reserve' and four days 'rest'. This system depended on many factors including the weather, the number of troops etc.

*Trench life – note the three men asleep.*

In close reserve the men were on short notice to return to the front line, depending on the circumstances. The time when they battalions rotated was always a trying time and noise was kept to a minimum for any noise usually drew enemy fire or shelling.

Other than when in battle, trench life tended to be boring, with hard physical work thrown in. Boredom often led to mistakes and an air of nonchalance, and any loss of concentration could lead to being exposed to a snipers bullet.

At dawn and dusk, the whole British line was ordered to 'stand to'. Which meant that for a short period, the whole trench was in readiness for an enemy attack?

All of the men posted to the fire trench and most of those in the support trench had to wear their equipment at all times. Men in the front line had to keep their bayonets fixed during hours of darkness or mist, or whenever there was an alert of enemy activity.

A man could not leave his post without permission of his immediate commander, and an officer had to approve him leaving the trench. One officer per Company was on trench duty at all times, and his NCOs had to report to him hourly. He was under orders to move continually up and down his assigned trenches, checking that the equipment was in good state, that the sentries were alert and that the men were as comfortable as the conditions allowed. The NCOs had to inspect the men's rifles twice daily and otherwise ensure that fighting equipment and ammunition was present and in good order. From mid-1915, every trench had some form of warning of gas attack. Often this was an empty shell casing, held up by wire or string, that would be hit (like a gong) with a piece of wood or similar. If the gas gong was heard, all officers and men would know that they had to put on their gas masks as soon as they could. Some of the gasses used were invisible, and if their delivery by gas shells popping on impact with the ground had not been heard, they could sometimes be detected by their distinctive smell.

***Cosy eh?***

Every day, the battalion holding the line would request from the nearby Brigade workshop a list of stores it needed. Some special items such as wire 'knife rests' (a wooden support for a barbed wire entanglement), signboards, boxes, and floor gratings would be made up at Brigade and brought to the trenches ready to use. Sandbags, wood, cement, barbed wire, telephone cable, and other supplies would also be sent up as needed. Men would be sent back to Brigade as a carrying party to fetch it.

Rations would be brought up through the communication trenches at night. This too would be when the all-important mail arrived. The British postal service was second to none. The letters from home could take a little as two days to reach a soldier in the trenches (better than today), and the lads would share the things they received in parcels (except socks – those they kept for themselves). They even shared their families, reading each other's letters.

It can be said that the British army went through four stages during the war.

The first was the British Expeditionary Force – the original standing army that was dispatched to France in 1914 – but by 1915 they were virtually all gone.

The second was the Territorial Army – reservists who at least had some training in the ways of the military – but by the end of 1915 they was nearly all gone too.

The third was Kitchener's Army – volunteers from 1914 who were now called up to fight – these had no experience and over 600,000 became casualties. It has been said it too two years to train but disappeared in the first two hours of the Battle of the Somme.

And fourthly came the conscript army who saw out the war.

**The dead.**

Almost one million British servicemen died in the Great War. Some were killed in their thousands in the great battles, other alone – from a shell, sniper or disease.

Thousands have no known grave.

This then is my small attempt to remember those local lads who fell......

# WILLIAM AINSCOE

**William Ainscoe** was born in Knutsford in 1893, the son of Samuel (a butcher) and Martha Ainscoe. He was a butcher living at 9, Minshall Street, Knutsford.

He enlisted in the army on the 4th September 1914 in the 12th Battalion of the Cheshire Regiment as Private no. 15610.

**Brief history of the Battalion:**

The 12th (Service) Battalion, Cheshire Regiment was raised in Chester on the 13th of September 1914 as part of Kitchener's Second New Army and joined 22nd Division as army troops. They trained at Seaford, spending the winter in billets in Eastbourne. In February 1915 they transferred to 66th Brigade, still with 22nd Division. They moved to Aldershot for final training in June and preceded to France on the 6th of September, landing at Boulogne, the division concentrating near Flesselles. In October they moved to Marseilles by train and embarked for Salonika on the 27th. 67th Brigade, 9th Borders, 68th Field Ambulance and the Advanced Divisional HQ saw their first action in the second week of December in the Retreat from Serbia. In 1916 the division fought in the Battle of Horseshoe Hill and Battle of Machukovo. In 1917 they were in action during the Battles of Doiran. They were in action at Doiran just before the Armistice with Bulgaria was signed at the end September 1918.

*Thanks to the Wartime Memories Project.*

He contracted malaria in 1916 and was hospitalised. On recovery he returned to his Battalion.
William was killed in action on the 31st March 1918.

**On that fateful day:**
The war diary for that day records no activity.

*William is buried in Karasouli Cemetery along with 1421 other servicemen. His grave is E1036. He also has a memorial in Knutsford Cemetery.*

> *Note:*
> *His mother received his property – I.D. disc, wallet, 2 gospels, photos, letters, watch with strap (broken) and a registered letter.*

# WILFRED CECIL ALCOCK

**Wilfred Cyril Alcock** was born in Knutsford in 1882, one of six children born to Frederick (a printer and stationer) and Harriet (printers assistant) of Caxton House, 95 King Street, Knutsford. He too was a printer working for his father.

Just prior to the war being declared Wilfred sailed for America, settling just outside Boston.

We also know he was a prominent Mason whilst in Massachusetts.

He joined the Royal Canadian Flying Corp as a cadet no. 74783 but was accidentally killed during his training on the 24th November 1917, aged 25.

**On that fateful day:**
There is no record of how he met his death, but it is believed it was in a 'flying acident'.

*Wilfred is buried in New Bedford (Oak Grove) Cemetery, Massachusetts, U.S.A*

# HERBERT ALDCROFT

**Herbert Aldcroft** was born in Mobberley, Cheshire in 1886, one of six children born to William (a farmer) and Ann Aldcroft of Moss farm, Moss lane Mobberley. Daniel was a farm labourer.

He enlisted in the army and became Private no 27612 of the 1st Battalion of the Cheshire Regiment.

### Brief history of the Battalion:

The 1st Battalion, Cheshire Regiment was a regular unit of the British Army and was in Londonderry when war broke out in August 1914 with 15th Brigade in 5th Division. They returned to England and proceeded to France with the British Expeditionary Force, landing at Le Havre on the 16th of August 1914. They saw action at The Battle of Mons, The Battle of the Marne, The Battle of the Aisne, The Battles of La Bassee, at Messines and in The First Battle of Ypres. Between the 3rd of March and 7th of April 1915 they were attached with 15th Brigade to 28th Division in in exchange for 83rd Brigade in order to familiarise the newly arrived troops with the Western Front. In 1915 they were in action in The Second Battle of Ypres and the Capture of Hill 60. In March 1916 they took over a sector in the front line in the southern edge of Vimy Ridge, in front of Arras. The 5th Division arrived on the Somme to relieve the British units who had suffered badly in the attack on the first of July and went into action at High Wood, being withdrawn in October.

Herbert died of wounds on the 2nd August 1916.

**On that fateful day:**
Herbert's service records no longer exist so I have found it impossible to locate where and when he received his wounds, but it is more than likely they were received during the Battle of the Somme.

*Herbert is buried in St. Sever Cemetery, Rouen along with 3,082 other servicemen. His grave is B. 29. 20.*

---

# WILLIAM PETER ALLEN

**William Peter Allen** was born in Chelford, Cheshire, one of six children born to Emma. They later moved to 1, Clifford Street, Patricroft, Lancashire. William was a slater's labourer.

He enlisted in the 10th Battalion of the Duke of Wellington (West Riding Regiment), becoming Private no. 16042.

He arrived in France on the 29th August 1915.

**Brief history of the Battalion:**

The 10th Battalion, Duke of Wellington's West Riding Regiment was raised at Halifax in September 1914 as part of Kitchener's Third New Army and joined 69th Brigade, 23rd Division. 23rd Division concentrated in Hampshire in September with 68th Brigade at Bullswater, 69th and 70th brigades at Frensham. The artillery units assembled at Mytchett Camp in November. As the winter set in, the Division moved to Aldershot, with CII and CIII Artillery Brigades moving to Ewshott. At the end of February 1915 they moved to Shorncliffe, Kent, and some of the infantry were engaged in constructing defences to the south of London in April and May, before the Division moved to Bordon, Hampshire at the end of the month. They proceeded to France in the third week of August, landing at Boulogne and concentrating near Tilques. On the 5th of September 23rd Division became attached to III Corps, moving to the Merris-Vieux Berquin area, for trench familiarisation under the guidance of the 20th (Light) and 27th Divisions. They took over front line sector between Ferme Grande Flamengrie to the Armentieres-Wez Macquart road in their own right on the 14th. During the Battle of Loos CIII and CV Brigades RFA were in action attached to 8th Division. With 23rd Division holding the front at Bois Grenier, they were relieved from that sector at the end of January 1916 and Divisional HQ was established at Blaringhem with the units concentrated around Bruay for a period of rest. On the 3rd of March they returned to the front line, taking over a sector between the Boyau de l'Ersatz and the Souchez River from the French 17th Division, with the Artillery taking over an exposed position between Carency and Bois de Bouvigny where it was subjected to heavy shelling. In early March a Tunnelling Company was established and men with a background in mining were transferred from the ranks to the Royal Engineers. In mid-April they returned to Bruay area for rest until mid-May when they again took over the Souchez-Angres front, just before the German Attack on Vimy Ridge on the 21st. The brunt of the attack fell on 47th (London) Division, to the right of 23rd Division and the 23rd Divisional Artillery went into action in support of the 47th. On the 1st of

June the Artillery supported 2nd Division as they undertook operations to recover lost ground. On the 11th of June the 23rd Division Infantry moved to Bomy and the artillery to Chamblain Chatelain and Therouanne to begin intensive training for the Battles of the Somme. They were in action in The Battle of Albert including the capture of Contalmaison, The Battles of Bazentin Ridge, Pozieres, Flers-Courcelette, Morval and The Battle of Le Transloy including the capture of Le Sars.

*Thanks to the Wartime Memories Project.*

William was killed in action on the 29th July 1916.

**On that fateful Day**
The war diary states:

*'29.7.16 BECOURT WOOD*
*The enemy was shelling the main road through village and was very near to doing some serious damage. The Battn was soon again in action. We sustained somewhat severe casualties which reads –*
*Officers – 2 killed, 4 wounded, 1 missing.*
*Other ranks – 31 killed, 124 wounded, 13 shell-shocked, 30 missing.'*

*William is remembered on the Thiepval Memorial along with another 72,208 other servicemen.*

# ALBERT ANDREW ARTHERN

**Albert Andrew Arthern** was born in High Legh, Cheshire in 1887, one of eleven children born to Thomas (a police officer) and Martha Arthern of High Legh. Albert was a farm labourer.

He enlisted in the Royal Irish Rifles at the beginning of the war, becoming Private no. 17550 of the 3rd Battalion. They were a 'Reserve Battalion' and did not serve abroad.

He died in Dublin on the 26th October 1914.

I have been in touch with the Royal Irish Rifles Museum in Belfast but they have no record as to how Albert died.

*Albert is buried in Grangegorman Military Cemetery, Co. Dublin.*

# ALBERT ATKINSON

**Albert Atkinson** was born in Knutsford in 1897, the son of James (a caretaker/postman) and Eliza Atkinson of Green Street, Knutsford. Albert initially enlisted in the 5th Battalion of the Cheshire Regiment but was transferred to the 21st Signals Company of the Royal Engineers, becoming Private no. 37837.

**Brief history of the Company:**
21st Divisional Signals Company, The Royal Engineers provided communications for 21st Division. The Division was established in September 1914, as part Kitchener's Third New Army. The Division concentrated in the Tring area, training at Halton Park before winter necessitated a move into local billets Chesham. In May 1915 they moved to Wendover and on the 9th of August they moved to Witley Camp for final training. They proceeded to France during the first week of September and marched across France to going into the reserve for the British assault at Loos on the 26th of September suffering heavy casualties. In 1916 they were in action in the Battles of The Somme, including The Battle of Morval in which the Division captured Geudecourt. In 1917 they were in action during The German retreat to the Hindenburg Line, the Arras offensive, the Third Battles of Ypres and The Cambrai Operations. In 1918 they fought on The Somme then moved north and were in action during the Battles of the Lys, the Battle of the Aisne, The Somme, the Battles of the Hindenburg

Line and the Final Advance in Picardy.

*Thanks to the Wartime Memories Project.*

Albert was killed in action on the 28th May 1918.

**On that fateful day:**
At the time of writing the Battalion War Diary was unavailable.

*Albert is buried in Harmonville Military Cemetery along with nearly 250 other servicemen. His grave is III. C. 2.*

# DANIEL BAILEY

**Daniel Simcock** was born in 1896, the son of Sarah, who married Enoch (a council roadman) and lived with her mother in Pepper

Street, Mobberley. By the age of 15 Daniel was using his mother's maiden name of Daniel.

His service records no longer exist but we know he enlisted sometime after 1915 in the Cheshire Regiment as Private no. 76625 and later transferred to the 2nd Battalion of the Oxford and Buckingham Light Infantry as private no. 24815.

**Brief history of the Battalion:**

In January 1916, the 2nd Ox and Bucks were at Cottes St.Hilaire; the 2nd Division was at that time taking its turn in the corps reserve. The Battalion later moved to Bethune and then returned to the Festubert trenches. The ¼th Ox and Bucks took part in the First Day of the Somme on 1 July 1916, in which the British Army suffered over 60,000 casualties – the largest number sustained in a day by the British Army. The battalions of the Ox and Bucks on the Western Front saw extensive service during the Battle of the Somme (1 July – 18 November), suffering heavily, including at Mametz Wood, Pozières and at Ancre, the last major subsidiary battle. On 28 July the 2nd Ox and Bucks moved to front-line trenches near Waterlot farm and sustained heavy casualties at the battle there on 30 July. The 2nd Ox and Bucks fought on the Somme battlefield at Delville Wood, Guillemont and on 13 November in the battle of Beaumont Hamel: a large attack on the Redan Ridge in the battle of the Ancre. The 2nd Ox and Bucks sustained many casualties during the battle of Beaumont Hamel, including Captain RB Kite who within the previous 12 months, had been awarded the Military Cross and twice mentioned in dispatches.

The New Year of 1917 brought with it a period of severe weather conditions on the Somme plain which led to an unofficial truce between the two sides. In March 1917, the Germans began the withdrawal to the Hindenburg Line (14 March – 5 April) and at the end of March the 2nd Ox and Bucks moved from the Somme to the back areas of Arras. The 2nd Ox and Bucks and other battalions of the regiment saw much involvement in the Arras Offensive (9 April – 16 May), including at the Battles of Scarpe and Arleux. The 2nd Ox and Bucks took part in the battle of Arras from 11 April and had a leading role in the battle of Arleux on 28–29 April: during the battle the battalion protected the right flank of the Canadian 1st Division which was critical to the capture of the village of Arleux and sustained more than 200 casualties. In the summer of 1917, the 2nd Ox and Bucks held the line at Bailleulemont, near Arras. The battalions of the Ox and Bucks saw further service in many of the subsidiary battles during the Battle of Passchendaele (also known as Third Ypres) that took place between 31 July-6 November. Some of the battles that the Ox and Bucks took part in included Menin Road and Polygon Wood in September and early October. The 2nd Ox and Bucks and the 6th (Service) Battalion, Ox and Bucks also took part in the Battle of Cambrai (20 November-3 December) that saw the first large-scale use of tanks by the British and was the last major battle of the year.

In January 1918, the 2nd Ox and Bucks marched to Beaulencourt, later that month they moved to Havrincourt Wood and then on 9 February to Metz-en-Couture. The 2nd Ox and Bucks were at Vallulart Camp, Ytres when on 21 March 1918 the Germans launched the last-gasp Spring Offensive (Operation Michael). The 2nd Ox and Bucks and other battalions of the regiment sustained heavy casualties as part of the defence of the Somme during the Battle of St. Quentin (21–23 March), the First Battle of Bapaume (24–25 March) and in subsequent battles that saw the Germans achieve significant gains. After that offensive lost its momentum, the Germans launched Operation Georgette in April which the Ox and Bucks defended against in the Battle of the Lys and subsequent actions. By August the German offensives had failed and the Allies had launched a counter-attack. In August the 2nd Ox and Bucks took part in the Battle of Albert (1918) (21–23 August) and the Second Battle of Bapaume (31 August – 3 September) while the 2/4th Ox and Bucks and the 2/1st Buckinghamshires took part in the advance into Flanders, with both offensives seeing the Allies advance to the Hindenburg Line by early September. The 2nd Ox and Bucks took part in the offensive against it that saw the Allies break through the defences, taking part in the Battle of Havrincourt (12 September), Battle of the Canal du Nord (27 September – 1 October) and the Second Battle of Cambrai (8–9 October). The Regiment then took part in the last actions of the war, taking part in the Battle of the Selle and the Battle of Valenciennes. The 2nd Ox and Bucks final battle of the war was the Battle of the Selle (17–25 October).

Daniel was killed in action on the 1st October 1918.

**On that fateful day:**

The war diary states:

*"1.10.18 CANAL du NORD area*

*From midnight 10th Sept until 5.30am 1st Oct enemy shelling was slight as was also machine gun fire. At zero hour (6am) our artillery opened on the initial barrage line for 6 minutes during which time the two front companies (C and D) moved out into 'worm formation', as close up to the barrage as possible so as to be ready to go forward at 6.06am. The barrage lifted and C and D companies advanced with A and B in support. They at once came under heavy machine gun fire from four distinct points and many casualties resulted. Our own shells falling short also caused casualties. The Coy advanced 400 – 500 yards when, owing to the extent of front to be occupied, to the losses sustained and to the fact that the left flank of the 3rd Division (co-operating on out right) had not got forward, our leading companies lost direction, with the result that the regiment covered only half its allotted frontage. About this time the support companies reinforced the front line and the whole pushed forward to the line of the railway, where they captured 3 German machine guns with their teams and several other prisoners. Further advance became impossible, as the enemy machine gun nests immediately opened very heavy fire on any movement. The senior officers present (Captain Eagle, D Company and Lt Cowell, C Company) ordered their men to dig in.*

*The situation remained unchanged throughout the day until 6.30pm whan an attack was made by the 24th R.F. and 2nd H.L.I. which surprised the enemy, who were evidently expecting to be attacked from another direction. The attack was successful and the Regiment became support Battalion.*

*Communication all day was very difficult, all ground over which orderlies had to move being in full view so they had to crawl for very long distances.*

*Casualties – Lt L. Bartlett and 33 OR killed, 3 officers and 125 OR wounded; and one man wounded and missing."*

**Daniel is buried in Anneux British cemetery, France along with 1013 other servicemen. His grave is IV. B. 36.**

# JOHN BAILEY

**John Bailey** was born in Knutsford, the son of Mr and Mrs J. Bailey of The Old Hall, Tatton Park, Knutsford.

His service record no longer exists but we know he enlisted in 'C' Company, 7th Battalion of the Kings (Shropshire Light Infantry).

**Brief history of the Battalion:**

A war-raised Service Battalion under Lt. Col. J.H. Barber, it was formed in Shrewsbury in September 1914 and joined the 76th Brigade of the 25th Division; landed at Boulogne on 28th September 1915 and served entirely on the Western Front.

7 KSLI first saw action in the Ypres Salient in the winter of 1915-16 and moved to the Somme in July 1916; fought at Bazentin Ridge and then at Serre on the Ancre later in the year.

It was in action at Arras and in the three severe battles of the Scarpe in April-May 1917. Back in the Ypres sector in 1917, the 7th took part in the fighting at Polygon Wood in September (3rd Battle of Ypres) and was back on the Somme for the battles of 1918.

After taking part in the offensives of summer-autumn of 1918, at Albert, Bapaume, the Canal du Nord and the Selle, the 7th ended the war as part of the 8th Brigade of the 3rd Division, at Romeries, near Solesmes, France. It was disbanded in Shrewsbury in June 1919.

The 7th suffered more casualties than any other KSLI battalion, with 1048 killed in action or died during the war, and earned more battle honours than any other KSLI battalion.

John was killed in action on the 25th April 1917.

**On that fateful day:**

The war diary has no specific entry for this day.

*John has no know grave but is remembered on the Arras Memorial, France along with the names of 34,791 other servicemen.*

# JOHN BAILEY

John was born in 1890 in Mobberley, the son of John and Charlotte Johanna Bailey of Barnshaw Cottage, Mobberley. John is a photographic student.

He enlisted in the army, becoming Private no. 27397 in the South Lancashire Regiment before transferring to the 1st Battalion of the Royal Inniskillings Regiment, becoming Private no. 49599. He went to France sometime after 1915.

**Brief history of the Battalion:**

The 1st Battalion was raised on the August 1914 in Trimulgherry, India. They were recalled to UK at the outbreak of the war and landed at Avonmouth on 10 January 1915. On the 10 January 1915 they came under command of 87th Brigade in 29th Division. They moved to Rugby. In March 1915 they sailed, going via Egypt, and landed at Cape Helles, Gallipoli, on 25 April 1915. In January 1916 they evacuated from Gallipoli to Egypt. On the 18 March 1916 the battalion landed at Marseilles for service in France. On the 5 February 1918 they transferred to 109th Brigade in 36th (Ulster) Division.

He was killed in action on the 15th October 1918.

**On that fateful day:**

The war diary states:

This action commenced on the 14th October 1918 – they had also been in heavy fighting at the beginning of the month too.

*"15.10.18*

*At 0900 the 2nd Battn. Royal Inniskilling Fusiliers attacked GULLEGHEM and the 1st Battn. moved forward behind the 9th Battn.*

*On reaching the line G.22 Central the 9th Battn. passed through the 2nd Battn. Royal Inniskillings Fusiliers and took HEULE. The 1st Battn moving up in support to them to G.22 Central reaching this position at 11.00. Headquarters established at XXXX*

*Information received form O.C. 9th Battn. Royal Inniskilling Fusiliers that his Battn. had captured HEULE and was in position on the railway to the east of it and in touch with the 29th on the left but his right flank was in the air. It was then discovered that the Brigade on the right was held up on the line. The O.C. 1ˢᵗ Inniskilling Fusiliers ordered 'B' and 'D' Companies men to cover the flank. 'D' Company to take up position along the bank of the HEULEBEKE . 'B' Company was ordered to move alongside of the GULLEGHEM – HEULE Road and attack the farms and occupy them.*

*The advance to the farms was carried out under heavy Machine Gun fire though no casualties occurred. While these movement were being carried out a message was received from the Brigade on the right that they were about to attack with artillery support.*

*The artillery was stopped in time and the Brigade on the right moved forward at the same time as 'B' Company and passed them.*

*At 15.45 orders were received that the 29ᵗʰ Division were about to advance on the left and that the 103ʳᵈ Brigade would capture the crossing on the LYS within the Divisional boundary and that the 1ˢᵗ Batt, Royal Inniskilling Fusiliers were to send forward two Companies at 1500 to clear the triangle formed by the HEULEBEEKE railway and the north Divisional boundary, keeping touch with the 29ᵗʰ Division and 108ᵗʰ Brigade. The O.C. 1ˢᵗ Battn. Royal Inniskillin Fusiliers immediately ordered 'C' & 'D; Companies forward to do this but at 16.30 a cancelling order was received and these Companies were stopped and sent back to their original positions. As the situation on the right flank was now cleared by the advance of the 2ⁿᵈ Royal Irish Rifles. 'B' Company was withdrawn in close support to the 9ᵗʰ Battn Royal Inn. Fusiliers. At 16.40 headquarters were moved to be in close touch with the 9ᵗʰ Battn.*

*At 17.40 further orders were received that the area previously ordered was to be cleared by the 1ˢᵗ The Royal Inniskilling Fusiliers.*

*'C' & 'D' Companies were ordered forward to do this. The Company Commanders of these two Companies went forward to make a personal reconnaissance and got in touch with the 29ᵗʰ Division who were advancing on the left and with the 2ⁿᵈ Royal Irish Rifles on the right who had come up to their line of the railway.*

*They advanced with these Companies and secured the line of the road, as it was reported that the 29th Division had reached the LYS. The O.C. 1st Battn. The Royal Innis. Fusiliers after reporting the situation ordered the success to be exploited and patrols were pushed out which reached the LYS. The bridge was blown up by the enemy just before the patrol reached the river.*

*At about 23.00 orders were received that all troops must be withdrawn behind the railway by 0500 as the 108th Brigade were to advance from there with a barrage at 05.50 and seize the crossing of the LYS. Communication was extremely difficult and the information that the Battalion was already patrols as far as the LYS could not be sent to the Brigade in time to stop this attack. 'C' & 'D' Companies had therefore to be withdrawn behind the railway which was held by the 9th Royal Inniskilling Fusiliers.*

*These two Companies were then billeted in the cellars in HEULE. "*

The Battalion was returned to billets on the 16th.

Their casualties for this action were 1 officer killed, 1 wounded. 25 O.R killed 116 wounded.

***John is buried in Dadizeele New British Cemetery, Belgium together with 1,029 other servicemen. His grave is VI. C. 28.***

# LIONEL ALGERNON BAYLEY

**Lionel Algernon Bayley** was born in Mobberley, Cheshire in 1893, one of eleven children born to Frederick William (a railway platelayer) and Elisabeth Bayley of Station Cottages, Mobberley.

On leaving school Lionel became a Nurseryman clerk

His service records still exists – and we see he attested on the 3rd September 1914 at Knutsford, becoming Private no. 15890 of the 10th Battalion of the Cheshire Regiment. He was called up in 1915.

Following his training, and on arriving in France on the 8th March 1915 he was transferred to the 17th Manchester Regiment becoming Private no. 9510.

He was wounded in action around Montauban on the 1-2 July 1916 – the notation stating it was a 'slight wound'.

He was admitted to the 45th Casualty Clearing Station on the 3rd July suffering from a gunshot wound to his leg – it is unclear if this is the same wound he received the day before.

He died of wounds on the 4th July 1916.

**On that fateful day:**
Unfortunately I have been unable to discover where and when he received his wounds.

*Lionel is buried at Daours Communal Cemetery Extension. Somme, along with 1231 other servicemen. His grave is II. B. 20.*

# VERNON BAILEY

**Vernon Bailey** came from Mobberley and at the outbreak of the war he enlisted in the Cheshire Regiment as private no. 76670 but later transferred to the 2nd Battalion of the Ox and Bucks Light Infantry as private no. 34817.

**Brief history of the Battalion:**
See Appendix Five for this.
     Vernon was killed in action on the 1st October 1918.

47

## On that fateful day:
The war diary states:

### 1.10.18 CANAL du NORD area
*From midnight 10th Sept until 5.30am 1st Oct enemy shelling was slight as was also machine gun fire. At zero hour (6am) our artillery opened on the initial barrage line for 6 minutes during which time the two front companies (C and D) moved out into 'worm formation', as close up to the barrage as possible so as to be ready to go forward at 6.06am. The barrage lifted and C and D companies advanced with A and B in support. They at once came under heavy machine gun fire from four distinct points and many casualties resulted. Our own shells falling short also caused casualties. The Coy advanced 400 – 500 yards when, owing to the extent of front to be occupied, to the losses sustained and to the fact that the left flank of the 3rd Division (co-operating on out right) had not got forward, our leading companies lost direction, with the result that the regiment covered only half its allotted frontage. About this time the support companies reinforced the front line and the whole pushed forward to the line of the railway, where they captured 3 German machine guns with their teams and several other prisoners. Further advance became impossible, as the enemy machine gun nests immediately opened very heavy fire on any movement. The senior officers present (Captain Eagle, D Company and Lt Cowell, C Company) ordered their men to dig in.*

*The situation remained unchanged throughout the day until 6.30pm whan an attack was made by the 24th R.F. and 2nd H.L.I. which surprised the enemy, who were evidently expecting to be attacked from another direction. The attack was successful and the Regiment became support Battalion.*

*Communication all day was very difficult, all ground over which orderlies had to move being in full view so they had to crawl for very long distances.*

*Casualties – Lt L. Bartlett and 33 OR killed, 3 officers and 125 OR wounded; and one man wounded and missing.*

***Vernon is buried in the Anneux British Cemetery along with 1.013 other servicemen. His grave is III. D. 9.***

# WILLIAM HENRY BAINBRIDGE

**William Henry Bainbridge** was born in Marston but later went to live in Knutsford.

He enlisted at Richmond, Yorkshire in the Household Cavalry. He became Private no. GS/6012 in the 1st Dragoons.

**Brief history of the Regiment:**
The regiment was formed in 1685 as The Queen's Regiment of Horse

and was renamed The King's Own Regiment of Horse in 1714. The regiment attained the title 1st King's Dragoon Guards in 1751.

At the outbreak of war in August 1914 the 1st King's Dragoon Guards were stationed in Lucknow, India with the Lucknow Cavalry Brigade. The regiment was ordered to France and arrived at Marseilles on 7th November 1914. They formed part of 1st Indian Cavalry Division and served on the Western Front.

*Thanks to the Wartime Memories Project.*

William was killed in action on the 13th May 1915.

**On that fateful day:**
The war diary records no action on this day.

The Commonwealth War Graves Commission has no record of William's grave.

# HARRY SEYMOUR BAIRD

**Harry Seymour Baird** was born in Knutsford, one of four children born to John William (a builder) and Annie Baird of High Town, Knutsford. On leaving school he became a joiner. He also served in the army during the Boer War.

He moved to Stafford and in 1912 married Miss Barge and together they had children.

He enlisted in the army, first as Private no. 227 in the Cheshire Yeomanry and then being transferred to the 10th Battalion of the Kings (Shropshire) Light Infantry as Private no. 230535.

He rose to the rank of Sergeant.

**Brief history of the Battalions:**

The 1/1st Battalion Cheshire Yeomanry were based in Chester in August 1914 when war broke out, serving with the Welsh Border Mounted Brigade in the Mounted Division. In November 1915 they converted to a dismounted unit and on the 3rd March 1916 they proceeded to Egypt, leaving from Devonport on His Majesty's Transport "Haverford", landing at Alexandria became part of the 4th Dismounted Brigade at to Beni Salama Camp. On the 18th of April 1916 the Cheshire Yeomanry entrained at Wardar and moved to Minia Lower Camp. From the 1st of June 1916 one Troop was posted to canal transport guard duties at Samalita and the remaining Troops manned this position in rotation until the regiment moved to El Alamein on the 14th of November 1916. In March 1917 the regiment merged with 1/1st Shropshire Yeomanry to form the 10th (Shropshire and Cheshire Yeomanry) Battalion, King's Shropshire Light Infantry transferring to 231st Brigade, 74th (Yeomanry) Division.

The 10th Battalion was formed at Cairo on 2nd March 1917 from the dismounted troopers of the Shropshire Yeomanry and the Cheshire Yeomanry. They served in Palestine in the 231st Brigade of the 74th "Broken Spur" Division.

*Thanks to the Wartime Memories Project.*

Harry was admitted to hospital on the 9th July 1917 and died as a result of pneumonia on the 22nd July 1917.

**Disease in the Mesopotamian campaign:**
Like Gallipoli, conditions in Mesopotamia defy description. Extremes of temperature (120 degrees F was common); arid desert and regular flooding; flies, mosquitoes and other vermin: all led to appalling levels of sickness and death through disease. Under these incredible conditions, units fell short of officers and men, and all too often the reinforcements were half-trained and ill-equipped. Medical arrangements were quite shocking, with wounded men spending up to two weeks on boats before reaching any kind of hospital. These factors, plus of course the unexpectedly determined Turkish resistance, contributed to high casualty rates.

- 11012 killed
- 3985 died of wounds
- 12678 died of sickness
- 13492 missing and prisoners (9000 at Kut)
- 51836 wounded

*Data from "Statistics of the Military Effort of the British Empire" (London: HMSO, 1920).*

*H is buried in the Port Said War Memorial Cemetery, along with 1,085 other servicemen, His grave is F. 8.*

# JAMES ROBINSON BARBER

**James Robinson Barber** was born in Blakely, Lancashire in 1886, the son of Richard R. (a farmer) and Sarah A. Barber who came to live in Mobberley.

James later moved to 8, Danube Street, Toxteth where he became a telegraph delivery boy. By 1911 he was a postman and had moved to lodge at 49, Collard Road, Speke.

He enlisted in the army in 1916 becoming Bombardier no. 24042 in 'D' Battery 165 Brigade of the Royal Field Artillery.

**Brief history of the Battery:**
James' battery joined the 36th Division in France in 1916.
See appendix two for the make-up of a Division.
James was killed in action on the 9th February 1918.

**On that fateful day:**
At the time of writing the war diary was unavailable.

*James is buried in Roclincourt Military Cemetery, France together with 916 other servicemen. His grave is IV. A. 14.*

# JAMES ROBINSON BARBER

**James Robinson Barber** was born in Knutsford in 1898, one of nine children born to Samuel (a butcher) and Mary Barber of 91, King Street, Knutsford.

On leaving school James entered the family business and he too became a butcher.

His service records no longer exist but we know he joined the 11th Battalion of the Cheshire Regiment in 1915, becoming Private no. 16993, and went with his Regiment to France on the 25th September 1915.

**Brief history of the Battalion:**

The 11th (Service) Battalion, Cheshire Regiment was raised in Chester on the 17th of September 1914 as part of Kitchener's Third New Army and joined 75th Brigade, 25th Division. They trained at Codford St Mary and spent the winter in billets in Bournemouth. They moved to Aldershot for final training in May 1915 and proceeded to France on the 26th of September, the division concentrating in the area of Nieppe. On the 26th of October they transferred to 7th Brigade still with 25th Division. Their first action was in defence of the German attack on Vimy Ridge in May 1916. They then moved to The Somme and joined the Battle just after the main attack, with 75th Brigade making a costly attack near Thiepval on the 3rd of July. The Division was in action at The Battle of Bazentin, The Battle of Pozieres and The Battle of the Ancre Heights. In 1917 they were in action at The Battle of Messines attacking between the Wulverghem-Messines and Wulverghem-Wytschaete roads. In the Third battle of Ypres were in action during The Battle of Pilkem. In 1918 they were in action on The Somme, in the Battles of the Lys suffering heavy losses. On the 17th of June 1918 the battalion was reduced to cadre strength with many troops transferring to the 1/6th Cheshires. On the 23rd of June the cadre transferred to 39th Division and on the 3rd of August was disbanded in France.

*Thanks to the Wartime Memories Project.*

Samuel died at home from pneumonia on the 26th October 1918.

*James is buried in Knutsford Cemetery.*

# THOMAS E. BARBER

**Thomas Edward Barber** was born in Goostrey, Cheshire in 1885, one of six children born to William (a hay dealer) and Emma Barber of Booth Beck, Goostrey. On the death of his parents Thomas moved to Ongarue, New Zealand as did his brother W. H. Barber.

Thomas took up the occupation of a bushman in the employ of his brother.

On the outbreak of was he enlisted as Private no. 12/3908 of 'A' Company of the 11th Reinforcement Auckland Infantry Brigade, later joining 2nd Battalion, Wellington Regiment of the New Zealand Expeditionary Force. He embarked from Wellington on the 1st April 1916, heading for Port Said, then on to the Western front.

Thomas was killed in action on the 17th September 1916.

**On that fateful day:**

The New Zealand Expeditionary Force diaries make no mention of any action on the day Thomas died – so once again it can be put down to 'casual shelling' or 'a sniper'.

*Thomas is remembered on the Caterpillar Valley (New Zealand) Memorial, Somme, France along with the names of 1205 fellow New Zealanders.*

# JOHN BARNES

**John Barnes** was born in Tabley, Cheshire in 1898, one of six children born to William (a blacksmith) and Mary Hannah Barnes of Mere, Knutsford.

John joined the army and became Private no. 15669 of the 1st Battalion, Cheshire Regiment in September 1914 at the age of 16 – a soldier had to be 19 years of age to serve abroad, but he went, arriving on the Western Front in early 1915.

**Brief history of the Battalion:**

The 1st Battalion, Cheshire Regiment was a regular unit of the British Army and was in Londonderry when war broke out in August 1914 with 15th Brigade in 5th Division. They returned to England and proceeded to France with the British Expeditionary Force, landing at Le Havre on the 16th of August 1914. They saw action at The Battle of Mons, The Battle of the Marne, The Battle of the Aisne, The Battles of La Bassee, at Messines and in The First Battle of Ypres. Between the 3rd of March and 7th of April 1915 they were attached with 15th Brigade to 28th Division in in exchange for 83rd Brigade in order to familiarise the newly arrived troops with the Western Front. In 1915 they were in action in The Second Battle of Ypres and the Capture of Hill 60. In March 1916 they took over a sector in the front line in the southern edge of Vimy Ridge, in front of Arras. The 5th Division arrived on the Somme to relieve the British units who had suffered badly in the attack on the first of July and went into action at High Wood, being withdrawn in October. The Division spent late autumn and winter near Festubert and in 1917 were in action in the Battles of Arras and the Third Battle of Ypres.

*Thanks to the Wartime Memories Project.*

John was killed in action on the 5th October 1917.

**On that fateful day:**
The war diary makes no mention of any action on this day.

*John has no known grave and is remembered at Tyne Cot Memorial, Belgium, along with the names of 34,952 other servicemen.*

# HARON BARONIAN

**Haron Baronian** was born in West Didsbury, Manchester in 1897 to Zarch (a merchant) and Shushan Baronian of Brae Cottage, Legh Road, Knutsford. His parents were both Turkish citizens (which might have caused a few problems when Turkey entered the war on the side of the Central Powers). He was one of six children who seemed to have had a privileged upbringing as the family had several servants. His father being a cotton merchant trading mainly with China.

He attended Manchester University and was studying Chinese, where he was a member of the Officer Training Corp.

In January 1916 and arrived at the front in July of that year. Haron joined the army, becoming Private no.33006 of the 8th Battalion of the Cheshire Regiment.

**Brief history of the Battalion:**

The 8th (Service) Battalion, Cheshire Regiment was raised in Chester on the 12th of August 1914 as part of Kitchener's First New Army and joined 40th Brigade, 13th (Western) Division which assembled on Salisbury Plain. 40th Brigade moved to Chiseldon and Cirencester in September 1914. Near the end of February the Division concentrated at Blackdown in Hampshire. They moved to the Mediterranean from the 13th of June 1915 landing at Alexandria then moving to Mudros, by the 4th of July to prepare for a landing at Gallipoli. The infantry landed on Cape Helles between the 6th and 16th of July to relieve 29th Division. They returned to Mudros at the end of the month, and the entire Division landed at ANZAC Cove between the 3rd and 5th of August. They were in action in The Battle of Sari Bair, The Battle of Russell's Top and The Battle of Hill 60, at ANZAC. Soon afterwards they transferred from ANZAC to Suvla Bay. They were evacuated from Suvla on the 19th and 20th of December 1915, and after a week's rest they moved to the Helles bridgehead. They were in action during the last Turkish attacks at Helles on the 7th of January 1916 and were evacuated from Helles on the 8th and 9th. The Division concentrated at Port Said, holding forward posts in the Suez Canal defences. On the 12th of February 1916 they moved to Mesopotamia, to join the force being assembled near Sheikh Sa'ad for the relief of the besieged garrison at Kut al Amara. They joined the Tigris Corps on the 27th of March and were in action in the unsuccessful attempts to relieve Kut. They were in action in The Battle of Kut al Amara, The capture of the Hai Salient, the capture of Dahra Bend and The passage of the Diyala, in the pursuit of the enemy towards Baghdad. Units of the Division were the first troops to enter Baghdad, when it fell on the 11 March 1917. The Division then joined "Marshall's Column" and pushed north across Iraq, fighting at Delli 'Abbas, Duqma, Nahr Kalis, crossing the 'Adhaim on the 18 April and fighting at Shatt al 'Adhaim.

*Thanks to the Wartime Memories Project.*

Haron was killed in action on the 11th April 1917.
Obituary in the Knutsford Guardian dated 27th April 1917:

*"Mr. and Mrs. Baronian of Brae Cottage, Legh Road, Knutsford had official news on Monday of the death in action of their second*

son, *Private Haron Baronian of the Cheshire Regiment. Private Baronian joined the Cheshire Regiment in January of last year. Five months later he was drafted to the Front. He developed an enthusiasm for military life and wrote most cheerfully of the conditions. On January 31ˢᵗ, he was wounded and one of the most treasured possessions of the family is a letter he wrote shortly after, describing the attack on the enemy defences during the course of which a bullet penetrated his hand "word was passed round on January 31ˢᵗ" he wrote, "that we were to charge the trenches the next day. On February 1ˢᵗ at 9.30 we went over the top – that it the popular name out here – but as the distance to the enemy's lines was too great to charge all the way we advanced at a steady pace. Of course, the bombardment which started before we went over continued as we advanced, and we could see the shrapnel sweeping ahead of us. We had got to within 30 yards of the enemy's frontline trench when I suddenly felt an awful pain like a stab through my left hand. I suppose I fell down. At any rate a friend called Alec Saunders stopped a little with me and bandaged me up roughly, stopping the bleeding. As I was lying on the ground I could see the enemy's prisoners being hurried back to our line in the open. Our fellows carried the trench easily, and after consolidating it, some of them went over. After a time, I saw a sergeant wounded in the arm and was able to bandage him up as best as I could with one hand. Then I crawled up to the enemy's trench, and after being with several wounded fellows sometime we got to a fairly safe place in the front. After a great deal of waiting we got back to our own line, and going through various dressing stations we went to the hospital at XXXXXX where we stopped the night. The next morning we got on the boat, arriving at XXXXXX about 4pm on February 3ʳᵈ."*

*Private Baronian was educated at Bowden College, then Manchester University and the School of Technology. A brilliant student, he was a great prize winner, especially in the French examinations. At the university he studied Chinese, the intention being for him to join his father in his business of cotton merchant trading with China. Of a sunny disposition, the young man was most popular among his school contemporaries. Shortly after the outbreak of the war he trained with the OTC, but later joined the army from the School of Technology as a private.*

*Two other sons of Mr. and Mrs. Baronian are on service, one being with the Marconi factory engaged on war work."*

> ## Note:
> *Despite the fact that Haron was an excellent scholar and obviously intelligent, and he was a member of the Officer Training Corp (OTC) – in the British army of the day he would have found it impossible for him, of Armenian extraction, to get a commission.*
>
> *The family commissioned a statute of Haron which now stands outside the Red Cross Headquarters in Knutsford. It was sculpted by Hamo Thornygate shortly after Haron's death.*

**Haron's statue in Knutsford**

*The likeness is amazing.*

*Haron has no known grave but is remembered on the Basra Memorial, along with the names of 40,682 other servicemen.*

# FRANK BARROW

**Frank Barrow** was born in Mobberley in 1893, one of six children born to John (a jobbing bricklayer) and Annie (a confectioner) of London Road, Alderley Edge, Cheshire. Frank worked as a warehouseman and also helped his mother with the confectionary.

He enlisted in the army in 1914, becoming Private no. 2305 of the 1/7th Battalion of the Cheshire Regiment.

He arrived in the Balkans on the 8th August 1915. He was promoted to Acting Corporal.

**Brief history of the Battalion:**
The 7th Battalion, Cheshire Regiment was a territorial unit of the British Army and was based in Macclesfield with Cheshire Brigade, Welsh Division when war broke out in August 1914. They were at once mobilised and moved to Shrewsbury and Church Stretton but by the end of August were at Northampton. In December 1914 they moved to Cambridge and by March 1915 were at Bedford preparing for service in India. On the 13th of May 1915 the Cheshire Brigade was renamed 159th Brigade, 53rd (Welsh) Division. On the 2nd of July orders arrived to re-equip for service in the Mediterranean and on the 14th they sailed from Devonport to Alexandria and made a landing at Suvla Bay Gallipoli on the 9th of August 1915. They were involved in operations in the Suvla Bay area suffering heavy losses. By the time they were evacuated

to Mudros on the 11th of December the Division stood at just 162 officers and 2428 men (approx.. 15%).

*Thanks to the Wartime Memories Project.*

James died on the 5th December 1915.
His remaining records merely state he 'died', so it would appear he succumbed to disease as opposed to dying as a result of wounds.

*James is buried in East Mudros Military Cemetery, Greece along with 885 other servicemen. His Grave is III. D. 119.*

# JOSEPH BARROW

**Joseph Barrow** was born in Knutsford, Cheshire in 1894, one of two children born to Thomas (a farm labourer) and Hannah of Blakeley Cottage, Mobberley. Joseph was an apprentice grocer.

He enlisted in the 16th Battalion of the Manchester Regiment as private no. 19321, and arrived in France on the 10th November 1915.

**Brief history of the Battalion:**

The 16th (1st City) Battalion, Manchester Regiment was raised in Manchester on the 28th of August 1914 by the Lord Mayor and City. Initially they trained at Heaton Park but moved in April 1915 to Belton Park, where they joined 90th Brigade, 30th Division. They to Larkhill in September 1915 for final training and proceeded to France on the 6th of November 1915. Concentrating near Amiens. In 1916 they were in action during the Battle of the Somme, in which the Division captured Montauban. In 1917 they took part in the pursuit of the German retreat to the Hindenburg Line, the Arras Offensive and The Battle of Pilkem Ridge.

Joseph was killed in action on the 23rd April 1917.

**On that fateful day:**

The war diary states:

*'At 4.40am on the 24th the 90th Brigade commenced its attack on the German position of CHERISY. 17th Manchester on the right and Royal Scots on the left. 16th Manchesters in close support. The attack was conceived as a leap-frog plan – the leading waves having objectives half the distance to the village. 2nd and 3rd waves to push to points in and around the village.*

*16th supplied specialist bombing parties for the advance.*

*The advance met extremely heavy machine-gun fire and destructive artillery fire.*

*Our troops fought hard and doggedly throughout the day and many parties succeeded in penetrating their objectives but by nightfall very little ground had been gained whilst the loss had been appalling. The German resistance had been very strong from the first and as indicated the advance had been at a heavy cost.*

(The Germans suffered heavily too in their counter-attacks) *Losses for the day 31 OR Killed 56 missing.*

*Joseph is remembered on the Arras memorial along with the names of 34791 other servicemen.*

# TOM BARROW

**Thomas Barrow** was born in Openshaw, Manchester in 1890, the son of John (a police officer) and Christina Barrow, who lived at 62, Carmen Street, Ardwick, Manchester. He had four siblings.

His mother was a native of Tabley, Knutsford and when his father retired as a Sergeant, having served for 26 years; the family moved back to Tabley and lived in a tithed house at Tabley brook, Over Tabley. His father had also served in the Indian army and his grand-father was killed at the Battle of Waterloo. So his father joined the Knutsford Volunteers, rising to the rank of Platoon sergeant.

It appears that Tom left home following numerous disagreement with his father who he thought to be 'overbearing'.

Eventually he found employment at The Cavendish Hotel on the Grand Parade in Eastbourne as a billiard marker.

Early in 1916 he enlisted at Eastbourne recruiting office in the 13th battalion of the Royal Sussex regiment, becoming Private no G/3283. (His number tells us he was a 'general service' recruit, not being given the prefix 'SD' indicating a local man from South Downs.

**Brief history of the Battalion:**

13th (3rd South Down) Battalion, The Royal Sussex Regiment was raised at Bexhill on the 20th of November 1914 by Lieut-Col. Lowther, MP and Committee. After initial training close to home, they moved to Maidstone in July 1915 and were adopted by the War Office. They moved to Aldershot in September and then to Witley to join 116th Brigade, 39th Division in October. They preceded to France, landed at Le Havre in March 1916, the division concentrating near Blaringhem and receiving five battalions from other divisions to replace those of 118th Brigade who had remained in England to complete their training. On the 30th June 1916 they were in action in an attack near Richebourg l'Avoue with the Sussex battalions suffered heavy casualties.

**The war diary states:**

*'29 June:*
*Day spent in collecting materials, and general organisation for the attack. In the afternoon, our artillery bombarded the enemy trenches*

*from 2pm to 5pm, cutting his wire and destroying his works. [Extract from Operation Order Number 23. Intention. The Battalion will assault and capture the enemy trenches as follows: Enemy front-line from Boar's Head to S.10.c.8.1. Enemy support line from S.16.a.5½. 6½ to S.16.a.9.9. The 12th battalion will assault on our left. The dividing line between battalions will be the ditch running from our front line parapet at S.10.c.5.3 to the enemy front-line parapet at S.10.c.8.0. Method of attack. Main attack from our front line between cinder track and the ditch near Vine Street. Flank attack from our own Fishtail Sap against the Boar's Head. Main attack will be delivered in four lines, each line consisting of 4 Platoons. Flank attack will be delivered by five bombing parties, each party consisting of one NCO and six men. Lewis guns: these will assemble in the old disused trench about 35 yards in front of trench between Bond Street and Vine Street. Carrying party. Carrying party will assemble in the Strand. As soon as the assaulting lines have advanced over the front parapet these parties will move to the company stores situated in our present front line. Their work will be to transfer SAA , bombs, rations and water from the stores to the company's stores in a new front line. Silence must be insisted on.]*

### 30 June: Report on Operations.

*1. The Battalion assembled at 1:30pm on the morning of 30 June in readiness for the assault with all 4 Platoons of each Company in the front line.*

*2. The preliminary bombardment on the morning of the attack opened at 2:50am and at 3.05am the leading wave of the battalion scaled the parapet, the remainder following at 50 yards interval. At the same time the flank attack under Lieutenants Whitley and Ellis gained a footing in the enemy trench. The passage across no man's land was accomplished with few casualties except in the left companies, which came under very heavy machine-gun fire. The two right companies succeeded in reaching the objective but the two left companies only succeeded in penetrating the enemy's wire in one or two places. Just at this moment a smoke cloud, which was originally designed to mask our advance, drifted right across the front and made it impossible to see more than a few yards ahead. This resulted in all direction being lost and the attack devolving into small bodies of men not knowing which way to go. Some groups succeeded in entering the support line, engaging the enemy with bombs and bayonets and organising the initial stages of a defence. Other parties swung off to the right and entered the trench where the flanking party was operating, causing a great deal of congestion. On the left the smoke and darkness made the job of penetrating the enemy wire so difficult that few if any succeeded in reaching the enemy trench. Some parties of the right company succeeded in reaching the enemy support line when they were subjected to an intense bombardment with HE and whizzbangs. Captain Hughes, who was wounded, seeing that his company was in danger of being cut off, gave the order for the evacuation of the enemy trenches and the remainder of the attacking force returned to our trenches. The enemy who was evidently thoroughly prepared now concentrated his energies on the front line and for the space of about two and a half hours our front and support lines were subjected to an intense bombardment with a bit heavy and light shells causing a large... [The diary disappears here and does not start again until after the attack].*

Tom was killed in action on the 30th June 1916.

This attack is not mentioned in the official history of the war, no doubt it was over-shadowed by the greater event that took place the following day (1st July 1916)

The battle of the 330th June lasted just over 5 hours leaving 17 officers and 349 other ranks dead or missing and over 1000 wounded or taken prisoner. This day became known locally as 'the day that Sussex died'.

Tom left the sum of £166.8s.6d to his mother in his will.

*Tom has no known grave and is remembered on the Loos Memorial, along with the names of 20,621 other servicemen*

# NATHANIEL JAMES MERRIMAN BARRY

**Nathaniel James Merriman Barry** was the son of Sir Jacob and Lady Mary Barry. He married Marion Boyd and lived at The Lodges, Overbury, Tewkesbury. He was a farmer at 'Rustenburg', Naivasha, British East Africa.

He became a captain in the General Service attached to the East Africa Transport Corp.

Unfortunately all the records have been destroyed so we know very little about Nathaniel.

He was killed in action on the 21ˢᵗ October 1917.

**On that fateful day:**
I have so far been unable to locate the war diaries for this regiment.

*Nathaniel is buried in Dar Es Salaam War Cemetery, Tanzania, along with 1764 other servicemen. His grave is I. A. 7.*

# GEORGE EDWARD BASKERVILLE
*(Brother of John)*

**George Edward Baskerville** was born in 1899, one of seven children born to John and Mary Ann Baskerville of Holly Cottage Marthall, Cheshire. He worked as a farm labourer.

He enlisted in the army becoming Private no. 3025 (later re-numbered to 290862) of the 1/7th Battalion of the Cheshire Regiment.

**Brief history of the Battalion:**

The 7th Battalion, Cheshire Regiment was a territorial unit of the British Army and was based in Macclesfield with Cheshire Brigade, Welsh Division when war broke out in August 1914. They were at once mobilised and moved to Shrewsbury and Church Stretton but by the end of August were at Northampton. In December 1914 they moved to Cambridge and by March 1915 was at Bedford preparing for service in India. On the 13th of May 1915 the Cheshire Brigade was renamed 159th Brigade, 53rd (Welsh) Division. On the 2nd of July orders arrived to re-equip for service in the Mediterranean and on the 14th they sailed from Devonport to Alexandria and made a landing at Suvla Bay Gallipoli on the 9th of August 1915. They were involved in operations in the Suvla Bay area suffering heavy losses. By the time they were evacuated to Mudros on the 11th of December the Division stood at just 162 officers and 2428 men ( approx. 15%). From Mudros they went on to Alexandria and to Wardan, where the the divisional artillery re-joined in February 1916. They were in action at The Battle of Romani in the Palestine campaign and in 1917 158th Brigade fought at The First Battle of Gaza and the whole Division were in action during The Second Battle of Gaza, The Third Battle of Gaza when they were involved in capture of Beersheba, Tell Khuweilfe, and The Capture of Jerusalem. In December they were in action in The Defence of Jerusalem. In March 1918 they fought at The Battle of Tell'Asur. On the 31st of May 1918 the 7th Cheshires left the Division and sailed for France, joining 102nd Brigade, 34th Division on the 1st of July. They returned to action, at The Battles of the Soissonais, the Ourcq and the capture of Baigneux Ridge. They took part in the Final Advance in Flanders and at the Armistice were at rest in the area east of Courtrai. 34th Division was selected to join the Army of Occupation and began to move towards Germany on the 14th of November.

*Thanks to the Wartime Memories Project.*

George was killed in action on the 23rd July 1918.

**On that fateful day:**
The war diary states:

***23.7.18 – Village of Parcy Tigny.***
*'Considerable opposition was met with from the enemy machine guns in BOIS de REUGNY and from the high ground on our right front. Owing to insufficient support on both flanks the Battalion was unable to advance any further and the ine was consolidated.. The support and reserve companies were moved up to the OLD PARIS TRENCH line. Throughout the day PARCY TIGNY was subjected to heavy bursts of enemy shell fire.*
*Approx casualties for the day 180.'*

*George is buried in Raperie British Cemetery, France along with over 600 other servicemen. His grave is IIIA. D. 6.*

74

# JOHN FRED BASKERVILLE
*(Brother of George)*

John Fred Baskerville was born in 1899, one of seven children born to John and Mary Ann Baskerville of Holly Cottage Marthall, Cheshire. He worked as a farm labourer. He later moved to Siddington, Cheshire.

He enlisted in the army, becoming Private no 12691 (later re-numbered to 242530) of the 2/6th Battalion of the Lancashire Fusiliers. He rose to the rank of Lance Corporal.

**Brief history of the Battalion:**
2/6th Battalion was formed at Mossborough on 29 September 1914 as a home service ("second line") unit. On the 8th February 1915 it was attached to 197th Brigade, 66th (2nd East Lancashire) Division. They moved to Crowborough in May 1915 and went on to Tunbridge Wells in October 1915 and Colchester in March 1916. The Battalion landed at Le Havre 26 February 1917. On the 21st January 1918 it was absorbed by 1/6th Bn.

*Thanks to The Long, Long Trail.*

John was killed in action on the 24th August 1917.

**On that fateful day:**
The war diary states:

**'21/8/17 to 27/8/17 BEACON TRENCH and BOCHE TRENCH**
*The Battn remained in the line during this time. A large amount of work was done on the trenches. We were heavily shelled by the enemy on the night of the 22nd and also the evening of the 26th. (No mention is made of any action on the 24th) Gas shells were used during these bombardments.'*

*John is buried at Ramscappelle Road Military Cemetery along with 841 other servicemen. His grave is II. C. 2.*

# GEORGE ARTHUR BEBBINGTON

**George Arthur Bebbington** was born in Knutsford in 18185, one of six children born to William Arthur (a music teacher) and Alice Bebbington of 26, Bexton Road, Knutsford.

George became a bank clerk at Parrs bank, Garston and lodged at 10, Island Road, Garston, Liverpool.

He attested at Liverpool on the 11th September 1914 as Private no. 21446 and joined the 5th Battalion of the Kings (Liverpool Regiment), later being transferred to the 19th Battalion.

**Brief history of the Battalion:**
19th (3rd City) Battalion, The King's Regiment (Liverpool) was raised by Lord Derby at the old watch factory, Prescott, Liverpool on the 29th of August 1914. After training in the Liverpool area, they joined 89th Brigade, 30th Division on the 30th of April 1915, which concentrated near Grantham. In the autumn they moved to Larkhill, Salisbury and proceeded to France on the 7th of November 1915 landing Boulogne, the division concentrating near Amiens. In 1916 they were in action during the Battle of the Somme, in which the Division captured Montauban.

*Thanks to the Wartime Memories Project.*

He was promoted to Lance corporal (unpaid) on the 17th November 1915.

George was killed in action on the 30th July 1916.

**On that fateful day:**
The war diary has no entry for this specific date.

***George is buried in Guillemont Road Cemetery, Somme, France along with 2,263 other servicemen. His grave is V. D. 2.***

# HAROLD BEBBINGTON

Harold Bebbington was born in Ollerton, Cheshire in 1897, one of five children born to Thomas (a gardener) and Agnes Bebbington of Ollerton. Harold became a farm labourer, working on a farm in Tabley, Cheshire.

He enlisted in the Royal garrison Artillery on the 8th December 1915, becoming Gunner no.85350.

His service records no longer exist so we don't know if he served aboard but on the 25th may 1917 he was discharged from the army through 'sickness' under Paragraph 392 XVI of the Kings Regulations that stated he was 'no longer fit for war service.

Harold died on the 31st January 1919 – more than likely with pneumonia.

***Harold is buried in Marthall (All Saints) Churchyard, Cheshire.***

# JOHN THOMAS BELL

John Thomas Bell was born in Plumley in 1895, one of seven children born to George (a farm labourer) and Elisabeth Bell of The Firs, Plumley, Cheshire. John was also a farm labourer.

He attested for the army on the 7th September 1914 and was called to serve in the 3rd Battalion of the Cheshire Regiment as Private no. 15488. He was later transferred to the 10th Battalion.

He went to France on the 25th September 1915.

**Brief history of the Battalion:**

The 10th (Service) Battalion, Cheshire Regiment was raised in Chester on the 10th of September 1914 as part of Kitchener's Third New Army and joined 75th Brigade, 25th Division. They trained at Codford St Mary and spent the winter in billets in Bournemouth. They moved to Aldershot for final training in May 1915 and proceeded to France on the 26th of September, the division concentrating in the area of Nieppe. On the 26th of October they transferred to 7th Brigade still with 25th Division. Their first action was in defence of the German attack on Vimy Ridge in May 1916. They then moved to The Somme and joined the Battle just after the main attack, with 75th Brigade making a costly attack near Thiepval on the 3rd of July. The Division was in action at The Battle of Bazentin, The Battle of Pozieres and The Battle of the Ancre Heights. In 1917 they were in action at The

Battle of Messines attacking between the Wulverghem-Messines and Wulverghem-Wytschaete roads. In the Third battle of Ypres were in action during The Battle of Pilkem. In 1918 they were in action on The Somme, in the Battles of the Lys suffering heavy losses.

*Thanks to the Wartime Memories Project.*

Thomas was killed in action on the 24th March 1918.

**On that fateful day:**
The war diary states:

*24.3.18 – Lagnycourt Sector*
*The company took the brunt of an attack on the trenches by the Germans – and suffered very heavy casualties'*

***John is remembered on the Arras Memorial, France along with 34,791 other servicemen.***

# PHILIP OSWALD BELL

**Philip Oswald Bell** was born in 1896 in Nether Peover, Cheshire one of nine children born to William (a brewer) and Alma Bell of the Warren de Tabley Arms, Peover.

Philip became a professional soldier.

Philip joined the Royal Field Artillery as Signaller no. 9888 of the 149th (County Palatine) Battery.

He arrived in France on the 28th November 1915.

**Brief history of the Battery:**

CXLIX Brigade, Royal Field Artillery served as divisional artillery with 30th Division. 30th Division was formed in April 1915 from units of Kitchener's 5th New Army and concentrated near Grantham. In the autumn they moved to Larkhill, Salisbury and proceeded to France in November, sailing to Le Havre and Boulogne and concentrating near Amiens. In 1916 they were in action during the Battle of the Somme, in which the Division captured Montauban.

*Thanks to the Wartime Memories Project.*

Philip died on the 10th May 1916, having been wounded eight days before.

**On that fateful day:**
It was reported in a letter from his commanding officer to his mother that a shell had come through the roof of his dugout while the men were asleep and exploded, killing several of them and wounding Philip, who died later at the field hospital.

*Philip is buried in the Suzanne Communal Cemetery Extension, Somme, France along with 155 other servicemen. His grave is F. 25.*

# ERNEST BENTLEY

**Ernest Bentley** was born in Knutsford in 1888, one of six children born to John (a house painter) and Elizabeth Ann Bentley of 3, Northwich Road, Knutsford. They later moved to 2, Egerton Terrace, Knutsford. The 1911 census states that Ernest 'worked form home'.

He enlisted in the Cheshire Regiment as Private no. 4707 but later was transferred to the 1st Battalion of the Kings Own Royal Lancaster Regiment as Private no. 30309

**Brief history of the Battalion:**

1ˢᵗ Battalion, The King's Own (Royal Lancaster Regiment) was in Dover serving with 12th Brigade, 4th Division when war broke out in August 1914. 4th Division was held back from the original British Expeditionary Force by a last minute decision to defend England against a possible German landing. The fate of the BEF in France and the lack of any move by the Enemy to cross the channel, reversed this decision and they proceeded to France, landing at Boulogne on the 23rd of August 1914, arriving in time to provide infantry reinforcements at the Battle of Le Cateau, the Divisional Artillery, Engineers, Field Ambulances and mounted troops being still en-route at this time. They were in action at the Battle of the Marne, The Battle of the Aisne and at The Battle of Messines in 1914. In 1915 they fought in The Second Battle of Ypres and moved south to The Somme. Between the 5th of November 1915 and 3 February 1916, 12th Brigade were attached to 36th (Ulster) Division, providing instruction to the newly arrived Division. The 1st Kings Own were in action during the Battles of the Somme in 1916. In 1917 they were at Arras, in action during the First and Third Battles of the Scarpe, before heading north for the Third Battle of Ypres, where they fought in The Battle of Polygon Wood, The Battle of Broodseinde, The Battle of Poelcapelle and The First Battle of Passchendaele.

Ernest was killed in action on the 12ᵗʰ October 1917.

**On that fateful day:**
The war diary for the above date states:

**'12.10.17 POLECAPPEL**
*Zero hour was 5.30 am. Enemy put down a heavy barrage on our front line, also great M.G. fire from POLCAPPEL (sic). Warwick's met with little opposition on the left, but household Battn suffered heavy casualties by flanking M.G. fire from the village. In spite of this they took REQUETE Farm. 18ᵗʰ Divn. Of our right made no progress in*

*the village, and so 12^(th) Bde. had to form a defensive flank. This was done by 1 Coy Kings Own and 1 Coy Rifle Bde.*

*Counter-attack forced line to retire slightly during the day near REQUETE Farm.*

*The line as held in the evening was as shown in the attached map C – in red.*

*2 Battns of the 34^(th) Divn. Were sent up at night to relieve front line troops, but owing to darkness, and state of the ground the relief was not to be completed'.*

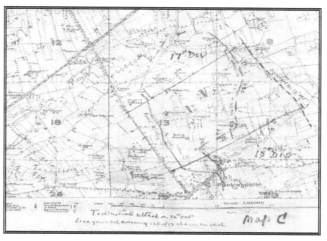

**Map as mentioned in the diary above.**

**Ernest is remembered on the Tyne Cot memorial, Belgium along with the names of 43,952 other servicemen.**

# ARTHUR JOHN BERRY M.M.

**Arthur John Berry** was born in Knutsford on the 18th February 1896, one of four children born to John (a railway worker) and Ellen Berry (nee Mills) of 289, Concrete Terrace, Cross Town, Knutsford. The family later moved to 8, Green Street, Knutsford.

By the age of 15, Arthur was in service as a Hall Boy at Toft Hall, Knutsford. The hall boy or hallboy was the lowest ranked male domestic worker on the staff of a great house. Usually a boy or young teenager, his name derived from the fact that his main duties were in the servants' hall, where he may also have slept.

Like his female counterpart, the scullery maid, the hall boy would have been expected to work up to 16 hours per day, seven days per week. His duties were often among the most disagreeable in the house, such as emptying chamber pots for the higher-ranking servants, and (in the absence of a boot boy) cleaning the boots.

***Toft Hall, Knutsford as it looked in Arthur's day.***

He enlisted at Manchester Recruiting Office in March 1915, becoming Private no. 3378 in 'A' Company of the 1/6th Battalion of the Manchester Regiment, later being promoted to Sergeant no. 250959.

He left Britain on the 3rd October and arrived in Gallipoli on the 23rd October 1915.

**Brief history of the Battalion:**

The 1/6th Battalion, Manchester were a Territorial unit, when war broke out in August 1914 they were based in Stretford Road, Hulme as part of the Manchester Brigade, East Lancashire Division. They were mobilized and moved to Rochdale to prepare for service overseas. They proceeded to Egypt arriving at Alexandria on the 25th of September to defend the Suez Canal from the Turkish forces in Palestine. They were in action in the Turkish attack on the Suez Canal on the 3rd of February 1915. In the first week of May the division embarked from Alexandria, landing at Cape Helles, Gallipoli, where they saw action in the attempts to capture the heights of Krithia and the Battle of Krithia Vineyard which was a diversionary attack for the British Landing at Suvla Bay. The much depleted division were evacuated from Gallipoli in the first week of January 1916, returning to Alexandria via Mudros. They returned to duty on the Suez Canal and were in action in the Battle of Romani in August. In early 1917 they were ordered to the Western Front, departing from Alexandria in February. They went into the front line at Ephey, moved to Havrincourt then were withdrawn to Albert for rest and training during July and August. In September they moved north to Flanders and were in action during the Third Battle of Ypres at Iberian, Borry Farm, Beck House Farm and Sans Souci. At the end of the month they moved to the coast at Nieuport until November when they moved to La Bassee Canal at Givenchy. On the 19th of February 1918 they transferred to 126th Brigade still with 42nd Division. In 1918 they saw action during The Battle of Bapaume, The First Battle of Arras, The Battle of the Ancre, The Battle of Albert, The Second Battle of Bapaume, The Battle of the Canal du Nord, The pursuit to the Selle and The Battle of the Selle.

*Thanks to the Wartime Memories Project.*

He arrived in France on the 1st March 1917, and on the 6th May he was promoted to Sergeant.

Shortly before his death Albert was awarded the Military Medal when, following and attack on the enemy lines and seeing that all the officers had fallen he took command and 'won through what was a very difficult situation, calling for no inconsiderable amount of resource and courage.'

Arthur was killed on the 22nd April 1918.

**On that fateful day:**

He was returning from a bombing raid on a German Machine-gun post when a bomb (possible a grenade) was accidentally dropped by one of his comrades – it went off killing him instantly.

There is no entry in the Battalion records of this incident. The awarding of his Military Medal is noted a couple of days before.

*Arthur is buried in Couin New British Cemetery, France, along with 360 other servicemen. His grave is C36. He also has a small memorial in Knutsford Cemetery.*

*Note:*
*His 1914/15 medal (Mons Star) was returned under regulation no. 1743 of the Kings Regs 1912 – for if a medal remained unclaimed for 10 years it was returned and 'broken up'.*

# ALBERT BESWICK

**Albert Beswick** was born in Plumley in 1895, the son of Albert (a general labourer) and Ann Beswick of Plumley Moor, Knutsford. He took up the occupation of domestic gardener.

He enlisted at Kendal in the 8th Battalion of the Border Regiment as Private no. 15089. His number showing he enlisted in September 1914

**Brief history of the Battalion:**
8th (Service) Battalion, The Border Regiment was raised in Carlisle in September 1914 as part of Kitchener's Third New Army. They joined 75th Brigade, 25th Division and moved to Codford for training in November 1914, being billeted in Boscombe. The Battalion moved to Romsey in May 1915 and then to Aldershot following in June.

They proceeded to France on the 27th of September 1915, landing at Boulogne. The 25th Division concentrated around Nieppe and saw action in 1916 on Vimy Ridge.

Albert was killed in action on the 21st October 1916.

**On that fateful day:**
The war diary for that day states:

*21.10.16*
*Attack on Regina Trench by the Battn and Coy of 11th Cheshire Regt. The Battn and 1 Coy of X1 Cheshire's took over the line in Hessian trench at 6am, the relief being completed by 8am. Border's on the right and Cheshire's on the left. The objective in Regina Trench was assigned to the Battn was roughly 330 yards. The 13th Cheshire's, 74th Bde. Being on our right and responsible for the sunken road, the 8th Lancers were on our left.*

*The attack was ordered in four waves, Border's being in ½ Coy Columns 'A; Coy and the Xith Cheshire's in column of platoon 30 paces in advance.*

*Our artillery barrage opened at 12.06pm, which was the signal to get out of the trench: the waves were not very good but there was no confusion, direction was well kept by the Border's, this was caused* by the communication trench running right obliquely across our front, a change of direction had also to be made.

The whole advanced too quickly, sufficient attention was not paid to the barrage orders, officers were few, but watches could not have been properly used.

The ground was not cut up by shell holes as much as expected and was easy to advance over, the leading wave reach the objective before the barrage lifted and suffered some casualties in consequence; the wire was well cut and presented no obstacle. The barrage was excellent, a few shells were short, but I think this must be expected, the attack was sudden and swift, had there been a slight check to allow the barrage to lift the Battn. would have got over almost without a casualty.

When the trench was reached on the left, the men got in so easily they did not realised they gained their objective, a gap was also left on the right owing to opposition from a large dugout on the right where a machine-gun fired a few rounds.

Some dug-outs and emplacement showed up plainly on the left of STUMP ROAD and Germans were seen coming out of them. Within a minute of reaching REGINA TRENCH some officers and about 80 men of whom 40 were Borders left the trench and made straight across for them. Among these men were about 20 of the 13$^{th}$ Cheshire's who had some across our front, some went through the barrage and occupied a trench some 600 yards in front of the line, they were withdrawn after dark. Capt. Stewart realised what was happening and stopped a good many from going forward and got them to work at once in the trench. He found he was in touch with the 8$^{th}$ S. Lancs on the left but the right was held up. He ordered a block to be made until he could collect more men as the line was thin and sent back a written report of the situation which was most useful as it arrived after a report came from Lt. Hibbard as to the situation on the right. He said the trench had not been cleared but was full of Borders and Cheshires, this turned out to be the bombers originally told off to clear the right and two details of Lewis Guns and about 30 men of the Cheshire Regt.

*Who were unable to go on. Lt. Binnie was then sent up with the last remaining squad of Battn. Bombers at Battn HQ to try and get (in) touch with Capt. Stewart by bombing up to the C.T. On arriving at the dug-out he found that the one just beyond the block was ablaze and he could not get on that way but under the cover of the smoke caused by it managed to get his squad and 10 others from the C.T. over man by man to Regina Trench to where Catt. Stewart was, only one man being hit on the way. He got to work at once in a very gallant manner, himself getting on to the parapet and sniping while his men worked up the trench, he accounted for at least 8 German killed, and within 20 minutes the remainder, about 60, surrendered. The trench was cleared and touch gained with the 13ᵗʰ Cheshire's*

*Consolidation proceeded without opposition and several patrols were captured during the night.*

*3 machine guns were captured, 1 by the Borders, 1 by the Xith Cheshire's and 1 by the S. Lancs. 251 Germans were captured and 50 killed were counted. The Coy of the Xith Cheshire Regt and the officers attacked from that Battn rendered very useful assistance. Also the platoon of carriers who did excellent work carrying bombs and ammunition. A Coy of the Xith Cheshire's were ordered to reinforce the front line their place in Hessian Trench being taken by a Coy Xith Cheshire's, FIELD TRENCH was dug during the night by 1 Coy of the R.Es. also the C.T. on the right was improved and made passable throughout. The trench was very heavily shelled very soon after the attack commenced, this was kept up intermittently for 24 hours until the Battn was relieved. The front line was thinned out on the morning of the 22ⁿᵈ, the Coy of the Xith Cheshire's being sent back to their H.Q. The bombers of the XI Cheshire's were kept in reserve and were not required.*

*Casualties Cap.t Miller and Capt. Weston killed, Lt. Le may wounded, 18 other ranks killed, 111 wounded, 30 missing.*

The following day the Battn was relieved by the 10ᵗʰ Worcester's and marched to a camp between Albert and Bouzincourt.

*Albert is remembered on the Thiepval Memorial along with the names of 72,203 other servicemen.*

# HARRY BIRCHALL

**Harry Birchall** was born in Miles Platting, the son of Mr and Mrs J Birchall of Moston, Lancashire.

Harry married Sophia and moved to Chelford Road, Ollerton, Cheshire.

Harry enlisted in the army and became Private no. 8439 in the 17th Battalion of the Manchester Regiment.

He was a 'bomb-thrower'.

He was killed in action on the 8th November 1915.

**Brief history of the Battalion:**

The 17th (2nd City) Battalion, Manchester Regiment was raised in Manchester on the 28th of August 1914 by the Lord Mayor and City. Initially they trained at Heaton Park but moved in April 1915 to Belton Park, where they joined 90th Brigade, 30th Division. They to Larkhill in September 1915 for final training and proceeded to France on the 6th of November 1915, concentrating near Amiens. In 1916 they were in action during the Battle of the Somme, in which the Division captured Montauban.

**On that fateful day:**

The war diary states:

*8.11.15*

*Arrived in France that day – spent the night in Boulogne.*

There is no report of any casualties – the Battalion didn't go into action until the 9th December.

**Harry is buried in Bernafay Wood British Cemetery, Montauban, along with 968 other servicemen. His grave is D. 3.**

# GEORGE J. BIRKENHEAD

**George J. Birkenhead** was born in Knutsford in 1881, the son of Peter (a boot maker) and Mary Ann Birkenhead who had resided in Princes Street, Knutsford.

George joined the army, becoming Private no. 1738 of the 1$^{st}$ Battalion of the Lancashire Fusiliers.

### Brief history of the Battalion:
The first Battalion, in August 1914 was in Karachi. It was immediately recalled to England, and landed on the 2 January 1915 and moved

*Lancashire Fusiliers landing at Gallipoli.*

94

to Nuneaton. They came under the direct orders of 86th Brigade, 29th Division, and on the 16 March 1915 sailed via Egypt and landed Gallipoli 25 April 1915. They were evacuated to Egypt January 1916. Landed at Marseilles March 1916.

George was killed in action on the 2nd May 1915.

**On that fateful day:**
The war diary states:

*2.5.15 Gallipoli Peninsular*
*11 p.m.*
*Heavy bombardment of out trenches by the enemy artillery.*

*Harry has no known grave but is remembered on the Hellas Memorial,*
*Turkey, along with the names of 20,885 other servicemen.*

# JOSEPH BOOTH

**Joseph Booth** was born in Knutsford in 1880. He enlisted as a regular soldier in 1908, joining the Cheshire Regiment.

When the war started Joseph was in the 2$^{nd}$ Battalion of the Cheshire Regiment, becoming Private no. 8851.

He arrived in France on the 6$^{th}$ January 1915.

**Brief history of the Battalion:**

The 2$^{nd}$ Battalion, Cheshire Regiment was a regular unit of the British Army and was in Jubbulpore, India when war broke out in August 1914. They returned to England, landing at Devonport on the 24$^{th}$ of December 1914. They joined 84$^{th}$ Brigade, 28$^{th}$ Division, at Winchester and proceeded to France, embarking at Southampton and landing at Le Havre on the 17$^{th}$ of January 1915. 28$^{th}$ Division concentrated in the area between Bailleul and Hazebrouck. They saw action in the Second Battle of Ypres, where casualties were high and The Battle of Loos.

**Thanks to the Wartime Memories Project.**

Joseph was killed in action on the 8$^{th}$ May 1915.

## On that fateful day:
The war diary states:

*8.5.15 Verlorenhoek.*
*'A heavy bombardment of the trench was commenced by the enemy about daybreak and was carried on incessantly until the line was broken by a fierce infantry attack, made with overwhelming numbers. Asphyxiating gas was used freely by the enemy. The positions occupied by the Btn HQ and no.1 and 4 coy were surrounded by the enemy and with very few exceptions the officers and men were killed or taken prisoner.*
*Killed 17 missing 182.*
*After the attack by the enemy the firing line was reformed in what had hither to been the support trench about 500 yards to the rear of the original trench. The two officers and the remaining OR were put under the command of Lt. Col. Marsden of the 1ˢᵗ Welsh – that Batt being also in occupation of the new firing line. '*

This is the same fighting in which Jack Rushton was killed.

*Joseph is remembered on the Menin Gate memorial, Belgium, along with 54,405 other servicemen.*

# MATTHEW OLLIER BOSTOCK

**Matthew Ollier Bostock** was born in Knutsford in 1896, one of five children born to William Bostwick (a bricklayer's labourer) and Elisabeth Bostwick. They lived at 44, Silk Mill Street, Knutsford, but later mover to 1, Bakehouse Yard, Knutsford. On leaving school Matthew started work as an apprentice plumber.

His service records no longer exist but we know he joined the army in 1914 and became Private 1551 in the 1st/5th Battalion of the Cheshire Regiment and arrived in France on the 15th February 1915.

**Brief history of the Battalion:**

The 1/5th (Earl of Chester's) Battalion, Cheshire Regiment was a Territorial unit based in in Chester with Cheshire Brigade, Welsh Division, when war was declared in August 1914. They were immediately mobilised and moved to Shrewsbury and Church Stretton, by the end of August they moved to Northampton and then in December to Cambridge for final preparations. They proceeded to France on the 15th of February 1915, landing at Le Havre to join 14th Brigade, 5th Division. They were in action in The Battle of Mons and the subsequent retreat, The Battle of Le Cateau, The Battle of the Marne, The Battle of the Aisne, The Battles of La Bassee and Messines and The First Battle of Ypres. In 1915 they were in action at The Second Battle of Ypres and the Capture of Hill 60. In autumn 1915, many units were exchanged with units from the newly arrived volunteer 32nd Division, to stiffen the inexperienced Division with regular army troops. On the 29th of November 1915 they became a Pioneer Battalion. On the 13th of February 1916 the 1/5th Chester's transferred to the newly reformed 56th (London) Division, in the Hallencourt area in February.

*Thanks to the Wartime Memories Project.*

The records show he 'DIED' on the 17th June 1915. I have been unable to locate how and where he met his death.

*Matthew is buried in Dickbusch New Military Cemetery, Leper, along with 624 other servicemen. His grave is F. 32.*

# SAMUEL BOWERS

**Samuel Bowers** was born in Knutsford, one of ten children born to Peter (a farm labourer) and Jane Bowers of 1, Leak's Terrace, Knutsford. Samuel worked as a general labourer.

He joined the Cheshire Yeomanry as private no. 910 before transferring to the 10th Battalion of the Kings (Shropshire Light Infantry) as Private no. 230674.

**Brief history of the Battalion:**

The Battalion was formed at Cairo on 2nd March 1917 from the dismounted troopers of the Shropshire Yeomanry and the Cheshire Yeomanry. They served in Palestine in the 231st Brigade of the 74th "Broken Spur" Division.

It took part in the second and third battles of Gaza, July-November 1917 and then in the operations for the capture of Jerusalem (December 1917) and in the capture of Jericho (February 1918). In the attack on Birj-el-Lisaneh, near Tel Asur, on March 10th 1918, Pte. Harold Whitfield won the only VC to a Shropshire regiment for the Great War.

In May 1918, the 10th went to France, serving on the Lys in August and then at Epehy and captured the notorious " Quadrilateral" in November.

Having captured Tournai – where the 53rd had been in action in 1794 – it ended the war near Ath in Belgium and was disbanded in Shrewsbury in June1919.

Samuel was killed in action on the 30ᵗʰ November 1917.

**On that fateful day:**

The war diary states:

*30.11.17 BEIT DUKKA*
*Night 29/30ᵗʰ, Battn advanced, and captured TEREH holding the line from BEIT DUKKA to HILL 1750, both exclusively – enemy counter attacked during afternoon and eventually rushed HILL 1750 (held by the 25 R.W.F.) & TEREH – Battn retired to original line.*
    *Casualties. 8 Officers 93 O.R. killed. 3 Off 14 O.R. wounded, 5 Off 63 O.R. wounded and missing. 2 O.R. missing believed killed, 9 O.R. Acc injured.*

***Samuel is buried in Jerusalem Military Cemetery along with 2515 other servicemen. His grave is F. 58.***

# HARRY BOWYER

**Harry Bowyer** was born in Knutsford in 1900, one of four children born to William (a builder) and Annie Bowyer of 131, Middlewich Road, Northwich.

He joined the 1/10th Manchester Regiment but was transferred to ¼[th] Battalion of the East Yorkshire Regiment, becoming Private no. 30805 on entering France on the 5th April 1918.

**Brief history of the Battalion:**

The ¼[th] Battalion, the East Yorkshire Regiment was a territorial battalion based at Londesborough Barracks, Hull as a territorial battalion. They served as part of York and Durham Brigade, Northumbrian Division. They had just departed for their annual summer camp when war broke out and they were at once recalled to Hull and then moved to Darlington to take up defensive positions with a number of men being detailed to guard the wireless station at Stockton on Tees. Over 75% of the men volunteered for service abroad at the first time of asking, by the end of October 1914 those who had not volunteered were transferred to other units and other volunteers took their place in the 4th battalion which moved to Newcastle to prepare for service overseas.

They proceeded to France on the 17th of April 1915 landing at Boulogne. Concentrating in the area of Steenvoorde just as the German army attacked Ypres, using poison gas for the first time. The 50th Division were rushed into the battle. On the 12th of May became 150th

Brigade of the 50th Division. They saw action in The Battle of St Julien, The Battle of Frezenburg Ridge and The Battle of Bellewaarde Ridge. In 1916 they fought on the Somme at The Battle of Flers-Courcelette, The Battle of Morval and The Battle of the Transloy Ridges. In 1917 they were in action at Arras during The First Battle of the Scarpe, The Capture of Wancourt Ridge and The Second Battle of the Scarpe before moving north for the Third Battle of Ypres. In 1918 they fought on the Somme, in the Battles of the Lys and The Battle of the Aisne, leaving the troops exhausted. On the 15th of July 1918 the battalion was reduced to cadre and transferred to Lines of Communication, and then on the 16th of August they transferred to 116th Brigade, 39th Division at Varengeville and took on a role supervising courses of instruction for newly arrived American troops.

*Thanks to the Wartime Memories Project.*

Harry died from Dysentery – that exact date of his death is unknown but recorded as sometime in August 1918.

*Harry is remembered on the Soissons memorial, France along with the names of 3,878 other servicemen.*

103

# JAMES BRACEGIRDLE
*(Brother of William)*

**James Bracegirdle** was born in Knutsford in 1892, one of seven children born to George (a labourer) and Sarah (a charwoman) of 10, Swinton Square, Knutsford. James took up the trade as a gardener.

He enlisted in the army as Private no. 433 of the Cheshire Yeomanry before transferring to the 10th Battalion of the Kings (Shropshire Light Infantry as Private no. 250548.

**Brief history of the Battalion:**

10th (Shropshire & Cheshire Yeomanry) Battalion was formed at Cairo on 2nd March 1917 from the dismounted troopers of the Shropshire Yeomanry and the Cheshire Yeomanry. Served in Palestine in the 231st Brigade of the 74th "Broken Spur" Division.

It took part in the second and third battles of Gaza, July-November 1917 and then in the operations for the capture of Jerusalem (December 1917) and in the capture of Jericho (February 1918). In the attack on Birj-el-Lisaneh, near Tel Asur, on March 10th 1918, Pte. Harold Whitfield won the only VC to a Shropshire regiment for the Great War.

In May 1918, the 10th went to France, serving on the Lys in August and then at Epehy and captured the notorious "Quadrilateral" in November.

Having captured Tournai – where the 53rd had been in action in 1794 – it ended the war near Ath in Belgium and was disbanded in Shrewsbury in June1919.

James was killed in action on the 10th March 1918.

**On that fateful day:**
The war diary shows no entry for this day.

*James is buried in Jerusalem War Cemetery along with 2515 other servicemen. His grave is F. 48.*

# GILBERT JOHN BRACEGIRDLE

**Gilbert John Bracegirdle** was born in Truro in Cornwall in 1896, one of three children born to John (a former sergeant in the Royal

Artillery) and Blanche Bracegirdle, who later resided at Barnshaw Cottage, Mobberley, Cheshire. Gilbert later moved to 135, Ashley Road, Hale, Cheshire.

He enlisted at Altrincham in 1914 and entered the Royal Garrison Artillery as Private no. 43696 initially with the 14th then the 199th Siege Battery. He went to the Balkans front.

He rose to the rank of Sergeant.

*Royal Garrison Siege Battery in action in 1915.*

### Brief history of the Battalions:

The Siege Batteries were deployed behind the front line, tasked with destroying enemy artillery, supply routes, railways and stores. The batteries were equipped with heavy Howitzer guns firing large calibre 6, 8 or 9.2 inch shells in a high trajectory.

*Royal Garrison Siege Battery in action in 1915.*

Gilbert died of wounds on the 6th February 1917.

**On that fateful day:**
Gilbert died of wounds when he was accidentally killed when a delayed-fuse detonator went off.

*Gilbert is buried in Guillemont Road Cemetery, Guillemont, France along with 2,263 other servicemen. His grave is I. J. 5.*

# WILLIAM BRACEGIRDLE
*(Brother of James)*

**William Bracegirdle** was born in Knutsford in 1891, one of seven children born to George (a labourer) and Sarah Ann Bracegirdle of Swinton Square, Knutsford. William was a milk-hand.

He joined the 1ˢᵗ Battalion of the Kings (Shropshire Light Infantry) in 1915 as Private no. 24336.

**Brief history of the Battalion:**

A Regular battalion, based in the UK and Ireland, 1903-14. In Tipperary in August 1914 when mobilised for war, when it joined 16ᵗʰ Brigade, 6ᵗʰ Division and landed at St.Nazaire, France, on September 10ᵗʰ. It took part in the early battles of the Aise and Marne and thereafter served entirely on the Western Front and in just about every major engagement.

It was present in the First Battle of Ypres in 1914 and in the Ypres salient, 1915, when it played a leading part in the attack on the Hooge pprox.s in August. In April 1916, again at Ypres, they took part in the severe fighting for the capture of positions on the Ypres-Langemarck road, losing their CO, Lt. Col. Luard in the process.

Saw service on the Somme in 1916 under Lt. Col. Murray (Morval and Transloy Ridges; breaking of the "Quadrilateral" at Cinchy during the battle of Flers-Courcelettes) and at Arras and Cambrai in 1917.

In January 1918, the battalion was serving with 5ᵗʰ Army and met the brunt of the great German Spring Offensive on March 21ˢᵗ, being just about annihilated at Lagnicourt – not one combatant officer was left and only 53 other ranks came out of action.

The battalion was completely re-formed under Lt. Col. Meynell and within ten days of being all but destroyed, was back in the line at Ypres and fought continuously in the salient until late August.

After taking part in the fighting on the Hindenburg Line in 1918 with 4ᵗʰ Army, including the desperate fighting around St. Quentin, 1 KSLI served through the final operations against the Germans right up until the Armistice in November.

1 KSLI then became part of the Rhineland occupation force.

They lost 53 officers and 986 other ranks killed during the war.

William 'died' on the 2ⁿᵈ May 1917 which seems to suggest he died of disease but as his records no longer exist it is impossible to know for certain.

*William is buried in Etaples Military Cemetery, France together with 10,771 other servicemen. His grave is XIX. O. 2.*

# JAMES BRADLEY M.C.
## *(Brother of Sephin)*

**James Bradley** lived at Mere Old Hall, Mere, Knutsford.

He enlisted in the Royal Fusiliers but was commissioned into the Suffolk Regiment on the 16th May 1915 as a Second Lieutenant in the 2nd Battalion.

He arrived in France on the 18th November 1915.

**Brief history of the Battalion:**

2nd Battalion, the Suffolk Regiment were at the Curragh in Ireland serving with 14th Brigade, 5th Division when war broke out in August 1914. They returned to England and proceeded to France landing at Le Havre on the 17th of August 1914. They were in action in The Battle of Mons and the subsequent retreat, after suffering heavy casualties at The Battle of Le Cateau the transferred to GHQ Troops. On the 22nd of October 1915 they transferred to 76th Brigade in 3rd Division. They took part in the Winter Operations of 1914-15, The First Attack on Bellewaarde and the Actions at Hooge. In 1916 they took part in The Actions of the Bluff and St Eloi Craters then moved to The Somme for The Battle of Albert, The Battle of Bazentin helping to capture Longueval, The Battle of Delville Wood and The Battle of the Ancre.

*Thanks to the Wartime Memories Project.*

James won the Military Cross for gallantry on the 1st March 1916 during a battle to take The Bluff on the Ypres-Comines canal.. His citation in the London Gazette states:

*'For conspicuous gallantry for operations when leading his men and consolidating the positions won. When his company commander was wounded he took charge and held on to a wrecked trench under heavy shell-fire for two days and two nights.'*

James was reported missing in action on the 21st July 1916.

**On that fateful day:**
The war diary states that the Battalion was in action in an attack on Longueval and Delville Wood.

James was one of eleven officers killed that day – the diary makes no mention of how many 'other ranks' were lost.

*James is remembered on the Thiepval Memorial. Along with the names of*
*72,208 other servicemen.*

# SEPHIN BRADLEY
*(Brother of James)*

**Sephin Bradley** was a career soldier. He was commissioned in the
1ˢᵗ Battalion of the Suffolk Regiment as a Second Lieutenant on the
20ᵗʰ September 1911

**Brief history of the Battalion:**
1st Battalion, The Suffolk Regiment were in Khartoum, Sudan when war was declared in August 1914. They returned to England as soon as a territorial unit arrived to take over the garrison. The 1st Suffolk's arriving home on the 23rd of October. On the 17th of November 1914 they joined 84th Brigade 28th Division, at Winchester. They proceeded to France from Southampton, landing at le Havre on 18th of January, the division concentrated in the area between Bailleul and Hazebrouck, being joined by additional Territorial units. In 1915 they were in action in The Second Battle of Ypres and The Battle of Loos.

*Thanks to the Wartime Memories Project.*

On the 24th May 1915 the war diary states:

*'Valuable information was obtained by Lt. S Bradley and 2/Lt Kemble, who carried out reconnaissance under the fire of the enemy.'*

The following day (25th May) Shephin was reported missing later confirmed as killed in action.

**On that fateful day:**
The Battalion war diary for the Battalion says that they were involved in an attack on Bellewarde Farm near Poperinghe on the day he was killed.

***He is remembered on the Menin Gate Memorial along with 54,405 other servicemen.***

*Note:*
*The 2/Lt Kemble mentioned with Sephin in the war diary was later promoted to Captain Henry Noel Kemble of 353, East 22nd Street, Flatbush, Brooklyn, New York, a native of Jamaica. He was killed in action on the 20th July 1916 aged 20. His brother Cyril Stewart Kemble was also killed in action on the 27th May 1918 also aged 20.*

# GEORGE H. BRANDRETH

George **Brandreth** was born in Toft, Knutsford in 1899, the son of George (a carter) and Ellen Brandreth of 34, Silk Mill Street, Knutsford. The later moved to Church Hill, Knutsford,
George enlisted in the 1/5th Battalion of the Manchester Battalion, becoming Private no. 57098.

**Brief history of the Battalion:**
The 1/5th Battalion, Manchester were a Territorial unit, when war broke out in August 1914 they were based at Bank Chambers, Wigan as part of the Manchester Brigade, East Lancashire Division. They were mobilized and moved to Rochdale to prepare for service overseas. They proceeded to Egypt arriving at Alexandria on the

25th of September to defend the Suez Canal from the Turkish forces in Palestine. They were in action in the Turkish attack on the Suez Canal on the 3rd of February 1915. In the first week of May the division embarked from Alexandria, landing at Cape Helles, Gallipoli, where they saw action in the attempts to capture the heights of Krithia and the Battle of Krithia Vineyard which was a diversionary attack for the British Landing at Suvla Bay. The much depleted division were evacuated from Gallipoli in the first week of January 1916, returning to Alexandria via Mudros. They returned to duty on the Suez Canal and were in action in the Battle of Romani in August. In early 1917 they were ordered to the Western Front, departing from Alexandria in February. They went into the front line at Ephey, moved to Havrincourt then were withdrawn to Albert for rest and training during July and August. In September they moved north to Flanders and were in action during the Third Battle of Ypres at Iberian, Borry Farm, Beck House Farm and Sans Souci. At the end of the month they moved to the coast at Nieuport until November when they moved to La Bassee Canal at Givenchy. On the 19th of February 1918 they transferred to 126th Brigade still with 42nd Division. In 1918 they saw action during The Battle of Bapaume, The First Battle of Arras, The Battle of the Ancre, The Battle of Albert, The Second Battle of Bapaume, The Battle of the Canal du Nord, The pursuit to the Selle and The Battle of the Selle.

*Thanks to the Wartime Memories Project.*

George was wounded (I have been unable to locate where or when) and discharged from the army as being medically unfit on the 22nd April 1918.

He died on the 30th August 1919.

*George is buried in Knutsford Cemetery.*

# RAYMOND ARTHUR BRERETON

**Raymond Arthur Brereton** was born in Shropshire in 1895, the son of Joshua (a piano tuner) and Ruth Brereton of Paddock Hill, Mobberley. They later moved to The Plough and Flail, Mobberley where Ruth became the publican on the death of her husband.

Raymond enlisted in 'B' Company of the 12th Battalion, Northumberland Fusiliers.

**Brief history of the Battalion:**

The 12th (Service) Battalion the Northumberland Fusiliers was formed at Newcastle in September 1914 as part Kitchener's Third New Army and joined 62th Brigade, 21st Division. The Division concentrated in the Tring area, training at Halton Park before winter necessitated a move into local billets in Tring, Aylesbury, Leighton Buzzard, High Wycombe and Maidenhead. The artillery was at High Wycombe and Berkhamsted, RE at Chesham, and ASC at Dunstable. In May 1915 the infantry moved to huts at Halton Park, whilst the artillery moved to Aston Clinton with one brigade staying at Berkhamsted and the RE to Wendover. On the 9th of August they moved to Witley Camp. They proceeded to France during the first week of September and marched across France their first experience of action being in the British assault at Loos on 26th September 1915, suffering heavy casualties, just a few days after arriving in France. In 1916 they were in action in the Battles of The Somme, including The Battle of Morval in which the Division captured Gueudecourt.

Raymond died of wounds on the 26th June 1916.

**On that fateful day:**

I have been unable to discover where and when he received his wounds.

*Raymond is buried at Mericourt-L'Abbe Communal Cemetery Extension, together with 411 other servicemen. His Grave is I. C. 2.*

# FREDERICK BRIERLEY

**Frederick Brierley** was born in Knutsford in 1898, the son of Sam (a plumber and painter) and Annie Brierley of 4, Church View, Knutsford.

Fred joined the 8th Battalion of the Cheshire Regiment, becoming private no 24426.

He arrived in the Balkans on the 4th October 1915.

**Brief history of the Battalion:**

The 8th (Service) Battalion, Cheshire Regiment was raised in Chester on the 12th of August 1914 as part of Kitchener's First New Army and joined 40th Brigade, 13th (Western) Division which assembled on Salisbury Plain. 40th Brigade moved to Chiseldon and Cirencester in September 1914. Near the end of February the Division concentrated at Blackdown in Hampshire. They moved to the Mediterranean from the 13th of June 1915 landing at Alexandria then moving to Mudros, by the 4th of July to prepare for a landing at Gallipoli. The infantry landed on Cape Helles between the 6th and 16th of July to relieve 29th Division. They returned to Mudros at the end of the month, and the entire Division landed at ANZAC Cove between the 3rd and 5th of August. They were in action in The Battle of Sari Bair, The Battle of Russell's Top and The Battle of Hill 60, at ANZAC. Soon afterwards they transferred from ANZAC to Suvla Bay. They were evacuated from Suvla on the 19th and 20th of December 1915.

*Thanks to the Wartime Memories Project.*

Fred was killed in action on the 27th November 1915 – just 38 days after arriving at the front.

**On that fateful day:**
There is no entry in the war diary for this date.

*Fred is remembered on the Helles memorial, along with the names of 20,885 other servicemen.*

# THOMAS BRITCLIFFE

**Thomas Britcliffe** was born in 1884 in Knutsford, the son of Robert (a gardener) and Amanda Britcliffe of Swinton Square, Knutsford. Thomas took up the trade as a basket maker. He married Mabel in 1911 and moved to 7, Green Street, Knutsford.

He enlisted in the 1ˢᵗ Battalion of the Kings (Liverpool Regiment) and arrived in France 12ᵗʰ August 1914.

It would appear Thomas joined the army prior to the outbreak of the war and was with the British Expeditionary force in France. He was killed in action on the 13ᵗʰ November 1914

**On that fateful day:**

The Battalion had been in action since the beginning of the month.

The written history of the Regiment in WW1 says of this day – 'Raining heavily, making the trenches worse than ever. Their boots had long since ceased to be water-proof. Their feet were benumbed. They were standing in water up to their knees – for many days they stood like this.'

The History of the Kings Regiment (Liverpool) Vol 1 – Everard Wyrall, Page 94.

The war diary for this date states:

### *13.11.14 POLDERHOEK WOOD*

*Very wet. Trenches are getting into a horrible state and the paths are frightfully muddy.*

*HLI (*Highland Light Infantry*) were ordered back to reinforce the 6ᵗʰ Bde and half of 'D' Company had to take over their trenches. This means holding about a mile of trenches with 500 men.*

*Casualties 7.*

***Thomas has no known grave and is remembered at the Menin gate memorial along with the names of 54,406 other servicemen.***

# ARTHUR CUTHBERT BROOKE-TAYLOR

**Arthur Cuthbert Brooke-Taylor** was born in Bakewell, Derbyshire in 1888, the con of Herbert (an army coronel) and Mary Taitt Brooke-Taylor of The Close, Bakewell. He resided with his aunt, Mary Tailor at 'Heathcote', St. Johns Road, Knutsford. He was a heating and ventilation engineer.

He enlisted in the army, becoming a Second Lieutenant in the 6th Battalion of the Manchester Regiment.

**Brief history of the Battalion:**

The 1/6th Battalion, Manchester were a Territorial unit, when war broke out in August 1914 they were based in Stretford Road, Hulme as part of the Manchester Brigade, East Lancashire Division. They were mobilized and moved to Rochdale to prepare for service overseas. They proceeded to Egypt arriving at Alexandria on the 25th of September to defend the Suez Canal from the Turkish forces in Palestine. They were in action in the Turkish attack on the Suez Canal on the 3rd of February 1915. In the first week of May the division embarked from Alexandria, landing at Cape Helles, Gallipoli, where they saw action in the attempts to capture the heights of Krithia and the Battle of Krithia Vineyard which was a diversionary attack for the British Landing at Suvla Bay. Arthur died of wounds on the 4th June 1915.

*Arthur is remembered on the Helles Memorial, Turkey, along with the names of 20,885 other servicemen.*

# JOHN BROOKS

**John Brooks** was born in Knutsford in 1890, one of four children born to George (a railway signalman) and Rebecca Brooks of 4, Hayton Street, Knutsford.

He enlisted at Sheffield in the Royal Field Artillery but was transferred into the 2/7th Manchester Regiment as Private no. 60534.

**Brief history of the Battalion:**
The Battalion was formed in August 1914 in Burlington Street, Manchester, becoming part of Manchester Brigade, East Lancashire Division. On the 25th September 1914 they landed at Alexandria in Egypt. Then on the 6th May 1915 they landed on Gallipoli. On the 26th May 1915 the formation became 127th Brigade, 42nd (East Lancashire) Division. On the 28th December 1915 they were evacuated from Gallipoli, landed on Mudros and preceded to Egypt. On the 2nd March 1917 the Battalion landed Marseilles and proceeded to the Western Front.

*Thanks to The Long, Long Trail.*

John was killed in action on the 21st March 1918.

**On that fateful day:**
The war diary gives no information for this date.

*John is remembered on the Pozieres Memorial, France along with 2,758 other servicemen.*

# JOHN HENRY BROWN

**John Henry Brown** was born in Knutsford, Cheshire in 1900, one of six surviving children of John Thomas (a foreman railway porter) and Sarah Ellen Brown of 3, King Street, Knutsford.

Due to his age, John enlisted late in the war. He did so at Altrincham recruiting centre, joining the Kings (Liverpool) Regiment as Private no. 87151, but soon was transferred into 'D' Company, No. 3 Section of the 46th Machine Gun Corp (Infantry) as Private no. 146739.

**Brief history of the Battalion:**

The 46th Machine Gun Company joined 15th (Scottish) Division on the 11th of February 1916. In spring 1916, they were involved in the German gas attacks near Hulluch and the defence of the Kink position. They were in action during the Battles of the Somme, including The Battle of Pozieres, The Battle of Flers-Courcelette and the capture of Martinpuich, The Battle of Le Transloy and the attacks on the Butte de Warlencourt. In 1917 they were in action in The First and Second Battle of the Scarpe, including the capture of Guemappe during the Arras Offensive. They then moved north to Flanders and were in action during the Battle of Pilckem and The Battle of Langemarck. In 1918 they fought in The First Battle of Bapaume, The First Battle of Arras. They joined with the other

Machine Gun Companies of the Division to form 15th MG Battalion on the 17th of March 1918. The 15th Machine Gun Battalion was formed on the 17th of March 1918 from the Machine Gun Companies of 15th (Scottish) Division. They were in action at The Battle of the Soissonnais and the Ourcq taking part in the attack on Buzancy, and The Final Advance in Artois.

*Thanks to the Wartime Memories Project*

John died of wounds on the 18th October 1918, just 24 days before the armistice was signed.

**On that fateful day:**
John's service records no longer exist so it has proven impossible to say when and where he was wounded. We do know that in the final days of the war his Battalion was engaged in the final push against the Germans in the Artois region of France. The family were told that John had 'been shot through the neck and died a few days later.

*John is buried in St. Sever Cemetery Extension, Rouen, Seine-Maritime, France, along with 8,647 other servicemen. His grave is S. II. J. 6.*

# LEONARD BROWN

**Leonard Brown** was born in Mobberley, Cheshire in 1887, one of six children born to Alfred (a hay-cutter) and Sarah (a laundress) of Brownedge, Mobberley. Leonard was a poulterer.

His service records no longer exist but we know he enlisted in the army at Salford sometime after 1915 and became Private no 11772 in the 16th Battalion of the Lancashire Fusiliers, later transferring to the 63rd company of the Machine Gun Corp as Private no. 14816.

**Brief history of the Company:**
The 63rd Machine Gun Company joined 21st Division on the 4th of March 1916. They were in action in the Battles of The Somme,

Leonard was posted 'missing presumed killed' on the 1st July 1916 – the infamous first day of the battle of the Somme when the British army lost almost 59,000 soldiers (19,000 killed or missing)

**On that fateful day:**
To-date I have been unable to locate the war diary for this infantry brigade.

*Leonard has no know grave but he is remembered on the Thiepval Memorial, Somme, France along with the name of 72,203 other servicemen.*

# WILLIAM BROWN

**William Brown** was born in Mobberley in 1881, the son of Joseph and Elizabeth who went on to reside at 94, Moss Lane, Hale, Cheshire. William continued to reside at Mobberley as a boarded in Pepper Lane and later at New Mill. William was a farm labourer.

He enlisted in the 9th Battalion of the Cheshire Regiment, becoming Private no. 12703.

He arrived in France on the 19th July 1915.

**Brief history of the Battalion:**
The 9th (Service) Battalion, Cheshire Regiment was raised in Chester on the 13th of September 1914 as part of Kitchener's Second New Army and joined 58th Brigade, 19th (Western) Division. They moved to Salisbury Plain for training and went into billets in Basingstoke in December 1914 for the winter, returning to Salisbury Plain in March 1915. They proceeded to France on the 19th of July 1915, landing at Boulogne, the division concentrated near St Omer. Their first action was at Pietre, in a diversionary action supporting the Battle of Loos. In 1916 they were in action during the Battle of the Somme, capturing La Boisselle and being involved in the attacks on High Wood, The Battles of Pozieres Ridge, the Ancre Heights and the Ancre.

*Thanks to the Wartime Memories Project.*

William was killed in action on the 4th July 1916.

**On that fateful day:**
The war diary states that the Battalion was 'resting' on this day.

*William is remembered on the Thiepval Memorial along with the names of 72,208 other servicemen who have no known graves.*

# JOHN ARTHUR BURGESS

**John Arthur Burgess** was born in Mobberley in 1898, one of eight children born to John (a labourer) and Elizabeth Burgess of Paddock Hill, Mobberley.

He enlisted in the army becoming Private no. 27609 of the 3$^{rd}$ Battalion of the Cheshire Regiment.

John was presumed drowned when the troop carrier RMS Transylvania was torpedoed and sunk by the German U Boat U63 with the loss of 412.

*RMS Transylvania.*

John was presumed drowned on the 4th May 1917.

*John is remembered on the Savona memorial, Italy.*

# SIDNEY BURGESS

**Sidney Burgess** was born in 1899 at Mere, Cheshire, one of three children born to Henry (a farmer) and Emily Burgess of Park Gate Farm, Mere, Knutsford.

He enlisted in the army becoming Gunner no. 230409 of the 51st battery of the 39th Brigade of the Royal Field Artillery.

**Brief history of the Brigade:**
XXXIX Brigade, Royal Field Artillery served with 1st Division. 1st Division was one of the first British formations to proceed to France in August 1914, and fought on the Western Front throughout the war, taking part in most of the major actions. In 1914 they were involved in The Battle of Mons and the subsequent retreat, The Battle of the Marne, The Battle of the Aisne, the First Battle of Ypres and the Winter Operations of 1914-15. In 1915 they were in action during The Battle of Aubers and The Battle of Loos. In 1916 they were in action in the Battles of the Somme. In 1917 they saw action in The German retreat to the Hindenburg Line and the Third Battle of Ypres. In 1918 the Battles of the Lys, the Second Battles of Arras, the Battles of the Hindenburg Line, The Battle of the Selle and The Battle of the Sambre, in which the Division fought the Passage of the Sambre-Oise Canal.

He was died of wounds on the 23rd September 1918. I have been unable to locate when and where he was wounded.

*Sidney is buried in Vadencourt British Cemetery, France along with over 750 other servicemen. His grave is II. B. 42.*

# SIDNEY BURGESS

**Sidney Burgess** was born in High Legh in 1897, one of nine children born to James (a concrete maker) and Mary Ann Burgess of Kirkmans Green, High Legh. Sidney was a labourer.

Sidney joined the army on reaching 19 and became Private no. 23905 of the 8th Battalion of the Kings (Shropshire Light Infantry).

**Brief history of the Battalion:**

The 8th was a war-raised Service Battalion, formed in Shrewsbury in September 1914. They joined the 66th Brigade of the 22nd Division and landed in France on 28th October 1915, heading for Amiens.

After only a few weeks on the Western Front, the Battalion was sent to Macedonia, arriving on November 6th 1915. It spent the remainder of the war on the Salonika front around Doiran, suffering severely from malaria as well as from its encounters with the enemy. Periods of routine trench work, in reserve, along the Struma or in the defences of Salonika were interspersed with some severe fighting, as at "Pip Ridge", near Lake Doiran, in February 1917 and again in September 1918.

8/KSLI took part in the final drives against the Bulgarian army in 1918 and after the Armistice was sent to Doiran and Dedeagatch and then into Bulgaria.

*Thanks to the S.K.L.I Museum.*

Sidney was killed in action on the 25th April 1917.

**On that fateful day:**
The war diary states:

*24.4.17*
*01.00 hrs.*
*The Liaison Officer from 11th Worcester's Regt. On right of 'B' Company reported that Batt had encountered very serious opposition & required urgent support. Orders were sent to the two platoons in support in Green Ravine to proceed without delay in accordance with the pre-arranged plan to reinforce the left flank of the 11th Worcester Regt. Under difficulties & (a) message was dispatched to the 66th Infantry Bde requesting 2 additional platoons to support 'B' Company on Hill 380.*

*01.38 hrs*
*'B' Company (right) estimated its casualties at about 20 including Capt. L. Profit killed.*

*02.45 hrs*
*A Bulgarian prisoner was brought in from 'D' Coy (centre) & reports received that number of enemy wounded were lying on MAMELON WORKS*

*02.53 hrs.*
*Heavy rifle fire was reported on PETIT COURONNE.*

*04.00 hrs*
*A Bulgarian prisoner was brought in. M.O. Captain BOWELL proceeded to JACKSON Ravine in front of MAMELON*

**04.05 hrs**
*One platoon South Lancs arrived from Bde Reserve & another platoon was also sent from Bde Reserve to Green Ravine.*

**04.45 hrs**
*2/Lt Austin reported that 11ᵗʰ Worcester's owing to very heavy losses had withdrawn to their original trench line and for that reason the right flank of HILL 380 was exposed.*

**05.00 hrs**
*Three Bulgarian prisoners were brought in.*

**05.30 hrs**
*'C' Coy (left) reported that enemy counter attack launched about 05.00 hrs and had been repulsed.*

**09.25 hrs**
*Another Bulgarian prisoner brought in. From this time forward with the exception of intermittent shelling of our trenches by the enemy no incident occurred worthy of record.*

**20.00 hrs**
*Red and green lights were sent up on PETIT COURONNE & at 20.40 hrs the centre Coy 'D' reported that the enemy were advancing to the attack. The barrage signal was accordingly sent up from Bn. H.Qrs and from the left Coy 'C', simultaneously with this a report was received that HILL 380 was being heavily shelled. Our barrage opened and at the same time that of the enemy was directed against out trench line. Two platoons under 2/Lt Fairer ('A' Coy) were ordered to reinforce the centre company.*

**21.00 hrs**
*Our barrage with that of the enemy died down & enemy counter-attack*

*was easily driven off, only a few of their attacking party reaching our new wire. 'D' Coy (Centre) detailed a bombing party which was sent forward and succeeded in driving the enemy out of a ravine in front of JACKSON Ravine.*

**21.35 hrs**
*Lt Lloyd who was wounded reported at H.Qrs & brought information concerning the recent enemy counter-attack*

**21.45 hrs**
*Two platoons from Bde reserve were detailed in Reserve.*

**23.35 hrs**
*Searchlights were operating on HILL 380.*

The diary makes no mention of casualties but the attacks by the enemy continued throughout the following day. He died in the same action as Henry Royle.

***Sidney is buried in Karasouli Military Cemetery, Greece along with 1421 other servicemen. His grave is F 1404.***

# JOHN BURNS

**John Burns** enlisted in the 10th Battalion of the Cheshire Regiment, becoming Private no. 65778 having previously been in Private no. 72631 in the Cheshire Yeomanry.

**Brief history of the Battalion:**
The 10th (Service) Battalion, Cheshire Regiment was raised in Chester on the 10th of September 1914 as part of Kitchener's Third New Army and joined 75th Brigade, 25th Division. They trained at Codford St Mary and spent the winter in billets in Bournemouth. They moved to Aldershot for final training in May 1915 and proceeded to France on the 26th of September, the division concentrating in the area of Nieppe. On the 26th of October they transferred to 7th Brigade still with 25th Division. Their first action was in defence of the German attack on Vimy Ridge in May 1916. They then moved to The Somme and joined the Battle just after the main attack, with 75th Brigade making a costly attack near Thiepval on the 3rd of July. The Division was in action at The Battle of Bazentin, The Battle of Pozieres and The Battle of the Ancre Heights. In 1917 they were in action at The Battle of Messines attacking between the Wulverghem-Messines and Wulverghem-Wytschaete roads. In the Third battle of Ypres were in action during The Battle of Pilkem. In 1918 they were in action on The Somme, in the Battles of the Lys suffering heavy losses. On the 21st of June 1918 the battalion was reduced to cadre strength with many troops transferring to the 9th Cheshires.

*Thanks to the Wartime Memories Project.*

John died of wounds on the 23$^{rd}$ June 1918 – I have been unable to discover where and when he received his wounds as his Army service record no longer exists.

*John is buried in Sezanne Communal Cemetery, France along with 127 other servicemen. His grave is B. 29.*

# ALBERT CASH

**Albert Cash** was born in 1895, one of nine children born to John (a bricklayers labourer) and Annie Cash of 3, White Bear Yard, Canute

Square, Knutsford. On leaving school Albert became a Post Office messenger boy.

His service records no longer exist but we know he joined the army in 1914, becoming Private no. 1628 in the 1st/5th Battalion of the Cheshire Regiment. He arrived in France on the 15th February 1915.

**Brief history of the Battalion:**

The 1/5th (Earl of Chester's) Battalion, Cheshire Regiment was a Territorial unit based in in Chester with Cheshire Brigade, Welsh Division, when war was declared in August 1914. They were immediately mobilised and moved to Shrewsbury and Church Stretton, by the end of August they moved to Northampton and then in December to Cambridge for final preparations. They preceded to France on the 15th of February 1915, landing at Le Havre to join 14th Brigade, 5th Division. They were in action in The Battle of Mons and the subsequent retreat, The Battle of Le Cateau, The Battle of the Marne, The Battle of the Aisne, The Battles of La Bassee and Messines and The First Battle of Ypres.

In 1915 they were in action at The Second Battle of Ypres and the Capture of Hill 60. In autumn 1915, many units were exchanged with units from the newly arrived volunteer 32nd Division, to stiffen the inexperienced Division with regular army troops. On the 29th of November 1915 they became a Pioneer Battalion. On the 13th of February 1916 the 1/5th Chester's transferred to the newly reformed 56th (London) Division, in the Hallencourt area in February. In 1916 they were in action on The Somme taking part in the diversionary attack at Gommecourt on the 1st of July.

*Thanks to the Wartime Memories Project.*

Albert was killed in action on the 1st July 1916 – the worst day the British army had ever suffered for they lost over 59,000 men, with over 19,000 dead, on the first day of the Battle of the Somme – many within the first two hours.

It was said at the time – "The army that took two years to train was lost in two hours."

**On that fateful day:**
The war diary states:

*' 1.7.16 – Gommecourt*
*Attack on FAIR FARM*
*Attack commenced at 7.30am*
*The attack went over by platoons in 3 waves behind LRB (London Rifle Brigade), QWR (Queens West Riding) QVR (Queen Victoria Rifles).*
*Owing to the intense bombing by the Germans many casualties were inflicted on the company which had to eventually withdraw from the enemy's position about 8am. No platoon commanders returned with their men.*
*Killed 4 officers 113 OR'*

***Albert has no known grave and is remembered on the Thiepval Memorial, France, along with the names of 72,230 other servicemen.***

# DONALD CASH

**Donald Cash** was born in 1895 in Knutsford, the son of Samuel (a woodman) and Jessie (a housekeeper) of Park Cottage, King Street, Knutsford. Donald became an insurance clerk.

He enlisted in the Royal Field Artillery as Bombardier no. L/9670 of 'B' Battery 149th Brigade.

**Brief history of the Battery:**
CXLIX Brigade, Royal Field Artillery served as Divisional artillery with 30th Division. 30th Division was formed in April 1915 from units of Kitchener's 5th New Army and concentrated near Grantham. In the Autumn they moved to Larkhill, Salisbury and proceeded to France in November, sailing to Le Havre and Boulogne and concentrating near Amiens. In 1916 they were in action during the Battle of the Somme, in which the Division captured Montauban. In 1917 they took part in the pursuit of the German retreat to the Hindenburg Line, the Arras Offensive and The Battle of Pilkem Ridge. In 1918 they were in action on The Somme and in the Battles of the Lys.

Donald died of wounds on the 13th June 1917. I have been unable to discover when and where he received his wound.

*Donald is buried at Hop Store Cemetery, Belgium. His grave is I. B. 42. There is also a memorial to him in Knutsford Cemetery.*

# GEORGE CASH

George Cash was born in Knutsford in 1897, the son on Robert (a labourer) and Annie of 11, Moordale Road, Knutsford. George became a farm labourer.

He joined the 4th Battalion of the South Wales Borderers as Private no. 44858.

**Brief history of the Battalion:**

4th (Service) Battalion, The South Wales Borderers was raised at Brecon in August 1914 as part of Kitchener's Third New Army and joined 40th Brigade, 13th (Western) Division which assembled on Salisbury Plain. 40th Brigade moved to Chiseldon and Cirencester in September 1914. Near the end of February the Division concentrated at Blackdown in Hampshire. They moved to the Mediterranean from the 13th of June 1915 landing at Alexandria then moving to Mudros, by the 4th of July to prepare for a landing at Gallipoli. The infantry landed on Cape Helles between the 6th and 16th of July to relieve 29th Division. They returned to Mudros at the end of the month, and the entire Division landed at ANZAC Cove between the 3rd and 5th of August. They were in action in The Battle of Sari Bair, The Battle of Russell's Top and The Battle of Hill 60, at ANZAC. Soon afterwards they transferred from ANZAC to Suvla Bay. They were evacuated from Suvla on the 19th and 20th of December 1915, and after a week's rest they moved to the Helles bridgehead. They were in action during the last Turkish attacks at Helles on the 7th of January 1916 and were evacuated from Helles on the 8th and 9th. The Division concentrated at Port Said, holding forward posts in the Suez Canal defences. On the 12th of February 1916 they moved to Mesopotamia, to join the force being assembled near Sheikh Sa'ad for the relief of the besieged garrison at Kut al Amara. They joined the Tigris Corps on the 27th of March and were in action in the unsuccessful attempts to relieve Kut. They were in action in The Battle of Kut al Amara, The capture of the Hai Salient, he capture of Dahra Bend and The passage of the Diyala, in the pursuit of the enemy towards Baghdad. Units of the Division were the first troops to enter Baghdad, when it fell on the 11 March 1917. The Division then joined "Marshall's Column" and pushed north across Iraq, fighting at Delli 'Abbas, Duqma, Nahr Kalis, crossing the 'Adhaim on the 18 April and fighting at Shatt al 'Adhaim. Later in the year they were in action in the Second and Third Actions of Jabal Hamrin and fought at Tuz Khurmatli the following April. By the 28th of May 1918, Divisional HQ had moved to Dawalib and remained there until the end of the war, enduring extreme summer temperatures.

*Thanks to the Wartime Memories Project.*

George 'died' on the 24th September 1918. It can be assumed he died of disease.

*He is buried in Baghdad (North Gate) War Cemetery, Iraq, along with 4,160 other servicemen. His grave is III. D. 8.*

# DANIEL CAUFIELD

**Daniel Caulfield** was born in 1873 and was married to Sarah Jane and had five Children. He was a general labourer and they all lived at 12, Old Market Square, Knutsford.

Daniel joined the Territorial Army in 1908, becoming part of the 3rd V.B. Cheshire. He was awarded the Territorial Efficiency Medal. On the outbreak of the war he enlisted in the 2nd Battalion of the Cheshire Regiment and became Private no. 11675.

**Brief history of the Battalion:**
The 2nd Battalion, Cheshire Regiment was a regular unit of the British Army and was in Jubbulpore, India when war broke out in August 1914. They returned to England, landing at Devonport on the 24th of December 1914. They joined 84th Brigade, 28th Division, at Winchester and proceeded to France, embarking at Southampton and landing at Le Havre on the 17th of January 1915. 28th Division concentrated in the area between Bailleul and Hazebrouck. They saw action in the Second Battle of Ypres, where casualties were high and The Battle of Loos.

Daniel arrived in France with his Battalion on the 10th March 1915 and he was killed in action on the 3rd October 1915. The remaining record show that his body was never found as it states 'Death Assumed'.

*Daniel is remembered on the Loos Memorial along with 20,603 others.*

# JOSEPH CHAPMAN

**Joseph Chapman** was born in Knutsford on the 27th November 1898. He was one of five children who resided with his widowed mother, Elizabeth, at 14, Gannon Square, before the family moved to 8, Silk Mill Street, Knutsford.

On leaving school he was employed at the soap works in Plumley, Cheshire as a labourer.

His service records still exist so we know he enlisted in the army in 1916 and was with the 65th Training Reserve Regiment then in January 1918 he was called into the 13th Battalion of the Welsh Regiment, becoming Private no. 63670. His service record makes reference to the poor state of his teeth.

He went to France, arriving on the 11th January 1918.

**Brief history of the Battalion:**

The 13th (2nd Rhondda) Battalion, Welsh Regiment was raised in Cardiff on the 23rd of October 1914. They joined 129th Brigade, 43rd Division at Rhyl. On the 29th of April 1915, the formation was renamed, 114th Brigade, 38th (Welsh) Division. They moved to Winchester in August 1915 for final training and proceeded to France, landing at Le Havre in December 1915. In July 1916 they were in action at Mametz Wood on The Somme, suffering severe casualties. The Division did not return to major action for more than 12 months. In 1917 they were in action in the Third Battles of Ypres. In 1918 they were in action on The Somme, in the Battles of the Hindenburg Line and the Final Advance in Picardy.

*Thanks to the Wartime Memories Project.*

Joseph died of wounds on the 8ᵗʰ October 1918 at the 2ⁿᵈ Northumberland Field Ambulance.

*Joseph is buried in the Faubourg D'Amiens Cemetery, Arras, France, together with 2,647 other servicemen. His grave is I. A. 17.*

# HARRY CLARK

**Harry Clark** was born in Stretton, Cheshire in 1885, the son of John Clark of Pool Lane, Lymm. He married Margaret Curry Johnson in

July 1914and set up home at 92, Mobberley Road, Knutsford. They had one son. Harry was a joiner.

He enlisted in the East Lancashire Regiment before transferring into the 8th Battalion of the Leicestershire Regiment as Private no. 37815.

**Brief history of the Battalion:**

The 8th Battalion, Leicestershire Regiment was raised at Leicester in September 1914 as part of Kitchener's Third New Army and joined 23rd Division as Divisional Troops. In April 1915 they transferred to 110th Brigade, 38th Division and proceeded to France on 29th of July 1915 the Division concentrating near Tilques. On the 8th of July 1916 they transferred with 110th Brigade to 21st Division. They were in action in the Battles of The Somme, including The Battle of Morval in which the Division captured Geudecourt. In 1917 they were in action during The German retreat to the Hindenburg Line, the Arras offensive, the Third Battles of Ypres and The Cambrai Operations.

Harry was killed in action on the 1st October 1917.

**On that fateful day:**

There is no specific entry for this day in the war diary.

*Harry is remembered on the Tyne Cot memorial along with the names of 34,952 other servicemen.*

# LEONARD CLARKE

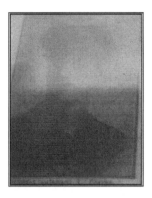

**Leonard Clarke** was born in Toddington, Leicestershire, one of seven children born to Thomas (a domestic coachman) and Isabella Clarke. The family came to live at Heathside, Albert Street, Knutsford.

Although Leonard's service record no longer exists, we know he joined the army sometime in 1916 and became a second Lieutenant

*Men of the 7th Battalion – just out of the trenches near Arras, March 1917. Photo courtesy of the Shropshire Military Museum.*

in the 4th Battalion of the Kings Shropshire Light Infantry, later to be attached to the 7th Battalion.

## Brief history of the Battalion:

A war-raised Service Battalion under Lt. Col. J.H.Barber, it was formed in Shrewsbury in September 1914 and joined the 76th Brigade of the 25th Division; landed at Boulogne on 28th September 1915 and served entirely on the Western Front.

The 7 KSLI first saw action in the Ypres Salient in the winter of 1915-16 and moved to the Somme in July 1916; fought at Bazentin Ridge and then at Serre on the Ancre later in the year.

It was in action at Arras and in the three severe battles of the Scarpe in April-May 1917. Back in the Ypres sector in 1917, the 7th took part in the fighting at Polygon Wood in September (3rd battle of Ypres) and was back on the Somme for the battles of 1918.

After taking part in the offensives of summer-autumn of 1918, at Albert, Bapaume, the Canal du Nord and the Selle, the 7th ended the war as part of the 8th Brigade of the 3rd Division, at Romeries, near Solesmes, France. It was disbanded in Shrewsbury in June 1919.

The 7th suffered more casualties than any other KSLI battalion, with 1048 killed in action or died during the war, and earned more battle honours than any other KSLI battalion.

*Thanks to the Shropshire Regimental Museum.*

Leonard died of wounds on the 4th October 1917.

## On that fateful day:

The war diary reports that the Battalion was based near St Omer and there was no action on that day but mentions that the shelling was heavy and several OR were lost to it. It would appear that Leonard was one of them.

*Leonard is buried in Dozinghem Military Cemetery, West-Vlaanderen,*
*Belgium along with 3,240 other servicemen. He is in grave VI. I. 11.*

# ROBERT CLARKE

**Robert Clarke** was born in Knutsford in 1891, the son of Mary Jane
Clarke (A dressmaker) of 4, Swinton Square, Knutsford. On leaving
school Robert became a hamper-maker.

His service record no longer exists but we know he joined the army at Altrincham and became Private S/18841 of the Seaforth Highlanders.

He later transferred to the 13th Company of the Labour Corp.

**Brief history of the Corp:**

The Labour Corps was raised in 1915 and disbanded in 1921; today their roles are undertaken by the Royal Logistics Corps.

The Corps grew to some 389,900 men (more than 10% of the total size of the Army) by the Armistice. Of this total, around 175,000 were working in the United Kingdom and the rest in the theatres of war. The Corps was manned by officers and other ranks who had been medically rated below the "A1" condition needed for front line service. Many were returned wounded. Labour Corps units were often deployed for work within range of the enemy guns, sometimes for lengthy periods.

In April 1917, a number of Infantry Battalions were transferred to the Corps. The Labour Corps absorbed the 28 ASC Labour Companies between February and June 1917. Labour Corps Area Employment Companies were formed in 1917 for salvage work, absorbing the Divisional Salvage Companies. In the crises of March and April 1918 on the Western Front, Labour Corps Units were used as emergency infantry. It became the 18th -19th Labour Corps in May 1917.

The Corps always suffered from its treatment as something of a second class organization: for example, the men who died are commemorated under their original Regiment, with Labour Corps being secondary. Researching men of the Corps is made extra difficult by this, as is the fact that few records remain of the daily activities and locations of Corps units.

*Thanks to the Wartime Memories Project.*

Robert was killed in action on the 18th June 1917.

**On that fateful day:**
To-date I have been unable to locate the war diary for this Battalion.

*Robert is buried in Poperinge New Military Cemetery, West-Vlaanderen, Belgium, along with another 948 servicemen. He is in grave II. F. 12.*

# WILLIAM TABERER CLAYTON

**William Taberer Clayton** was born in Rostherne, Knutsford, Cheshire in 1895, one of four children (he was a twin with his sister Dorothy) of Thomas (an estate clerk) and Nellie Clayton of The Old Hall, Rostherne.

Originally Williams joined the 9th Battalion of The Lancers but transferred, becoming Rifleman no. 11643 of the 1st Battalion of the Rifle Brigade (The Prince Consort's Own).

**Brief history of the Battalion:**
1st Battalion, The Rifle Brigade were at Colchester with 11th Brigade, 4th Division when war broke out in August 1914. 4th Division was held back from the original British Expeditionary Force by a last minute decision to defend England against a possible German landing. The fate of the BEF in France and the lack of any move by the Enemy to cross the channel reversed this decision and they proceeded to France, landing at Le Havre on the 23rd of August 1914 in time to provide infantry reinforcements at the Battle of Le Cateau. They were in action at the Battle of the Marne, The Battle of the Aisne and at The Battle of Messines in 1914. In 1915 they fought in The Second Battle of Ypres.

William was killed in action on the 6th July 1915.

**On that fateful day:**
The war diary for this day goes on for numerous pages and is reproduced as an appendix.

*William is buried in Talana Farm Cemetery, Belgium along with 520 other servicemen. His grave is I. C. 11.*

# JOHN BROOKS CLOSE-BROOKS M.C.

John Brooks Close-Brookes was born in Eccles, Lancashire in 1895.One of five children born to John (a banker) and Emily Close-Brooks. He resided at Birtles Hall, Chelford. He was a master cotton spinner. He married Frances Mary Brown (1890-1989) in April 1912 and later to Glenham Grove, Saxmundham, Suffolk.

He was a Captain in the 3rd Battalion of the Manchester Regiment. He was later attached to the 2nd Battalion:

**Brief history of the Battalion:**
2nd Battalion, The Manchester Regiment were in Curragh serving with 14th Brigade, 5th Division when war broke out in August 1914. They mobilised and proceeded to France landing at Le Harve on the 17th of August 1914 and entrained to La Cateau. They went into action on the 23rd forming a defensive line near Wasmes on the Mons-Conde canal at The Battle of Mons and the subsequent retreat. They were also in action at The Battle of Le Cateau, The Battle of the Marne, The Battle of the Aisne, at La Bassee, Messines and The First Battle of Ypres. In 1915 they were in action at The Second Battle of Ypres and the Capture of Hill 60. In autumn 1915, many units from 5th Division were exchanged with units from the newly arrived volunteer 32nd Division,

to stiffen the inexperienced Division with regular army troops and the 2nd Manchesters moved with 14th Brigade to 32nd Division.

*Thanks to the Wartime Memories Project.*

It was here at Ypres that he won his Military Cross – his citation reads:

*'For conspicuous gallantry at Ypres on the 10th June 1915, in attempting to rescue an N.C.O. belonging to his regiment. The N.C.O. was lying 35 yards in front of the enemy's trench when Lieutenant Close-Brooks crawled out to him in broad daylight. When finding that he was already dead he attached a cord to his body, which was recovered.'*
*London Gazette 1917*

Arthur died of wounds at the No. 8 British Field Ambulance on the 10th January 1917, and despite him being an officer I have been unable to discover how and where he was wounded.

***Arthur is buried in Amara Military Cemetery, Iraq along with 3,621 other servicemen. His grave is XXVIII. A. 2.***

**Note:**
*He left £63,103 3s 4d in his will.*

# JAMES COLLIER

**James Collier** was born in Swinton, Lancashire in 1884. He lived as a boarder with Mr and Mrs Peers at 17, Moordale Road, Knutsford. He was a sorting clerk/telephonist. He married Sarah Ann and they lived at 41, Mount Street, Swinton.

He enlisted at Knutsford in the 74th Signal Company of the Royal Engineers, becoming Sapper no. 182734.

**Brief history of the Company:**
74th Field Company, The Royal Engineers served with 15th (Scottish) Division. 15th (Scottish) Division was formed in September 1914, as part of Kitchener's Second New Army. They proceeded to France in the second week of July 1915. They were in action in the Battle of Loos in 1915. In spring 1916, they were involved in the German gas attacks near Hulluch and the defence of the Kink position. They were in action

*Signaller in action*

155

during the Battles of the Somme, including The Battle of Pozieres, The Battle of Flers-Courcelette and the capture of Martinpuich, The Battle of Le Transloy and the attacks on the Butte de Wallencourt

In 1917 they were in action in The First and Second Battle of the Scarpe, including the capture of Guemappe during the Arras Offensive. They then moved north to Flanders and were in action during the Battle of Pilckem and The Battle of Langemarck. In 1918 they fought in The First Battle of Bapaume, The First Battle of Arras, The Battle of the Soissonnais and the Ourcq taking part in the attack on Buzancy, and The Final Advance in Artois.

*Thanks to the Wartime Memories Project.*

James died of wounds on the 2nd November 1918 (just nine days before the armistice was signed) at the 1st Australian Casualty Clearing Station. I have been unable to discover where and when he received those wounds.

***James is buried in Fretin Communal Cemetery, France, along with 25 other servicemen. His grave is no. 9.***

# JOSEPH CONSTERDINE

**Joseph Consterdine** was born in 1893 in Manchester and raised by his grandfather. By 1911 he had move to be a grocers assistant at Chorley, nr. Mobberley, Cheshire.

He enlisted in the 4th Battalion of the Grenadier Guards in 1914, become Guardsman no. 21831 he and arrived in France on the 13th October 1915.

**Brief history of the Battalion:**
The 4th Battalion, Grenadier Guards was formed at Marlow. They proceeded to France on the 14th of July 1915 and joined 3rd Guards Brigade, Guards Division on the 19th of August. They were in action in The Battle of Loos. In 1916 they fought on The Somme in The Battle of Flers-Courcelette and The Battle of Morval, capturing Lesboeufs.

*Thanks to the Wartime Memories Project.*

Joseph was killed in action on the 16th September 1916.

**On that fateful day: The war diary records no action on this day.**

*Joseph has no know grave and he is remembered on the Thiepval Memorial along with the names of 72,203 other servicemen.*

# WILLIAM COOPER

**William Cooper** was born in Mobberley in 1894, where he resided with his aunt in Newton Hall Lane, Mobberley.

He enlisted in the 10th Battalion of the Cheshire Regiment in September 1914 as Private no. 15670.

He died at home on the 27th September 1914.

*William is buried in Codford (St Mary's) Churchyard, Wiltshire.*

# EDWARD CONNOR

**Edward Connor** was born in Northenden, Cheshire in 1900 one of five children born to John Connor (a coachman) of 36, Cranford Avenue, Knutsford.

Edward enlisted in the army but being too young to go abroad (under 19) he joined the 10th Training Battalion before transferring to the 24th Battalion of the Royal Fusiliers (City of London) as Private no. G/81505.

**Brief history of the Battalion:**

24th (2nd Sportsman's) Battalion, The Royal Fusiliers (City of London Regiment) was raised at the Hotel Cecil in the Strand, London, on the 25th of September 1914 by E.Cunliffe-Owen. In June 1915 they joined 99th Brigade, 33rd Division at Clipstone camp near Mansfield in Nottinghamshire in July 1915. In August they moved to Salisbury Plain for final training and firing practice. In November they received orders to prepare to proceed to France and the Divisional Artillery and Train were replaced by the units raised for the 54th (East Anglian) Division. By the 21st of November the 33rd Division had concentrated near Morbecque. On the 25th of November 1915 The Battalion transferred to 2nd Division as part of an exchange to strengthen the inexperienced 33rd Division. They took part in the Winter Operations 1914-15 and in 1915 saw action at The Battle of Festubert and The Battle of Loos. In 1916 they fought in the Battles of the Somme and the Operations on the Ancre. In 1917 they were in action during The German retreat to the Hindenburg Line, the Battles of Arras and The Battle of Cambrai. In 1918 they fought on the Somme, in the Battles of the Hindenburg Line.

Edwards died of wounds on the 20th July 1918. But as with almost all ordinary ranks (OR) it is almost impossible to locate where and when they were wounded.

*Edward is buried in Bac Du Sud Cemetery, Bailleulval, France along with 723 other servicemen. His grave is II. E. 20.*

# THOMAS CORK

**Thomas Cork** was born in Plumley in 1899, one of two children born to Thomas (a labourer) and Hannah Cork of Lower Peover, Cheshire.

He enlisted in the army but was unable to go abroad until he was nineteen so he became Private no.32433 of the Training Battalion. He later became Private no. 13518 of the 1ˢᵗ Battalion of the Royal Dublin Fusiliers.

**Brief history of the Battalion:**

1ˢᵗ Battalion, The Royal Dublin Fusiliers were in Madras when war broke out in August 1914. They returned to Britain landing at Plymouth on the 21ˢᵗ of December 1914. They went into to billets in Torquay, moving in January 1915 to Nuneaton to join 86ᵗʰ Brigade, 29ᵗʰ Division. On the 16ᵗʰ of March 1915 they sailed from Avonmouth for Gallipoli, via Alexandria and Mudros. They landed at Cape Helles on the 25ᵗʰ of April 1915 suffering heavy casualties and on the 30ᵗʰ of April they merged with the 1ˢᵗ Royal Dublin Fusiliers forming a unit nick named the 'Dubsters'. They resumed their own identity on the 19ᵗʰ of May 1915. They were evacuated from Gallipoli in the first week of January, returning to Egypt. On the 13ᵗʰ of March 1916 they sailed from Port Said for Marseilles, travelling by train to concentrate in the area east of Pont Remy by the end of March. In July they went into action in the Battles of the Somme. In 1917 they were in action in the First, Second and Third Battle of the Scarpe during the Arras Offensive, then moved to Flanders and fought in the The Battle of Langemarck. On the 19th of October they transferred to 48th Brigade in 16th (Irish) Division. On the 10th of February 1918 they absorbed 200 men from the disbanding 8/9th Battalion. In 1918 they were in action on the Somme 1918 suffering very heavy casualties and on the 14th of April 1918 the battalion amalgamated with 2nd battalion. On the 26th of April 1918 the 1dt Dublin Fusiliers transferred to 86th Brigade, 29th Division. They were involved in The Action of Outtersteene Ridge, The capture of Ploegstreert and Hill 63 during the Advance in Flanders.

Thomas was killed in action on the 13th May 1918.

**On that fateful day:**
The war diary states:

*13.5.18 PAPOTE*
*Immediate orders given by Commanding Officer for men to evacuate gas-affected areas. Batt. Therefore accommodated in bivouacs S.W. of PAPOTE. 2 O.R. killed by shellfire.*

***Thomas is buried in Cinq Rues British Cemetery, Hazebrouck along with 226 other servicemen. His grave is D. 10.***

# CHRISTOPHER CORK

**Christopher Cork** was born in Middlewich, Cheshire in 1878, one of seven children born to Thomas (a farmer) and Mary Cork of Allostock, nr. Knutsford. He was a straw and hay dealer.

At the outbreak of the war Christopher joined the 4th Battalion of the Grenadier Guards as Guardsman no. 21356.

He died from illness on the 12th March 1915 while still in England.

*Christopher is buried in Streatham Park Cemetery, Surrey.*

# ALFRED COTTRELL

**Alfred Cottrell** was born in Pickmere, Knutsford in 1895. One of twelve children born to Joseph (a labourer/horse breeder) and Alice Cottrell of Yew Tree Cottage, Knutsford Road, Pickmere. They later moved to 6, Hart Street, Altrincham, where Alfred became an assistant at a milliner's shop.

He enlisted in the 11th Battalion of the Cheshire Regiment, becoming Private no.33035.

He arrived in France on the 5th March 1917 and on the 28th March 1917 he was transferred to the 13th Battalion.

On the 28th June 1917 he was appointed Lance Corporal (unpaid).

**Brief history of the Battalion:**

The 13th (Service) Battalion, Cheshire Regiment was raised at Port Sunlight on 1 September 1914 by Gershom Stewart, MP. They moved to Chester and joined 74th Brigade, 25th Division in Kitchener's Third New Army. The Division assembled in the area around Salisbury for training and the 13th Cheshires spent the winter in billets in Bournemouth. The division moved to Aldershot in May 1915 for final training. They proceeded to France on the 25th of September 1915 and concentrated in the area of Nieppe. Their first action was in defence of the German attack on Vimy Ridge in May 1916. They then moved to The Somme and joined the Battle just after the main attack, with 75th Brigade making a costly attack near Thiepval on

the 3rd of July. The Division was in action at The Battle of Bazentin, The Battle of Pozieres and The Battle of the Ancre Heights. In 1917 they were in action at The Battle of Messines attacking between the Wulverghem-Messines and Wulverghem-Wytschaete roads. In the Third battle of Ypres were in action during The Battle of Pilkem.
*Thanks to the Wartime Memories Project.*

Alfred was killed in action on the 10th August 1917.

**On that fateful day:**
The war diary has no entry for this day.

*Alfred is remembered on the Menin Gate memorial along with the names of 54,405 other servicemen.*

*Note:*
*His service record still exists and shows that his mother committed suicide on the 30th March 1916 by 'hanging herself whilst temporarily insane'. – Albert was granted compassionate leave but was fined 3 days' pay when he 'overstayed' his leave entitlement.*

# DONALD CRAGG
### *(Brother of Harry)*

**Donald Cragg** was born in Knutsford in 1893, one of eight children born to George (A draper) and Esther (a dress-maker), who lived at Hayton Street, Knutsford. On leaving school he became a bookstall clerk.

He attested in September 1914 and was posted straight away, becoming Private 16413 of the 10th Battalion of the Loyal North Lancashire Regiment. He arrived in France on the 3rd July 1915.

**Brief history of the Battalion:**

10th (Service) Battalion, The Loyal North Lancashire Regiment was raised at Preston in October 1914 as part of Kitchener's Third New Army joined 22nd Division as army troops. They trained on the South Downs, spending the winter in Eastbourne. In April 1915 they transferred to the newly forming 112th Brigade, 37th Division, which was concentrating at Cholderton on Salisbury Plain. They proceeded to France, landing at Boulogne on the 1st of August, the division concentrating near Tilques. They went into action in The Battle of the Ancre. In 1917 they fought in The First Battle of the Scarpe, including the capture of Monchy-le-Preux, The Second Battle of the Scarpe and The Battle of Arleux. They were in action during the Third Battles of Ypres.

*Thanks to the Wartime Memories Project.*

On the 16th October 1916 he was awarded 7 days Field Punishment for being 'improperly dressed'. (See Appendix Three)

Donald was wounded on three occasions, once when he was shot in the foot, and twice he was 'gassed' whilst in the trenches.

He was promoted to Corporal on the 11th April 1917.

Donald was killed in action on the 13th August 1917.

**On that fateful day:**

The war diary makes no mention of any casualties for that day – it states:

*'13.8.17 IN THE TRENCHES.*

*Patrol of 'A' Coy goes out and obtains useful information.*
*We are heavily shelled.'*

*Donald has no known grave and is remembered on the Menin Gate Memorial along with the names of 54,406 other servicemen.*

# HARRY CRAGG
## *(Brother of Donald)*

**Harry Cragg** was born in Knutsford, one of eight children born to George (A draper) and Esther (a dress-maker), who lived at Hayton Street, Knutsford. On leaving school Harry became a plumber.

He married Lucy Hurst in 1913 and they and their future children moved in with his now widowed mother.

His service records no longer exist but we know he joined the army early in the war and became Private no. 17226 of the Loyal North Lancashire Regiment before transferring to the East Lancashire Regiment as Private no. 16418.

**Brief history of the Battalion:**

The 8th (Service) Battalion, East Lancashire Regiment was raised at Preston in September 1914 as part of Kitchener's Third New Army and joined 74th Brigade, 25th Division. They trained at Codford and spent the winter in billets in Bournemouth from November 1914, when they became Divisional Troops with 25th Division. In March 1915 they transferred to the newly formed 112th Brigade, 37th Division at Ludgershall and proceeded to France in late July, concentrating near Tilques. They went into action in The Battle of the Ancre.

*Thanks to the Wartime Memories Project.*

Harry was killed in action on the 15th July 1916.

**On that fateful day:**
The war diary states:

**'*15.7.16 POZIERS***
*At 9.20 am after heavy bombardment of POZIERS for one hour, the Battalion led a Brigade attack on the village. 'A' & 'B' Coys in the front line, 'C' & 'D' Coys in support. Owing to artillery barrage and machine gun fire the Battalion was unable to achieve its objective but was joined by other units of the Brigade and consolidated existing trenches to east ans south east of POZIERS. At 5 p.m. a further bombardment of POZIERS was carried out and the Battalion with remainder of the Brigade attempted another assault of POZIERS at 6-8 PM, this assault was again held up by machine guns and the wire not being cut in the hedges surrounding the village. The Battalion handed over the trenches to the 10th Bn Loyal North Lancashire Regt. At 2.30 am and proceeded to trenches in close support.*
*Casualties*
*officers 1 killed 8 wounded*
*Other ranks 56 killed 276 wounded 33 missing.'*

***Albert has no known grave and is remembered on the Thiepval Memorial, France, along with the names of 72,230 other servicemen.***

# HARRY CUMMINS

**Harry Cummins** was born in Manchester in 1887 and resided at 21, Cranford Avenue, Knutsford with his wife Bridget Margaret and his two step children.

He enlisted in the army in 1916 becoming a sapper in the 488th Field Company of the Royal Engineers, later transferring to Special Brigade Depot as Sapper no. 204176.

He was injured, suffering severe damage to his knee when he fell from a ladder, resulting in him being discharged from the army as 'unfit'.

He died in the 11th January 1921.

*Harry is buried in Knutsford Cemetery – his grave tended by the Commonwealth War Graves Commission.*

# JAMES CUMMINS

**James Cummins** was born in Mobberley in 1896, one of three children born to James (a baker) and Mary Ann Cummins who moved to Rusholme, Manchester and later to 56, Layton Road, Blackpool. James was a labourer.

He enlisted in the 13th Battalion of the Cheshire Regiment, becoming Private no. 10331.

He arrived in France on the 15th January 1915.

**Brief history of the Battalion:**

The 13th (Service) Battalion, Cheshire Regiment was raised at Port Sunlight on 1 September 1914 by Gershom Stewart, MP. They moved to Chester and joined 74th Brigade, 25th Division in Kitchener's Third New Army. The Division assembled in the area around Salisbury for training and the 13th Cheshires spent the winter in billets in Bournemouth. The division moved to Aldershot in May 1915 for final training. They proceeded to France on the 25th of September 1915 and concentrated in the area of Nieppe. Their first action was in defence of the German attack on Vimy Ridge in May 1916. They then moved to The Somme and joined the Battle just after the main attack, with 75th Brigade making a costly attack near Thiepval on the 3rd of July. The Division was in action at The Battle of Bazentin, The Battle of Pozieres and The Battle of the Ancre Heights.

James was killed in action on the 7th July 1916.

**On that fateful day:**
The war diary states:

*7.7.16*
*'Over the parapet at 8.05am and after suffering severe casualties we reached out objective and consolidated.*
*Casualties killed 10 Officers 243 Other Ranks.*

*James is remembered on the Thiepval Memorial, along with the names of 72,208 other servicemen.*

# ALBERT E. CURBISHLEY

**Albert E. Curbishley** was born in Knutsford in 1898, one of ten children born to Joseph (an estate labourer) and Alice Curbishley of Toft Road, Knutsford. The family later moved to Moor Head, Bexton, Knutsford.

After leaving school he became a postman.

His service records still exist. At the outbreak of was Albert signed up on the 3rd September 1914, falsely stating that he was 19 years. He became Private no. 15609 in the 10th Battalion of the Cheshire Regiment

On the 7th October 1914 his father wrote to his commanding officer, informing him that Albert was under age and asking for him to be released or assigned duty at home.

His commanding officer said –

'This man is of 17 years of age. He will be held to serve."

So on the 26th September 1915, aged 18 years, he duly went to France with his Battalion.


**Boy Soldiers:**

When war was declared in 1914 it was thought that 'it would all be over by Christmas', so lads by the thousands thronged the recruiting offices throughout the country – many of them under age.

The rules were that to enlist and then fight abroad a recruit had to be over nineteen years of age. He could enlist at eighteen but only when he turned nineteen could he leave the UK and fight abroad. NO ONE could join the army under eighteen – but these rules were formulated years before the First World War and no one could have foreseen the urgent need for more men in a mechanised war – though just looking back 50 years to the American Civil War might have given those in power some inkling.

The rush that followed Lord Kitchener's appeal could not have been anticipated either with few of the recruiting officers scrutinized the enlistment form too carefully and so if the lad volunteered to fight and he was fit and healthy then why not take him?

It is thought that, in the patriotic fervour pervading the times, as many as a quarter of a million under aged lads joined-up.

These young lads, not only lied about their age – they also gave a false name, making it almost impossible for their worried parents tracking them down and bringing them home.

So – all in all, tracing these young lads is a difficult task but Ernest is an exception – he gave his correct name.

The first of the boy soldiers arrived at the front in early 1915. The first major battle that involved 'Kitchener's Volunteers' was the Battle of Loos. It did not go well for the British and they suffered 50,000 casualties killed and wounded. 3,600 of these were under the age of nineteen – an age when they should not even have been in the trenches.

On the first day of the Battle of the Somme in 1916, 500 'Boy Soldiers' were killed and 2,000 wounded. BY the time the battle had

*Officer to young boy of thirteen – "Do you know where young boy go who tell lies?"*
*Young boy – "To the front, Sir."*
*F.H. Townsend Punch 11ᵗʰ August 1916*

ended, 18,000 'Boy Soldiers' had been killed or wounded. It was rumored that a boy as young as twelve was involved in this battle.

There were those who opposed the use of underage soldiers. Across the nation, these were parents whose sons had frequently joined up without their knowledge. Many turned to the one man who found fame by fighting for the return to the UK of these 'Boy Soldiers' – Liberal MP for Mansfield Sir Arthur Markham.

Markham was born on August 25th 1866 into a successful coal mining family. In 1900, Markham was elected MP for Mansfield. Accusations that he was anti-war were false. Markham gave one of his homes in Folkestone, Kent, to the government to house overseas officers and paid for packages to be sent to British POW's. He also feared that industry would be left short of workers if too many youths left to fight.

Markham used the platform of the House of Commons to openly question the War Office about its recruitment policy. His principal opponent in this chamber was the Under-Secretary of State for War, Harold Tennant. Within the House, many sided with Tennant as they saw that the wellbeing of the army was more important than what many MP's viewed as nothing more than a legal nicety. Markham accused the War Office of dishonesty. In a statement to the House he said:

"There has been fraud, deceit and lying practiced by the War Office."

Tennant claimed that the War Office was, in fact, the victim of deceit as it had been the boys who had lied about their age, not the War Office enticing in underage soldiers. Markham accused the government of issuing confidential instructions to the Army to ignore age. Tennant denied this and stated that nothing regarding this had been brought to his attention. Tennant put the case of the government plainly:

"In this country no boys under the prescribed age as laid down by regulations have been enlisted with the knowledge of the War Office. Boys under that age are not wanted either with or without the consent of their parents."

As the war proceeded, Markham became inundated with requests from parents who wanted to know where their sons were. Those who had enlisted under false names were all but impossible to contact. Markham concerned himself with those boys aged between fourteen and sixteen. Tennant responded by issuing War Office directives to senior Army officers that 'Boy Soldiers' should be returned to the UK but that the onus for carrying this through lay with senior army commanders in France and Belgium. However, senior officers were not keen to lose trained men and the War Office was not keen to force their directives through.

Markham was seemingly out on a limb and the strain of it was too much for him. He died in August 1916 aged just 50. The number of 'Boy Soldiers' recruited fell drastically after the Battle of the Somme had ended when conscription was brought in. Anyone conscripted aged eighteen or over had to bring proof of their age with them.

No official figures were ever kept for the recruitment of 'Boy Soldiers'. In fact, it would have been impossible to do so with so many youths lying about their age. The record books would have stated 'aged 18' for someone who may have been fifteen. The gravestone of Rifleman V J Strudwick in a CWG cemetery just outside of Ypres does have his true age on it – 15 – but very many clearly do not.

***Information courtesy of The History Learning Site.***


On the 25th November 1915 he received a gunshot wound to his shoulder, resulting in him being hospitalised at the 77th Field hospital. He returned to England aboard the hospital ship SS Cambria, a converted P&O liner and spent 33 days in hospital, before returning to his unit in France.

He was transferred to the 9th Battalion on the 3rd March 1916

**Brief history of the 10th Battalion:**

The 10th (Service) Battalion, Cheshire Regiment was raised in Chester on the 10th of September 1914 as part of Kitchener's' Third New Army and

joined 75th Brigade, 25th Division. They trained at Codford St Mary and spent the winter in billets in Bournemouth. They moved to Aldershot for final training in May 1915 and proceeded to France on the 26th of September, the division concentrating in the area of Nieppe. On the 26th of October they transferred to 7th Brigade still with 25th Division
.

**Brief history of the 9th Battalion.**
Their first action was at Pietre, in a diversionary action supporting the Battle of Loos. In 1916 they were in action during the Battle of the Somme, capturing La Boisselle and being involved in The attacks on High Wood, The Battles of Pozieres Ridge, the Ancre Heights and the Ancre.

*Thanks to the Wartime Memories Project.*

Albert was killed in action on the 5th November 1916.

**On that fateful day:**
These is no entry for this day in the war diary.

*Albert has no known grave and is remembered on the Thiepval Memorial,*
*Somme, France, together with the names of 72,203 other servicemen.*

# EDWARD CURBISHLEY

**Edward Curbishley** was born in Knutsford in 1889, one of thirteen children born to Joseph (a railway platelayer) and Amelia Curbishley of 6, Malt Street, Knutsford.

After leaving school he was employed a general labourer.

His service records no longer exist but we know he enlisted in the army sometime after 1915, becoming Private no. 31510 in the 2/4th Battalion of the Prince of Wales (South Lancashire) Regiment.

**Brief history of the Battalion:**

The Battalion was formed in Warrington in September 1914 and on the 8th February 1915 moved to Ashford in Kent and was attached to the 172nd Brigade in the 57th (2nd West Lancashire) Division.

In June 1916 they moved again, this time to Mytchett (Aldershot) and went on to Blackdown.

On the 16th February 1917 they landed at Boulogne, France. The 57th took part in the following engagements:

Second Battle of Passchendaele (eighth phase of the Third Battle of Ypres)

Battle of the Scarpe (first phase of the Second Battles of Arras 1918, also known as the Second Battle of the Somme)

Battle of Drocourt-Queant (second phase of the Second Battles of Arras 1918)

Battle of the Canal du Nord (third phase of the Battles of the Hindenburg Line)

Battle of Cambrai (sixth phase of the Battles of the Hindenburg Line) Edwards was killed in action on the 28th August 1918.

**On that fateful day:**
There is no record of any specific action on this day recorded on the war diary.

*Edward has no known grave but is remembered on the Vis-En-Artois Memorial, France along with the names of 9847 other servicemen.*

# OLIVER CURBISHLEY

**Oliver Curbishley** was born in Knutsford in 1894, the son of William (A gardener/labourer at Tatton Estate) and Emma Curbishley of

19, Stanley Road, Knutsford. When his father died Emma took up employment as a school caretaker.

On leaving school he became a general labourer.

He attempted to join the Territorial Army in July 1914 but was rejected after a few days.

He joined the army sometime in 1916, becoming Private no. 18649 in the 10th Battalion of the Cheshire Regiment.

**Brief history of the Battalion:**

The 10th (Service) Battalion, Cheshire Regiment was raised in Chester on the 10th of September 1914 as part of Kitchener's Third New Army and joined 75th Brigade, 25th Division. They trained at Codford St Mary and spent the winter in billets in Bournemouth. They moved to Aldershot for final training in May 1915 and proceeded to France on the 26th of September, the division concentrating in the area of Nieppe. On the 26th of October they transferred to 7th Brigade still with 25th Division. Their first action was in defence of the German attack on Vimy Ridge in May 1916. They then moved to The Somme and joined the Battle just after the main attack, with 75th Brigade making a costly attack near Thiepval on the 3rd of July. The Division was in action at The Battle of Bazentin, The Battle of Pozieres and The Battle of the Ancre Heights. In 1917 they were in action at The Battle of Messines attacking between the Wulverghem-Messines and Wulverghem-Wytschaete roads. In the Third battle of Ypres were in action during The Battle of Pilkem.

*Thanks to the Wartime Memories Project.*

Oliver was killed in action on the 13th April 1917.

**On that fateful day:**
The war diary states:

**13.4.17 Batt in Training at the rear.**
*Later relieved the North Lancs at 8pm*
    *Unfortunately a salvo of 5.9 between La Bizet Church and Motor Car Corner killed 2 OR.*

*Oliver is buried in Tancrez Farm Cemetery, Hainaut, Belgium along with 333 other serviceman. His grave is II. F. 7.*

# CHARLES HENRY DANIEL

**Charles Henry Daniel** was born in Knutsford in 1891, one of four children born to Edwin (a butcher) and Emma Daniel. The family moved from Hazel Grove to live at 26, Richmond Hill, Cross Town, Knutsford when Edwin died.

On leaving school Charles took up his father's trade and became a butcher.

At the outbreak of war Charles enlisted at the Altrincham Recruiting Office, becoming Private no. 11145 of the 1st Battalion of the Cheshire Regiment on the 31st August 1914.

**Brief history of the Battalion:**

The 1st Battalion, Cheshire Regiment was a regular unit of the British Army and was in Londonderry when war broke out in August 1914 with 15th Brigade in 5th Division. They returned to England and proceeded to France with the British Expeditionary Force, landing at Le Havre on the 16th of August 1914. They saw action at The Battle of Mons, The Battle of the Marne, The Battle of the Aisne, The Battles of La Bassee, at Messines and in The First Battle of Ypres. Between the 3rd of March and 7th of April 1915 they were attached with 15th Brigade to 28th Division in in exchange for 83rd Brigade in order to familiarise the newly arrived troops with the Western Front. In 1915 they were in action in The Second Battle of Ypres and the Capture of Hill 60.

*Thanks to the Wartime Memories Project.*

Charles was killed in action on the 6th May 1915.

**On that fateful day:**

There is no entry in the war diary for this day except to say the Battalion was in the area of Hill 60

*Charles has no known grave so is remembered at the Menin Gate Memorial, Ypres, along with the names of 54,406 other servicemen who likewise have no know grave.*

# THOMAS DANIEL

**Thomas Daniel** was born in Mobberley in 1897, the son of Henry (a publican) and Annie of Mobberley.

He joined the 1/5th Royal Warwickshire Regiment as Private 29135.

**Brief history of the Battalion:**

1/5th Battalion, The Royal Warwickshire Regiment was a territorial with HQ in Thorp Street, Birmingham in 1914, serving with the Warwickshire Brigade, South Midland Division. The units of the Division had just departed for their annual summer camp when war broke out in August 1914 and they were at once recalled. They mobilised for war service on 5 August 1914 and moved to concentrate in the Chelmsford area by the second week of August 1914 and commenced training. They proceeded to France, from Southampton, landing at le Havre on the 22$^{nd}$ of March 1915. The Division concentrated near Cassel. On the 13$^{th}$ of May 1915 the formation was renamed 143$^{rd}$ Brigade, 48$^{th}$ (South Midland) Division. In 1916 they were in action in the Battle of the Somme, suffering heavy casualties on the 1$^{st}$ of July in assaulting the Quadrilateral (Heidenkopf). They were also in action at The Battle of Bazentin Ridge, capturing Ovillers, The Battle of Pozieres Ridge, the Battle of the Ancre Heights and The Battle of the Ancre. In 1917 the Division occupied Peronne during the German Retreat to the Hindenburg Line and were in action in the Third Battles of Ypres.

*Thanks to the Wartime Memories Project.*

Thomas was killed in action on the 4$^{th}$ October 1917.

**On that fateful day:**
The war diary (Appendix II) states:

*4.10.17*
*The enemy opened a heavy fire along our forming up line at twenty minutes before zero, & 'B' Coy suffered 7 casualties (O.R's) and 1 officer before zero.*

**Right Company ('A') Coy)**
*No. 1 platoon under 2/Leiut. W. Shadbolt got to VALE HOUSE with only a few casualties & consolidated the flanks.*

*No. 2 platoon passed through No. 1, had some severe fighting around WINZIG took twenty prisoners & consolidated.*

*No. 3 & 4 platoons cane through No's 1 & 2 but the NEW ZEALANDERS (1 AUKLAND BN.) lost direction & pushed our men over to the left.*

*No. 3 platoon under 2?Leiut. A. F. Foreman got on to the high ground about D.2. central and consolidated with the 1/6<sup>th</sup> R.War. R. on the left and the NEW ZEALANDERS on the right, he had about 10 men remaining.*

*No.4 platoon after casualties from M.G. fire on the left reached D.".c 7.1 & dug in.*

*About zero plus 50 minutes heavy shelling of VALE HOUSE commenced, almost wiping out No.1 platoon, wounding the platoon commander & killing or wounding all of the forward H.Q. which had moved up there.*

*(Capt. E. Holt, 2/Leiut. S.G. Mincher, & 2/leiut. W. Shadbolt, wounded).*

### *'B' Coy (left front company)*

*As soon as the leading platoons started moving forward heavy M.G. fire was opened from the front from about XXXXXX , iun all about 5 (light pattern) M.G's. and many snipers. These places were eventually cleared up but the company was only about 30 strong. Leiut. C.E. CARRINGTON with about 10 men worked across to D.2. central & consolidated there. The remainder of the Coy consolidated in the positions they had taken.*

### *'C' Company (right support company).*

*Moved up at zero plus 20 minutes and some of the leading men became somewhat involved in the fighting around WINZIG.*

*The pressure from the NEW ZEALANDERS on the right pushed the Coy over and 2/Leiut. F.W. HALE with the No. 9 platoon got to about D.2. central & consolidated just in the rear of the NEW ZEALANDERS.*

*No. 10 & 11 lost direction & I found them about 9.15 a.m. about XXXX but apparently they crossed the STRONBEEK about XXXX & working to the left consolidated behind the NEW ZEALANDERS about XXXX.*

### 'D' Coy (left support company)

*Moved up at zero plus 20 minutes & soon lost all its officers & 3 platoon sergeants from shell fire & snipers who still held out at about XXX*

*The remains of 2 platoons I found about XXX where they dug in close to the 2 M.G's. of 'A' Section (Lt. WHYTE) the other 2 platoons were in shell holes when I arrived up at 9.30 a.m. and I ordered C.S.M. SCOTT to dig in along the line of the STROONBEER about XXX.*

*About 100 prisoners, wounded and unwounded were taken by the Bn.*

*During the day Lieut. C.E. CARRINGTON was ordered to withdraw and form a support Coy about ALBATROSS FARM. Also in the afternoon the NEW ZEALANDERS moved to the right, thereby leaving about 30 men of the 1/5th R.War.R under 2/Leiut. F.W. HALE & 2/Leiut. A.F. FOREMAN betwwen D.2. central & WELLINGTON FARM. This thinning out was very necessary as there were too many men in the area & it was being heavily shelled.*

*About 4.45 p.m. 3 Coys of the 1/5th Gloucesters advanced to advance our line but although Capt. E.P.Q. CARTER & 2/Leiut. G.T. GAUNTLET directed them on to our front the high ground D.2. central & the fact of having to cross the stream diagonally if they kept in the right direction attracted them towards D.2. central where they dug in.*

The war diary says that this action went on for a further 3 days and concludes:

| CASUALTIES | KILLED | MISSING | DIED OF WOUNDS | MISSING | TOTAL |
|---|---|---|---|---|---|
| *Officers* | *3* | *–* | *1* | *–* | *10 (?)* |
| *O. Ranks* | *55* | *9* | *6* | *7* | *254* |
| **TOTALS** | **58** | **9** | **7** | **7** | **264** |

**WOUNDED**
*Officers ~ 6*
*O. Ranks ~ 177*
**Total ~ 183**

*Thomas is remembered on the Tyne Cot Memorial along with 34,952 other servicemen.*

# SAMUEL DANIEL

**Samuel Daniel** was born in Mobberley in 1881, one of eleven children born to James (a farmer) and Sarah of Dubbed Hedge, Mobberley. Samuel was a wagoner on a farm.

He joined the army as Private no. 268051 in the 1/6th Battalion of the Cheshire Regiment.

**Brief history of the Battalion:**

The 1/6th Battalion, Cheshire Regiment was a Territorial unit based in Stockport with Cheshire Brigade, Welsh Division when war broke out in August 1914. They proceeded to France on the 10th of November 1914 joining 15th Brigade, 5th Division on the 17 December 1914. On the 1st of March 1915 they transferred to GHQ and took over guard and other duties at Rouen, Abbeville and Dieppe. On the 9th of January 1916 they transferred to 20th Brigade, 7th Division then on the 29th of February 1916 to 118th Brigade, in the newly arrived 39th Division to replace units who had remained in England to complete their training. On the 30th June 1916 they were in action in an attack near Richebourg l'A'oue with the Sussex battalions suffered heavy casualties. They were in action during the Battles of the Somme, including, the fighting on the Ancre, The Battle of Thiepval Ridge, The Battle of the Ancre heights and the capture of Schwaben Redoubt and Stuff Trench as well as The Battle of the Ancre. In 1917 they fought in The Battle of Pilkem Ridge, The Battle of Langemarck, The Battle of the Menin Road Ridge, The Battle of Polygon Wood and The Second Battle of Passchendaele. In 1918 they were in action at The Battle of St Quentin, The actions at the Somme crossings, The Battle of Bapaume and The Battle of Rosieres before moving to Flanders. They took part the fighting on Wytschaete Ridge, The First and Second Battle of Kemmel and The Battle of the Scherpenberg.

*Thanks to the Wartime Memories Project.*

Samuel was killed in action on the 21st March 1918.

**On that fateful day:**
The war diary states:

*212.3.18*
*Heavy bombardment of the German defences started about 4am. At 5 the Battalion stood ready to move. At 6 the Batt marched to*

*LONGAVESNES and in conjunction with the remainder of the brigade dug a trench during the night which was to serve as a defensive flank. Shelling by both sides during the night fairly slight.*

**Samuel is buried in Heath Cemetery, Harbonnieres along with 1860 other servicemen. His grave is II. I. 8.**

# FREDERICK DARLINGTON

**Frederick Darlington** was born in Knutsford in 1898, the son of Robert (a bricklayer) and May Darlington of 110, King Street, Knutsford.

Frederick joined the Royal Flying Corp as Pilot no. 3295. He was died of wounds on the 23rd February 1918.

**On that fateful day:**
Frederick's casualty record shows that a report was received from Somers Town Police Station, London, stating that he was injured when a bomb was dropped from a 'hostile aircraft' at 'Euston Road/ St Pancras Railway Station'.
He subsequently died at home.

*Frederick is buried in Knutsford Cemetery.*

# FRED DARLINGTON
(Brother of Harry)

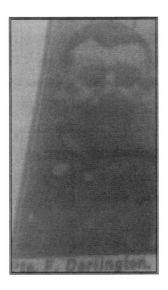

Fred Darlington was born in 1879 in Knutsford, one of five children born to John (a house painter) and Mary Jane Darlington of 9, Tatton Street, Knutsford. On leaving school he took up the trade as a pork butcher.

His service records no longer exist but we do know he enlisted in the army at the outset of the war, becoming Private no. 15845 of the 10th Battalion of the Cheshire Regiment.

**Brief history of the Battalion:**
The 10th (Service) Battalion, Cheshire Regiment was raised in Chester on the 10th of September 1914 as part of Kitchener's' Third New Army and joined 75th Brigade, 25th Division. They trained at Codford St Mary and spent the winter in billets in Bournemouth. They moved to Aldershot for final training in May 1915 and proceeded to France on the 26th of September,

the division concentrating in the area of Nieppe. On the 26th of October they transferred to 7th Brigade still with 25th Division. Their first action was in defence of the German attack on Vimy Ridge in May 1916. They then moved to The Somme and joined the Battle just after the main attack, with 75th Brigade making a costly attack near Thiepval on the 3rd of July. The Division was in action at The Battle of Bazentin, The Battle of Pozieres and The Battle of the Ancre Heights.

*Thanks to the War Memories Project.*

Fred died of wounds on the 12th October 1916.

**On that fateful day:**
Unfortunately I have been unable to discover how and where Fred was wounded.

*Fred is buried in Contay British Cemetery, France, together with another 1133 servicemen. His grave is III. B. 26.*

# HARRY DARLINGTON
## *(Brother of Fred)*

**Harry Darlington** was born in 1884 in Knutsford, one of five children born to John (a house painter) and Mary Jane Darlington of 9, Tatton Street, Knutsford. On leaving school he took up his father's trade as a house painter.

In 1908 he married Sarah and moved to 9, Canute Place, Knutsford and in 1911 they had a baby girl that they named Mabel.

He joined the army at the outset of the war, becoming Private no. 16222 of the 7th Battalion of the Loyal North Lancashire Regiment.

**Brief history of the regiment:**
10th (Service) Battalion, The Loyal North Lancashire Regiment was raised at Preston in October 1914 as part of Kitchener's' Third New Army joined 22nd Division as army troops. They trained on the South Downs, spending the winter in Eastbourne. In April 1915 they transferred to the newly forming 112th Brigade, 37th Division, which was concentrating at Cholderton on Salisbury Plain. They proceeded to France, landing at Boulogne on the 1st of August, the division concentrating near Tilques. They went into action in The Battle of the Ancre.

*Thanks to the Wartime Memories Project.*

Harry was killed in action on the 21ˢᵗ October 1915.

**On that fateful day:**
There is no specific action recorded in the war diary for this date.

*Harry is buried in Le Touret Military Cemetery, Richebourg-L'Avoue, along with 908 other servicemen. His grave is III. B. 4.*

# TOM DARLINGTON MM. MC

**Tom Darlington** was born in 1891, one of four children born to Edwin (a gardener) and Hannah Elisabeth of 2, Sparrow Lane, Knutsford.

On leaving school Tom became a law clerk.

On the outbreak of war he enlisted in the 20th (Service) Battalion of the Manchester Regiment at Belle Vue, Manchester, becoming Private no. 18125

He went to France on the 8th November 1915.

He rose to the rank of Sergeant.

**Brief history of the Battalions:**

The 20th (5th City) Battalion, Manchester Regiment was raised in in Manchester on the 8th of November 1914 by the Lord Mayor and City. They moved to Morecambe for training and in April 1915 moved to Grantham to join 91st Brigade, 30th Division. In September 1915 they moved to Larkhill, Salisbury Plain for final training and proceeded to France in November 1915, landing at Boulogne. On the 20th of December 1915, 91st Brigade transferred to 7th Division the 20th Manchesters then transferred to 22nd Brigade still with 7th Division. In 1916 They were in action during the Battles of the Somme, including the capture Mametz, The Battle of Bazentin, the attacks on High Wood, The Battle of Delville Wood, The Battle of Guillemont and the Operations on the Ancre.

On the 6th November he was commissioned into the 11th Queens (Royal West Surrey Regiment).

The 11th Battalion moved north and in 1917 were in action at Arras in The First Battle of the Scarpe, The Battle of Arleux and The Third Battle of the Scarpe. They remained in the Arras sector until the 30th of October when they moved to Hesdin for the Cambrai offensive in which the Division suffered heavy losses. In March 1918 they moved by motor lorry from Busnes to Albert and were in action in The Battle of Bapaume and spent the spring engaged in heavy fighting a the enemy advanced across the old Somme battlefields. On the 1st of July 1918, they attacked Bouzincourt. But were repelled by the enemy. They were relieved on the 10th and moved to the area south of Amiens. They were in action in The Battle of Amiens and were engaged in heavy fighting from the 22nd pushing the enemy back and capturing Meaulte, Mametz, Carnoy, Hardecourt and Faviere Wood within a week. In September they were in action in a successful attack on Nurlu and pursued the enemy back to Sorel Wood. They were in action during the battles of the Hindenburg Line, including The Battle of Epehy and The Battle of the St Quentin canal. In October they fought in The Final Advance in Artois reaching the Scheldt Canal by the 27th. They were withdrawn for rest on the 30th

Having already won the Military Medal earlier in the war – he was awarded the Military Cross in 1918.

The citation reads:

"For conspicuous gallantry and devotion to duty. When shelters were blown in by enemy shelling and several men were buried, this officer and four men after nearly three hours digging under heavy shellfire which necessitated them in taking refuge several times, succeeded in rescuing one man alive. This rescue was due to his example of energy and determination."

Tom was reported 'missing believe killed' on the 1st October 1918.

**On that fateful day:**
The war diary states:

*1.10.18 YPRES*
*Orders received at 1am for Bde to move by march route at 7am to YPRES-MENIN ROAD via xxxx and AMERICA. The Battalion moved at 6.35am. On reaching xxx the Bde halted owing to the advance guards of xxx Brigarde being checked at AMERICA. At 4.25 am orders were received for the Battalion to attack with the 23 Middlesex on the right and make good the railway VERVICQ MENIN*

*VERVICQ MENIN RAILWAY# The Battalion assembled on the line at 5.15am and advances at 5.45am (C &D in front B & A in support). After advancing about 1500 yards it came under heavy machine gun fire from tall chicory field in Q and owing to casualties and darkness it was not possible to go further and dug in on the line.*

*During the march to the place of assembly the battalion came under very heavy shell fire and severe casualties ensued.*

*Tom is buried at Hooge Crater Cemetery, Belgium along with 5,923 other servicemen. His grave is XVII. G. 17.*

# HUGH MERCER DAVIES D.C.M.

**Hugh Mercer Davies** was born in 1883 and was living with his wife Laura at 65, Brook Street, Macclesfield.

He enlisted in the army in August 1914, rising to the rank of Second Lieutenant in the 430th Company of the Royal Engineers. He served in Egypt and Gallipoli.

**Brief history of the Company:**
The 430th Company moved independently until it joined the 48th Division in 1915.

He receive the Distinguished Conduct Medal when a Sergeant Major – the citation reads –

*'For exceptional ability and good work. He turned out a large quantity of grenades to meet an urgent demand'.*
*London Gazette 21st June 1916.*

Hugh was killed in action on the 12th October 1918.

**On that fateful day:**
As yet I have been unable to gain access to the war diary

*Hugh is buried in Maurois Communal Cemetery, France along with over 80 other servicemen. His Grave is no. 43.*

# REGINALD ALEXANDER FORBES DOWNIE
*(Brother of Robert)*

**Reginald Alexander Forbes Downie** was born in Scotland in 1899, one of five children born to Robert Manners (an importer) and Elisabeth Henderson Downie who came to reside at Cornbrook, Knutsford.

He enlisted in the 1st Battalion of the Cameron Highland Regiment as a Lieutenant. He was later attached to the 5th Battalion.

He arrived in France on Christmas Eve 1917.

**Brief history of the Battalion:**
The 5th (Service) Battalion, Queen's'Own Cameron Highlanders was raised at Inverness in August 1914 as part of Kitchener's'First New Army; they joined 26th Brigade in 9th (Scottish) Division. The Battalion moved to Aldershot for training and in February 1915 went to Bordon. They proceeded to France and landed at Boulogne on the 10th of May 1915. They saw action in The Battle of Loos in 1915, the Battles of the Somme in 1916, the Arras Offensive, the Third Battle of Ypres and the last phase of the Cambrai operations in 1917. In 1918 the Battalion was in action on the Somme, the Battles of the Lys and The Final Advance in Flanders. The 9th (Scottish) Division was withdrawn for rest in late October and was in billets at the Armistice

on the 11ᵗʰ of November. The Division then advanced to the Rhine as part of the occupation force.

*Thanks to the Wartime Memories Project.*

Reginald was killed in action on the 24ᵗʰ March 1918.

**On that fateful day:**
Neither the 5ᵗʰ Battalion nor the 1ˢᵗ Battalion war diary makes any reference to Reginald's death.

The 5ᵗʰ Battalion states:

*'24.3.18*
*An inter Company relief was carried out. 'C' Coy from HAALEN and 'D; Coy from HILLSIDE relieved 'A' and 'B' Companies. In the front line.*
    *During this tour 2 officer patrols were sent out nightly.*
    *Enemy posts were found but no identification were got. Work on the posts were carried out.'*

***Reginal has no known grave and is remembered on the Pozieres memorial along with the names of 14,656 other servicemen.***

# ROBERT THEODORE MANNERS DOWNIE
*(Brother of Reginald)*

**Robert Theodore Manners Downie** was born in Scotland in 1891, one of five children born to Robert Manners (an importer) and Elisabeth Henderson Downie who came to reside at Cornbrook, Knutsford.

Robert spent his early years in India.

He enlisted in the 3$^{rd}$/5$^{th}$ Battalion of the Highland Light Infantry as a Second Lieutenant.

He contracted cerebrospinal fever while on home leave in Leeds and died on the 24$^{th}$ January 1916.

# ARTHUR LANCELOT DAWSON

**Arthur Lancelot Dawson** was born in Knutsford, one of three children born to John (a labourer) and Sarah of Chelford Road, Knutsford. Arthur took up the trade of domestic gardener.

He joined the Royal Field Artillery as Gunner 172735 of 45 Battery of the 5ᵗʰ Brigade.

Brief history of the Battery:

This was a unit of Britain's'pre-war regular army. It is also sometimes shown as 5 Brigade RFA. Comprising numbers 45, 64, 73 and 81 Batteries, this brigade came under command of the 7ᵗʰ (Meerut) Division of the Indian Army. It moved to the 3ʳᵈ (Lahore) Division on 22 November 1914.When the Division left France, the brigade remained and eventually came under command of the 3ʳᵈ Canadian Division (between 20 March and 13 July 1916) before going to the 4ᵗʰ Canadian Division in September 1916, with which it served until July 1917At that point it became an Army Brigade and served with the following: Second Army in October 1917, Third Army in December 1917, First Army in February 1918, Fifth Army in July 1918 and finally returned to Fourth Army in October 1918

*Thanks to the Long, Long Trail.*

Arthur died in Germany on the 28ᵗʰ March 1918

*Arthur is remembered on the Loos Memorial along with 20,603 others.*

202

# PETER DRINKWATER

**Peter Drinkwater** was born in Rostherne, Cheshire in 1875. He married Lizzie Howard in 1898 and they lived at New York Cottage, Hoo Green, Knutsford. He was an Osler.

He enlisted in the army on the 28th December 1914, becoming Driver no. T/4/039028 of the 23rd Reserve Park, Royal Service Corp.

**Brief history of the Regiment:**
The Army Service Corps can be traced back to the Corps of Waggoner's formed in 1794. The main role of the ASC was transport; they were responsible for the movement of all supplies required by the Army, including food, fuel, ammunition, horses, clothing and equipment. During the Great War 1914-1918 supplies were moved by horse drawn, steam and motor powered vehicles as well as by rail and waterways. The abbreviation MT stands for Motorized Transport and HT for Horse Transport.

The Army Service Corps was organised into Companies and provided men for the Divisional Train, Divisional Supply Column and Divisional Ammunition Park for each Division of the British Army. The Remounts Service was responsible for the supply of trained horses, whilst the Labour Corps provided men skilled in manual labour, who under took tasks such as loading and unloading supplies from trains and ships. The Pioneer Battalions took care of repairing roads and railways and army buildings.

The Army Service Corps numbered over ten thousand officers and a third of a million men, as well as employing huge numbers of labourers from China, India and Africa along with locals. The Army Service Corps became The Royal Army Service Corps in 1918 and their descendant unit today is the Royal Logistic Corps.

The 6th Divisional Train consisted of 17, 19, **23** & 24 Companies ASC. 6th Div. Proceeded to France on the 10th of September 1914, landing at St Nazaire. Marched to the Aisne to reinforce the hard-pressed BEF. They moved north to Flanders and were in action at Hooge in 1915. In 1916 they were again in action at Battle of Flers-Courcelette on The Somme, and again in The Battle of Morval and The Battle of Le Transloy, in 1917 they were in action at Hill 70 and Cambrai. In 1918 they saw action in the Battle of St Quentin, The Battles of the Lys, The Advance in Flanders, Battles of the Hindenburg Line and The Pursuit to the Selle.

*Thanks to the Wartime Memories Project.*

Peter 'died at sea' on the 6th February 1918 – it is not known if he was wounded or died of illness.

***Peter is buried in Altrincham, Bowden and Hale (Altrincham) Cemetery.***

# WILLIAM HENRY DUTTON

**William H Dutton** was born in Allostock, Cheshire in 1890, one of seven children born to Frederick (a market gardener) and Elisabeth Dutton of Allostock.

He enlisted in 'A' Company of the 122 Brigade of the Royal Field Artillery, becoming Driver 4453.

**Brief history of the Brigade:**
CXXII (Howitzer) Brigade, Royal Field Artillery, served as Divisional artillery with 38th (Welsh) Division from August 1915. The Division was formed from volunteer units that had already been raised by public subscription and private projects. They proceeded to France between in late November and early December 1915. In July 1916 they were in action at Mametz Wood on The Somme, suffering severe casualties. The Division did not return to major action for more than 12 months. In 1917 they were in action in the Third Battles of Ypres.

*Thanks to the Wartime Memories Project.*

William was killed in action on the 21st August 1917.

**On that fateful day:**
I have been unable to gain access to the war diary.

*William is buried in the Canada Farm Military Cemetery, along with 907 other servicemen. His grave id II. C. 21.*

# WILLIAM EDEN

**William Eden** was born in Whitchurch, Salop in 1888, the son of Nancy Eden, the publican of the Bulls Head, Mobberley. He assisted his mother with the running of the pub.

He enlisted in the 14th (Reserve) Battalion of the Cheshire Regiment as Private no. 35732.

**Brief history of the Battalion:**

14th (Reserve) Battalion was formed in Birkenhead in October 1914 as a Service Battalion of K4 and came under orders of

105th Brigade of original 35th Division on the 10 April 1915. They became a Reserve Battalion and moved in July 1915 to Kimnel Camp at (Rhyl) and in August 1915 to Prees Heath. They never went abroad.

William died at home of illness on the 5th May 1916.

*William is buried in Whitchurch Cemetery, Shropshire.*

# FRED EDGE EDWARDS

**Fred Edge Edwards** was born in Marbury, Cheshire in 1893, one of eleven children born to John (a gamekeeper) and Jane Edwards of Long Lane, Over Peover.

Fred enlisted in the 10th Battalion of the Cheshire Regiment, becoming private no. 24575.
He arrived in France on the 20th December 1915.

### Brief history of the Battalion:

The 10th (Service) Battalion, Cheshire Regiment was raised in Chester on the 10th of September 1914 as part of Kitchener's'Third New Army and joined 75th Brigade, 25th Division. They trained at Codford St Mary and spent the winter in billets in Bournemouth. They moved to Aldershot for final training in May 1915 and proceeded to France on the 26th of September, the division concentrating in the area of Nieppe. On the 26th of October they transferred to 7th Brigade still with 25th Division. Their first action was in defence of the German attack on Vimy Ridge in May 1916. They then moved to The Somme and joined the Battle just after the main attack, with 75th Brigade making a costly attack near Thiepval on the 3rd of July. The Division was in action at The Battle of Bazentin, The Battle of Pozieres and The Battle of the Ancre Heights.

*Thanks to the Wartime Memories Project.*

Fred died of wounds on the 17th July 1916 and as his service record no longer exists I have been unable to discover where and when he received those wounds.

*Fred is buried in Puchevillers Military Cemetery along with 1,763 other servicemen. His grave is I. E. 9.*

# JOHN EYRES

**John Eyres** was born in Peover, Cheshire in 1899, one of three children born to William and Lucy Eyres of Fox Cover Cottage, Lower Peover. John was a labourer.

John joined the 10th Battalion of the Cheshire Regiment, becoming Private no. 18345.

**Brief history of the Battalion:**

The 10th (Service) Battalion, Cheshire Regiment was raised in Chester on the 10th of September 1914 as part of Kitchener's'Third New Army and joined 75th Brigade, 25th Division. They trained at Codford St Mary and spent the winter in billets in Bournemouth. They moved to Aldershot for final training in May 1915 and proceeded to France on the 26th of September, the division concentrating in the area of Nieppe. On the 26th of October they transferred to 7th Brigade still with 25th Division. Their first action was in defence of the German attack on Vimy Ridge in May 1916.

*Thanks to the Wartime Memories Project.*

He arrived in France on the 19th December 1915.
John was killed in action on the 21st May 1916.

**On that fateful day:**
The war diary states:

## '21.5.16

*The CT suffered and some damage caused by shell fire and minenwerfer. At 3.45 an intense bombardment by all CT and supports. The fire was particularly heavy to the left of our sector. The bombardment continued with unabated violence for 4 hours and at the end of that time most of our trenches had been levelled and a very large proportion of our men had been killed or wounded.*

*At 7.45 the enemy attacked and took our outpost with little resistance as there was nobody left to oppose them.*

*A counter attack was delivered at 2am which was successful in retaking the line.*

*33 OK killed.'*

This was the same action in which Henry Taylor was killed.

---

**Note:**
*His medals were never collected.*

---

**John is buried at Ecoivres Cemetery with 1715 other servicemen.**

# JAMES FAGAN

**James Fagan** was born in Tabley, Cheshire in 1891, one of eight children born to Harry Daniel (a council roadman) and Martha Dean of Tabley.

He joined the 18th Battalion of the Lancashire Fusiliers, becoming Private no. 16307.

**Brief history of the Battalion:**

The 18th Battalion, Lancashire Fusiliers was raised as a Bantam Battalion (troops who were under the normal regulation minimum height of 5 feet 3 inches – in Bury on the 13th of January 1915 by Lieut-Col. G. E. Wike and a Committee. After initial training close to home, they moved to Garswood Park, Ashton in Makerfield on the 8th of April 1915. On the 21st of June they joined 104th Brigade, 35th Division at Masham, North Yorkshire. They moved to Cholderton, Salisbury Plain for final training in August and the Battalion was formally adopted by the War Office on the 27th. They were ordered to Egypt in late 1915, but the order was soon cancelled and they proceeded to France landing at Le Havre on the 29th of January 1916, the division concentrated east of St Omer. They were in action during the Battles of the Somme at Bazentin Ridge, Arrow Head Copse, Maltz Horn Farm and Falfemont Farm. The division received new drafts of men to replace losses suffered on the Somme, but the CO. soon discovered that these new recruits were not of the same physical standard as the original Bantams, being men of small stature from the towns, rather than the miners and farm workers who had joined up in 1915. A medical inspection was carried out and 1439 men were transferred to the Labour Corps. Their places being taken by men transferred from the disbanded yeomanry regiments, who underwent a quick training course in infantry methods at a Divisional depot set up specifically for that purpose. In 1917 they were in action during the pursuit to the Hindenburg Line, at Houthulst Forest and The Second Battle of Passchendaele.

*Thanks to the Wartime Memories Project.*

James was killed in action on the 22nd October 1917.

**On that fateful day:**
The war diary states:

*'22.10.17*
*The Battalion formed up immediately S of ANGLE POINT, S of HOUTHULST WOOD ay 2.30 am in close support to the 23rd Man R on right 17th Lan Fus on left. 'X' Coy on right 'Y' Coy on left of front line. 'W' support to 'X' Coy and 'Z' in support to 'Y'. The attack was in four waves. 25' between lines 75y between waves.*
*The line of the advance of the 7th LF, 23rd Man R were slightly (words illegible) and it was the duty of the 18th LF to fill up the gap thus formed and to keep touch with both of these two Battn.*
*While waiting for zero hour a light barrage was put down by the enemy between the Battn and HQ but there were no casualties.*
*At zero hour – 5.35 am Battn moved off keeping close to our barrage which was found too slow (8' for 100Y) and in consequence we suffered several casualties. In addition the barrage was very*

*ragged. One shot in four falling short, this was probably due to the bad gun platforms. Lts PRITCHETT & BOWERS were conspicuous in their efforts to keep their men back.*

*Shortly after the attack started, the Manch R suffered very heavy casualties and were held up. Our line continued to advance but owing to its right flank being unprotected began to suffer heavy casualties. At about 6.16 am Capt. MR WOOD M.C. who was in command of the two leading companies realised that he had worked too far over to the left so moved his own Coy ('X') back a short way and then over to the right in order to try and re-establish touch with the Man R and also to attack the wood from the south. He failed to gain touch with the Manch but moved forward to attack the wood under heavy fire M.G. and rifle from his front and right flank. On approaching the wood Lt. TORRANCE saw an active M.G. in front of him. He sent his men around each flank and charged the gun himself, capturing the gun + team. 'X' Coy entered the wood but taking their right flank unprotected and were almost surrounded by the enemy and after a hard fight were compelled to withdraw to the outskirts. Lt. TORRENCE was wounded and as he was about the last man, was not brought in. It is hopeful that he was taken prisoner with his servant who stayed with him. Capt. Wood who had fought most gallantly throughout the day fell in the wood.*

*The left half of the leading wave was on its objective a little in advance of a road called CONTER DRIVE which was roughly the general line of the objective at this point, and in touch with the 17th LF. At about 11 am two Companies of the 20th LF were sent up to fill the gap in our right flank and took up a position on the ANGLE POINT. Patrols pushed out well into VIC to get in touch with the Division on our right which had also been held up.*

*In the late afternoon orders were sent to 'Y' Coy to refuse his right flank and to establish contact with 20 LF.*

*At 3.45 pm word was received from Lt's FOX and HOBSON that the enemy were massing for a counter-attack in the woods.*

*The artillery were informed and they at once opened slow fire. At 4 pm the enemy moved to the attack. At 4.03 pm the S.O.S. was sent up and very many of the enemy were mown down by artillery, rifle, Lewis Guns + M.G. fire. The troops on the left of the 17th LF however were forced to retire slightly and the 17th LF and ourselves readjusted our line to conform. The enemy did not know where our line was and in consequence his barrage was too far to the rear to be effective.*

*The night passed quietly except for continuous M.G. fire and occasional heavy shelling in the neighbourhood of EGYPT HO.*

*Casualties:*
*Officers Killed 3 Wounded 7 Wounded and Missing 1*
*Other ranks Killed 27 Wounded 174 Wounded and missing 42.'*

***James is remembered on the Tyne Cot memorial, along with the names of 34,952 other servicemen.***

# JAMES FINN

James Finn was born in County Mayo, Ireland in 1883 and came to work as a farm labourer in Northwich.

He joined the 12th Battalion of the Prince of Wales Own (West Yorkshire Regiment) as Private no. 51789.

**Brief history of the Battalion:**
The 12th (Service) Battalion, West Yorkshire Regiment (Prince of Wales's'Own) was raised at York on the 16th if September 1914 as part of Kitchener's'Third New army and joined 63rd Brigade, 21st Division. The Division concentrated in the Tring area, training at Halton Park before winter necessitated a move into local billets in Tring, Aylesbury, Leighton Buzzard, High Wycombe and Maidenhead. In May 1915 the infantry moved to huts at Halton Park. On the 9th of August they moved to Witley Camp. They proceeded to France during the first week of September, landing at Le Havre and marched across France to going into the reserve for the British assault at Loos on the 26th of September suffering heavy casualties. On the 16th of November 1915 the Battalion transferred to 9th Brigade, 3rd Division. In 1916 they took part in The Actions of the Bluff and St Eloi Craters then moved to The Somme for The Battle of Albert, The Battle of Bazentin helping to capture Longueval, The Battle of Delville Wood and The Battle of the Ancre. In 1917 they were

at Arras, seeing action at Battles of the Scarpe and The Battle of Arleux. They moved north to the Flanders and were in action during The Battle of the Menin Road and Battle of Polygon Wood during the Third Battle of Ypres. Then moved south and were in action at The Battle of Cambrai.

*Thanks to the Wartime Memories Project.*

James was killed in action on the 21st November 1917.

**On that fateful day:**
The Battalion went into the front line on the 18th November 1917 at Faveuril.
The war diary for the 21st states:

*'21.11.17 TRENCHES*
*Occasional hostile shelling all day. 2 O.R. killed + 3 wounded.*
*4 O.R. joined from base.'*

***James is buried in Favreuil British Cemetery along with 385 other servicemen. His grave is II. C. 3.***

# BENJAMIN FORD

**Benjamin Ford** was born in mere, Cheshire in 1893, one of ten children born to Joseph (a farmer) and Ann Eliza Ford of Hulse Heath Farm, Mere. Benjamin worked on his father's farm.

He enlisted in the army in 1914 and arrived in France as Private no. 15059 of 8th Battalion of the Scots Fusiliers on the 20th September 1915. Then in November of that year the Regiment moved to Salonika.

**Brief history of the Battalion:**
8th (Service) Battalion was formed at Ayr on 1 October 1914 as part of K3 and came under orders of 77th Brigade, 26th Division. It moved to Codford St Mary and went into billets in Bristol in November 1914. They moved again, this time to Sutton Veny in April 1915. On the 20th September 1915 they landed at Boulogne but soon moved and by November 1915 were at Salonika.

*Thanks to the Long, Long Trail.*

217

Benjamin was killed in action on the 19th September 1918.

**On that fateful day:**
The official war history of the Regiment states:

*18.9.18*
*5.20 am*
*The attack began and in the face of a heavy artillery and machine-gun barrage it carried the point known as 'The Tongue'. But the enemy at once counter-attacked, and the Greeks on the right were driven from the objective they had won, while the French on the left had apparently never moved from their place of assembly. The result was that the Brigade had both flanks in the air, and as the enemy was pushing forward enveloping attacks, it was compelled, about 10.30 am slowly to withdraw. The commanding officer of the Scots Fusiliers, Lt. Col. G. G. Lindesay was wounded and most of the officers were already casualties. Accordingly the Battalion was retired to a ravine, where it was re-organised under two subalterns. It was a day of heavy losses – over 400.*

*The Scots Fusiliers took no part in what is described as 'the second fruitless assault on the 19th – the day Benjamin was listed as killed in action.*

***Benjamin has no known grave and is remembered on the Dorian memorial along with 1338 other servicemen.***

218

# JAMES FOSTER

**James Foster** was born on Tabley, Cheshire in 1896, one of four children born to George (a teamsman on a farm) and Elizabeth (a laundress) of 41, Cross Town, Knutsford. On leaving school James became a telegraph boy.

He enlisted in the army and became Private no. 14238 in the 10th Battalion of the Cheshire Regiment, and went to France on the 27th September 1915.

**Brief history of the Battalion:**

The 10th (Service) Battalion, Cheshire Regiment was raised in Chester on the 10th of September 1914 as part of Kitchener's Third New Army and joined 75th Brigade, 25th Division. They trained at Codford St Mary and spent the winter in billets in Bournemouth. They moved to Aldershot for final training in May 1915 and proceeded to France on the 26th of September, the division concentrating in the area of Nieppe. On the 26th of October they transferred to 7th Brigade still with 25th Division.

Their first action was in defence of the German attack on Vimy Ridge in May 1916. They then moved to The Somme and joined the Battle just after the main attack, with 75th Brigade making a costly attack near Thiepval on the 3rd of July. The Division was in action at The Battle of Bazentin, The Battle of Pozieres and The Battle of the Ancre Heights.

*Thanks to the Wartime Memories Project.*

James was killed in action on the 3rd May 1916.

**On that fateful day:**
The war diary states:

*'3.5.16*
*Things very quiet during the day. Our snipers did some very useful work accounting for several of the enemy who exposed themselves whilst working on or near new water in front of our right sector. A mine was exploded on our right at 8pm – there was considerable machine gun activity afterwards but little artillery fire. Rifle grenades were freely used during the night by the enemy and some casualties were caused by these.'*

***James is buried in Ecoivres Military Cemetery, Mont St Eloi, France, together with 1,508 other servicemen.***

# JOHN GEORGE FOWLES

**John George Fowles** was born in Knutsford in 1892, one of eleven children born to John George (an engineer at a paper plane) and Ada Gertrude Fowles of Booth Mill, Mobberley Road, Knutsford. John George Jr was a labourer. He married Nellie Groves on the 15th May 1915 and moved to 14, King Street, Knutsford.

He joined the Royal Engineers on the 30th August 1916, becoming Pioneer no 226636 of the 333rd Road Construction Company.

**Brief history of the Company:**
In 1914, the General Headquarters of the BEF in France and Flanders incorporated a GHQ Signals Company, two Corps Signals Companies (one each for I and II Corps), and specialist units for railways and printing. GHQ always maintained certain engineering units, including the Special Companies RE whose job was gas warfare, Meteorological, Special Works Park (camouflage) and other specialists.

As the army grew in size, the number of Corps increased and were organised into Armies. At Army level, several different types of Engineers units developed, and Corps were left with only one Company-sized unit, in motor and cable sections. Each of the five Armies on the Western Front contained the following, with the establishment varying between Armies and over time.

- Advanced RE Parks (responsible for stores and dumps of goods and equipment)
- Road construction.
- Pontoon Parks (looking after bridging equipment)
- Electrical and Mechanical Companies (responsible for machinery, including underground boring)
- Army Workshops (for repairs and maintenance of equipment)
- Anti-Aircraft Sections (searchlight operations)
- Army Troops Companies (established similar to Field Companies, but for behind-the-lines bridging and water work)
- Transportation Works Companies (maintaining vehicles)
- Forestry Companies

*Thanks to the Long, Long Trail.*

John died of a shell wound to the abdomen on the 30th November 1917. I have been unable to discover when and where he received the wound.

***John is buried in Lebucquiere Communal Cemetery Extension, France, along with 774 other servicemen.***

*Note:*
*Nellie received the sum of 13/9 (70p) pension.*

# GEORGE WALTON GARFT

**George Walton Garft** was born in Urmston in 1893, the son of Harry (a hotel Keeper) and Jessie of The Legh Arms, Chelford Road, Knutsford. He was an Insurance clerk. They later moved to 22, Manchester Road, Altrincham.

George joined the 17th Battalion of the Manchester Regiment, becoming Private no. 8588.

**Brief history of the Battalion:**

The 17th(2nd City) Battalion, Manchester Regiment was raised in Manchester on the 28th of August 1914 by the Lord Mayor and City. Initially they trained at Heaton Park but moved in April 1915 to Belton Park, where they joined 90th Brigade, 30th Division. They to Larkhill in September 1915 for final training and proceeded to France on the 6th of November 1915, concentrating near Amiens. In 1916 they were in action during the Battle of the Somme, in which the Division captured Montauban.

*Thanks to the Wartime Memories Project.*

George was wounded on the 1st July 1916.

**On that fateful day:**

George was with a party laying wire to consolidate their position close to Montauban when he was sit in the arm by a machine-gun bullet. He was taken to No. 5 General Hospital, Rouen where part of his arm was removed.

He was discharged from the army on the 3rd August 1917. George died on the 26th November 1918.

*George is buried in Sale Cemetery.*

# HERBERT GARNER

**Herbert Garner** was born in Altrincham in 1891, one of three children born to James (a domestic Gardener) and Sarah Garner of

14, Rostherne Street, Altrincham. Herbert was a house painter. He married Polly and raised a family of three children at 4, Wharf Road Altrincham before moving to Knutsford.

He enlisted in the Royal Regiment of Artillery as Gunner W/4933 before transferring to the 12th Battalion of the West Yorkshire Regiment as Private no. 47294.

**Brief history of the Battalion:**

The 12th (Service) Battalion, West Yorkshire Regiment (Prince of Wales's' Own) was raised at York on the 16th if September 1914 as part of Kitchener's' Third New army and joined 63rd Brigade, 21st Division. The Division concentrated in the Tring area, training at Halton Park before winter necessitated a move into local billets in Tring, Aylesbury, Leighton Buzzard, High Wycombe and Maidenhead. In May 1915 the infantry moved to huts at Halton Park. On the 9th of August they moved to Witley Camp. They proceeded to France during the first week of September, landing at Le Havre and marched across France to going into the reserve for the British assault at Loos on the 26th of September suffering heavy casualties. On the 16th of November 1915 the Battalion transferred to 9th Brigade, 3rd Division. In 1916 they took part in The Actions of the Bluff and St Eloi Craters then moved to The Somme for The Battle of Albert, The Battle of Bazentin helping to capture Longueval, The Battle of Delville Wood and The Battle of the Ancre. In 1917 They were at Arras, seeing action at Battles of the Scarpe and The Battle of Arleux. They moved north to the Flanders and were in action during The Battle of the Menin Road and Battle of Polygon Wood during the Third Battle of Ypres. Then moved south and were in action at The Battle of Cambrai.

*Thanks to the Wartime Memories Project.*

Herbert was killed in action on the 5th June 1917.

225

## On that fateful day:
The war diary states:

### '5.6.17 BROWN LINE
*5 officers and 210 O.R. employed on carrying duties + working parties.*
*Great air activity. Enemy plane brought down in flames W of BROWN LINE.*
*No casualties'.*

Perhaps the date of Herbert's death is wrong for the only casualties that the Battalion suffered around that date was the following day:

### '6.6.17 BROWN LINE
*10p.m.*
*Relieved the 4th Bn. Royal Fusiliers – Bde Support in LANCER LANE. Companies marched independently. Enemy put up a very heavy barrage just as the Coy got on the move, which delayed the relief considerably. Throughout the night enemy displayed great nervousness and continued intermittent shelling.*
*Casualties: 2 killed 6 wounded. Weather hot and dry.'*

***Herbert has no know grave but is remembered on the Arras Memorial,***
***France, along with 34,791 other servicemen.***

# JOHN GARNER

John Garner was born in Knutsford. He was one of five children born to George (a carter) and Annie Garner of 29, Tatton Street, Knutsford. John or Jack as he was known was first employed at Knutsford's Steam Laundry before going to work at the Royal George Stables.

His service records no longer exist but we know that he enlisted in the Cheshire Regiment in February 1916, becoming Private no. 35415, before transferring to the 2nd Battalion of the East Lancashire Regiment, becoming Private no. 28294.

**Brief history of the Battalion:**

2nd Battalion East Lancashire Regiment was in Wijnberg, South Africa when war broke out in August 1914. They returned to England, landing at Southampton on the 30th of October 1914 and joined 24th Brigade in 8th Division at Hursley Park, Winchester. They proceeded to France, landing at Le Havre on the 6th November 1914 a much needed reinforcement to the BEF and remained on the Western Front throughout the war. In 1915 they were in action at The Battle of Neuve Chapelle, The Battle of Aubers and The action of Bois Grenier. On the 18th of October 1915 they transferred with 24th Brigade to 23rd Division to instruct the inexperienced troops. In March 1916 23rd Division took over the front line between Boyau de l'E'satz and the Souchez River in the Carency sector from the French 17th Division, an area exposed to heavy shelling. In mid-April they withdrew to Bruay returning to the Carency sector in mid-May just before the German attack on Vimy Ridge, in the sector to their right. On the 15th of June 1916 24th Brigade returned to 8th Division. They were in action at the Battle of The Somme. In 1917 they fought in The German retreat to the Hindenburg Line and then moved to Flanders and were in action in The Battle of Pilkem and The Battle of Langemarck.

John was killed in action on the 15th March 1917.

**On that fateful day:**
The official history of the Battalion tells of an action that commenced on the 4th March 1917.

*'The casualties on the 4th March (1917) and the following days amounted to 11 other ranks killed and 4 officers and 39 other ranks wounded.*

*The Battalion remained at ASQUITH FLATS until the 14th when it relieved the 2nd Northants in FRITZ and PALLAS trenches. The relief was particularly difficult: a thaw accompanied by heavy rain had succeeded the frost and the whole shell pitted area was a quagmire in which some men were so firmly bogged that they were not pulled out until the following morning.*

*The enemy withdrew slowly on the 15th and 16th covered by snipers, and by the night of the 16th/17th the 24th Brigade line was advanced to the BREMEN WOOD lane and BACCHUS trenches. That night the Battalion was relieved until March 25th, when it moved to MOISLAINS, now cleared of the enemy.'*

The Knutsford Guardian of the 6th April 1917 states:

*'Mr and Mrs George Garner, 29, Tatton Street, Knutsford, have been officially informed of the death in action of their son, Private John (Jack) Garner. He was 26 years of age and for several years worked at the Knutsford Steam Laundry, and afterwards for Messrs G. Hard and Sons, of the Royal George Stables, by whom and their customers he was regarded as a efficient and obliging workman. He enlisted in February last year in the Cheshire Regiment and went to the front on October 4th and was then transferred to the Lancashers.*

*He was in several engagements and after a spell in the trenches always made a point of writing home. The last letter so written was dated February 15th having then come from trench duty covering a period of 16 days. The official communication states he was killed in action on March 15th'*

The article goes on to tell of his other two brothers who were serving in the army.

*John's 'Death Plaque' and scroll – picture coutosy of Gt. Neice Pam Evans*

*John is buried in Fins New British Cemetery, Sorel-Le-Grand, France along with 1289 other servicemen. His grave is VII. B. 13.*

# ARTHUR EWAN GIDMAN

**Arthur Ewan Garner** was born in Knutsford, son of Arthur (a cooper and basket manufacturer) and Gertrude Garner of Rose Bank, Stanley Road, Knutsford. They later moved to 38, Bexton Road, Knutsford.

Arthur joined the Loyal North Lancashire Regiment, becoming Private no. 29123 of the 1/¼ Battalion.

**Brief history of the Battalion:**

1/¼ Battalion, The Loyal North Lancashire Regiment was a territorial unit based in in Preston with the North Lancashire Brigade in West Lancashire Division. They had just arrived at the annual summer camp when war broke out in August 1914. They were at once recalled to base and moved to Swindon on the 22nd of August, in November they moved to Sevenoaks. In April the Brigade transferred to the Highland Division. They proceeded to France on the 4th of May, landing at Boulogne, on the 12th the formation was renamed 154th Brigade, 51st (Highland) Division. The Division concentrated in the area of Lillers, Busnes and Robecq and were rushed to the defence of Ypres, being in action until the 19th of May when they moved to Estaires on the River Lys. They were in action in the Battle of Festubert and The Second Action of Givenchy before moving south to The Somme taking over the line near Hamel. On the 7th of January 1916 they transferred to the reforming 164th Brigade, 55th (West Lancashire) Division. On the 16th of February, the Division relieved the French 88th Division south of Arras, they moved to The Somme in late July taking over a section of front line near the village of Guillemont. They were in action at the Battle of Guillemont, The Battle of Ginchy, The Battle of Flers-Courcelette and The Battle of Morval. The Division moved to Flanders in October 1916 and took over the front line between Wieltje and Railway Wood. In 1917 they were in action at Pilkem Ridge and Menin Road Ridge during the Third Battle of Ypres. They moved south to Cambrai where they suffered very heavily during the German Counter Attacks on the 30th of November 1917. In the spring of 1918 they were in action in the Battle of the Lys including the Defence of Givenchy on the 9th to the 17th of April.

*Thanks to the Wartime Memories Project.*

Arthur was killed in action on the 9th April 1918.

**On that fateful day:**
There is nothing recorded in the war diary for this date.

*Arthur is buried in Vielle-Chappelle Memorial Cemetery, Lacouture along with nearly a thousand other servicemen. His Grave is III. E. 10.*

# JOSEPH GIDMAN

**Joseph Gidman** was born in Knutsford in 1893, one of five children born to Hugh (a hamper maker) and Elizabeth Hannah Gidman of Bakehouse Yard, Knutsford. Joseph was also a hamper maker.

He joined the 18th Battalion of the Manchester Regiment, becoming Private no. 31382.

**Brief history of the Battalion:**
The 18th (3rd City) Battalion, Manchester Regiment was raised in

Manchester on the 28th of August 1914 by the Lord Mayor and City. Initially they trained at Heaton Park but moved in April 1915 to Belton Park, where they joined 90th Brigade, 30th Division. They to Larkhill in September 1915 for final training and proceeded to France on the 6th of November 1915, concentrating near Amiens. In 1916 they were in action during the Battle of the Somme, in which the Division captured Montauban.

*Thanks to the Wartime Memories Project.*

Joseph was killed in action on the 30th July 1916.

**On that fateful day:**
The war diary states:

**'TRONES WOOD**
*The attack on GUILLEMONT was carried out despite the fact that during the early hours there was a heavy ground frost.*
*Artillery barrage did not materialise only the 18 pounders.*
*18th and two companies of the 17th entered village but those that got in were taken prisoner and the majority of the casualties were the missing*
*Battalion casualties for July 32 officers and 1300 OR killed or missing.'*
Those who fell in the advance lay where they fell until September 15th – some six weeks later.

*Joseph is remembered on Thiepval Memorial along with 72,208 others*

233

# THOMAS GILLETT

**Thomas Gillett** was born in Lostock Garlem, Cheshire in 1899, one of four children born to Peter (a railway signalman) and Hannah Gillett of Lostock Garlem. He went to live with his sister at 17, Queens Street, Knutsford.

He enlisted in February 1917 in the 7th Battalion of the Prince of Wales (South Lancashire Regiment) as Private no. 39941.

**Brief history of the Battalion:**
The 7th (Service) Battalion, South Lancashire Regiment was raised at Warrington in September 1914 as part of Kitchener's' Second New Army and joined 56th Brigade in 19th (Western) Division. They trained at Tidworth and moved in billets in Andover in December 1914. They moved to Clevedon in February 1915 then returned to Tidworth in March for final training. They proceeded to France, landing at Boulogne on the 18th of July 1915, the division and concentrating near St Omer. Their first action was at Pietre, in a diversionary action supporting the Battle of Loos. In 1916 They were in action during the Battle of the Somme, capturing La Boisselle and being involved in The attacks on High Wood, The Battles of Pozieres Ridge, the Ancre Heights and the Ancre. In 1917 they were in action in The Battle of Messines and the Third Battles of Ypres.

Thomas died of wounds on the 6th October 1917

*Thomas is buried in Voomezeele Cemetery, Belgium – his grave is I. K. 5.*

# GEOFFREY MARCUS ERSKINE GIRARD

**Geoffrey Marcus Erskine Girard** was born in Knutsford in 1900, the son of H. E and Isobel Mary Girard (a lady of 'private means') who went to live in Chaucer Road, Bedford. His father later made a request for his son's medals whilst living at 48, Burlington Road, Bayswater, London.

Geoffrey joined the 28th London Regiment, becoming Private no. 3607. He was commissioned into the 7th Battalion of the Prince of Wales Leinster Regiment (Royal Canadians), on the 19th April 1917, becoming a Temporary Second Lieutenant.

**Brief history of the Battalion:**

7th (Service) Battalion, The Leinster Regiment was raised at Fermoy in October 1914 as part of Kitchener's Second New Army and joined 47th Brigade, 16th (Irish) Division. They moved to Kilworth in January 1915 and crossed to England in September 1915, undertaking final training at Blackdown. They proceeded to France on the 18th of December 1915 landing at Le Havre and concentrating in the Bethune area. In 1916 they were in action on the Somme during the Battle of Guillemont in which the Division captured the village and The Battle of Ginchy. In 1917 they fought at the Battle of Messines and The Battle of Langemarck, during the Third Battles of Ypres.

*Thanks to the Wartime Memories Project.*

He arrived in France 9th May 1915.
Geoffrey was killed in action on the 16th November 1917.

**On that fateful day:**
The war diary for this date states:

**'16.11.17 IN THE FIELD**
*Under the most unfortunate circumstances 2nd/Lt G.M.E. Girard accidentally met his death whilst firing a rifle in the front line.'*

*Geoffrey is buried in Croisilles Railway Cemetery along with 181 other servicemen. His grave is I. C. 2*

# WILLIAM GOTT

**William Gott** married Elsie Harriman in 1915 and they lives at Bollin House, Mobberley, later moving to 1, John Street, Altrincham. They had two children but his daughter Elsie Rene died of heart failure on the 1st January 1917 aged just 13 days.

He enlisted in the 8th Battalion of the Royal Welsh Fusiliers, becoming Private no. 16217.

**Brief history of the Battalion:**

8th (Service) Battalion, The Royal Welch Fusiliers was raised at Wrexham in August 1914 as part of Kitchener's'First New Army and joined 40th Brigade, 13th (Western) Division which assembled on Salisbury Plain. 40th Brigade moved to Chiseldon and Cirencester in September 1914. Near the end of February the Division concentrated at Blackdown in Hampshire. They moved to the Mediterranean from the 13th of June 1915 landing at Alexandria then moving to Mudros, by the 4th of July to prepare for a landing at Gallipoli. The infantry landed on Cape Helles between the 6th and 16th of July to relieve 29th Division. They returned to Mudros at the end of the month, and the entire Division landed at ANZAC Cove between the 3rd and 5th of August. They were in action in The Battle of Sari Bair, The Battle of Russell's Top and The Battle of Hill 60, at ANZAC. Soon afterwards they transferred from ANZAC to Suvla Bay. They were evacuated from Suvla on the 19th and 20th of December 1915, and after a week's rest they moved to the Helles bridgehead. They were in action during the last Turkish attacks at Helles on the 7th of January 1916 and were evacuated from Helles on the 8th and 9th. The Division concentrated at Port Said, holding forward posts in the Suez Canal defences. On the 12th of February 1916 they moved to Mesopotamia, to join the force being assembled near Sheikh Sa'a' for the relief of the besieged garrison at Kut al Amara. They joined the Tigris Corps on the 27th of March and were in action in the unsuccessful attempts to relieve Kut. They were in action in The Battle of Kut al Amara, The capture of the Hai Salient, the capture of Dahra Bend and The passage of the Diyala, in the pursuit of the enemy towards Baghdad. Units of the Division were the first troops to enter Baghdad, when it fell on the 11 March 1917.

*Thanks to the Wartime Memories Project.*
William was killed in action on the 16th February 1917.

**On that fateful day:**
The war diaries for the R.W.F were unavailable at the time of writing.

*William is remembered on the Basra memorial along with the names of 40,682 other servicemen.*

*Note:*
*It is interesting to know that Elsie stated on her pension request form that she 'did not know any particulars of her husband's family'. She was awarded 18/9 (92p) pension.*

# ERNEST GOUGH

**Ernest J. Gough** was born in Barnton, Cheshire in 1900, the only surviving child of Richard (a labourer) and Edith (a laundress) of 6, Moorside, Knutsford.

Ernest joined the Royal Devon Yeomanry as private no. 49181 but was later attached to the 1/1ˢᵗ Ox and Bucks Regiment. This became a 'composite' Battalion and sent to Russia in May 1919.

Ernest was killed on the 27ᵗʰ June 1919 whilst serving in Russia.

**Brief history of why he was lost in Russia:**
In December 1918 the battalion moved to Grammont but it was not till February 1919, when 150 all ranks returned to England, that demobilization began in earnest for the 16ᵗʰ.

In March 5 officers and 102 men transferred to the 2ⁿᵈ/4ᵗʰ Oxford and Bucks. Light Infantry, destined for the Army of Occupation in Egypt. It is clear that Ernest was one of these.

However the records show that instead of Egypt, the 1ˢᵗ Battalion of the Ox. And Bucks was despatched to Northern Russia to become a Composite Battalion, consisting of headquarters and A Company, (Oxfordshire and Buckinghamshire Light Infantry) B Company

(Royal Warwickshire Regiment), C Company (Devonshire Regiment) and D Company (Royal Berkshire Regiment). However, the War Office officially designated this unit as 1st Battalion, Oxfordshire and Buckinghamshire Light Infantry on 24 April 1919.

The reason for sending an allied expedition to North Russia was to protect a large store of war material given to the Russians in the early part of the war as it was feared these stores would fall into the hands of the enemy and also allow them to establish submarine bases at Archangel and Murmansk. The Battalion, as part of the allied force, sailed for Murmansk on 12 May 1919. The limited campaign that followed was a tragic-comic affair worthy of a Gilbert and Sullivan operetta. There appear to have been few minor skirmishes and I have not been able to establish the manner of Ernest's death.

*See also Appendix Eight.*

*Ernest is remembered on the Archangel Memorial, Russia, along with the names of 222 other servicemen.*

# WILLIAM GREAR M.M

**William Grear** was born in Mobberley in 1889, one of five children born to John (a grocer's assistant) and Elizabeth Grear of 7, Chapel Grove, Mobberley. They emigrated to Australia, where he became a farmer, and lived at 'Brighton', Station Street, Bowral, N.S.W.

All Mrs Grear's sons joined up – four went into the army and one into the navy. One of his brothers was killed at Gallipoli.

He enlisted in the 45th Battalion of the Australian Infantry as Private no. 218, attesting on the 23rd March 1916. He rose to the rank of Lance Corporal on the 22nd June 1917.

William was accidentally wounded on the left side of his scalp on the 17th March 1917 during live grenade practice. The was wounded in action on the 7th June the same year, when he received a gunshot wound to his buttocks.

William was killed in action on the 14th October 1917, having received severe injuries to his thigh, arm and leg. He died at the 3rd Canadian Casualty Clearing Station.

He is listed in the London Gazette of 26.4.17 stating that he had been awarded the Military Medal.

*William is buried in Lijssenthoek Military Cemetery along with 10,785 other servicemen. His grave is XII. C. 20A.*

# GEORGE GREGORY

**Photograph courtesy of *The Knutsford Guardian***

**George Gregory** was born in 1892 and lived with his parents Joseph, a railway platelayer, and Elizabeth and his two siblings in Back Lane, Plumley, Cheshire. He was a joiner and a wheelwright on the estate and a long-standing member of the Territorial Army and at the outbreak of the war he enlisted in the Cheshire Yeomanry, service number 1356 – a regiment raised by the ancestor of Lord Tabley, on whose land he was now a tenant.

Prior to going overseas he transferred to the 2nd Battalion of the Prince of Wales Volunteers (South Lancashire) Regiment and given the service number 31581. It is not known why he transferred but he did have two nephews in that regiment at the time.

**Brief history of the Battalion:**
2nd Battalion, The South Lancashire Regiment was based at Tidworth with 7th Brigade, 3rd Division when war was declared in August 1914. They proceeded to France with the BEF and landed at Le Havre on the 14th of August 1914. They saw action in The Battle of Mons and the rear-guard action at Solesmes, The Battle of Le Cateau, The Battle of the Marne, the Battle of the Aisne, at La Bassee, Messines and the First Battle of Ypres. They took part in the Winter Operations of 1914-15, The First Attack on Bellewaarde and the Actions at Hooge. On the 18th of October 1915 they transferred with 7th Brigade to 25th Division and on the 26th they transferred to 75th Brigade, 25th Division. They were in action in defence of the German attack on Vimy Ridge in May 1916. On the 21st of June 1916 they transferred to 64th Brigade in 21st Division and were in action in the Battles of The Somme, including The Battle of Morval in which the Division captured Gueudecourt.

*Thanks to the Wartime Memories Project.*

George was killed in action on the 21st October 1916.

**On that fateful day:**
The 2nd and 8th South Lancashires and 8th and 9th Loyals were involved in operations to clear the northern end of the Thiepval Ridge, in

particular successfully storming the Stuff and Regina trenches there on 21ˢᵗ October in the battle of the Ancre Heights.

---

**Note:**
*A letter was received from Private E. Lea (who later went on to win the Military Medal), of the same regiment confirming the news. He writes:*
*"I regret to inform you that George was killed in action on Saturday 21ˢᵗ Oct. He is sadly missed by all of us as we were all very fond of him. He was a good pal and his comrades and chums join with me in sending heartfelt sympathy to his mother."*

---

It was common practice for lads at the from to make a pact with one or more of their mates so that in the event of a death the survivor would write to the loved ones – I wonder if that was the case here?

*George is remembered on the Thiepval Memorial, along with the names of 72,203 other servicemen.*

# ERIC WALTER GRESWELL
## *(Brother of Harold)*

**Harold George Greswell** was born in Marthall, Cheshire in 1896, the son of Walter (a clergyman) and Catherine Greswell late of The Vicarage, Marthall, who transferred to Milton Abbas Vicarage, Blandford, Dorset, but by the end of the war his father was living at Chalet du Buissin, Canford Cliffs, Bournemouth.

He enlisted in the army, becoming a Lieutenant in the 8th Battalion of the Cheshire regiment, before transferring, in early 1915, to the Royal Flying Corp, which became the Royal Air Force becoming a pilot in the 111th Squadron, flying SE5A aeroplanes.

*The type of aircraft Eric flew.*

He was hospitalised on the 13th December 1915 with myalgia (severe muscle pain) and later rheumatism. He was transferred to a hospital in Gibraltar and later returned to England to convalesce. He returned to duty on the 5th March 1917.
He was killed on the 9th June 1918.

**On that fateful day:**
His surviving records show that he went 'missing in action' on the 9th June 1918 when:

*'He never returned from an E.A. (enemy aircraft) patrol.'*

On the 3rd September 1918, 2/Lt. Sarkorsky gave evidence that:

*'Eric was killed instantly when he was shot down in the neighbourhood of ET TIREH. He was buried in an olive grave close-by and a small cross was placed as a marker.'*

***Eric is re-buried at Ramleh War Cemetery, along with 3,502 other servicemen.***
***His grave is Y. 9.***

# HAROLD GEORGE GRESWELL
## *(Brother of Eric)*

**Harold George Greswell** was born in Snetterton, Norfolk in 1889, the son of Walter (a clergyman) and Catherine Greswell of The Vicarage, Marthall. He joined the army, in the Royal Engineers and went to India.

On the outbreak of was his regiment returned and they fought with the B.E.F. in France.

He was promoted to Captain and transferred to the 154th Field Battery.

**Brief history of the Battery:**

154th Field Company, The Royal Engineers served with 37th Division. The Division was formed in early 1915, in April the Division concentrated at Cholderton on Salisbury Plain and proceeded to France in July, concentrating near Tilques. They went into action in The Battle of the Ancre.

George died of wounds on the 18th August 1916.

**On that fateful day:**

Unfortunately there is no record of how and where Harold received his wounds.

*George is buried in Lapugnoy Military Cemetery, France, along with 1324 other servicemen. His grave is I. F. 66.*

# JAMES GRIFFITHS

**James Griffiths** was born in Knutsford in 1896, the son of James (a joiner and undertaker) and Catherine Griffiths of 29, King Street, Knutsford.

James became a motor mechanic and chauffeur, working in the family business.

He enlisted in the army sometime after 1915, becoming Driver no. 706914 'B' Battery 70 Bde of the Royal Field Artillery.

**Brief history of the Battery:**
LXX Brigade, Royal Field Artillery, served with 15th (Scottish) Division.
15th (Scottish) Division was formed in September 1914, as part of
Kitchener's' Second New Army. They proceeded to France in the second
week of July 1915. They were in action in the Battle of Loos in 1915. In
spring 1916, they were involved in the German gas attacks near Hulluch
and the defence of the Kink position. They were in action during the
Battles of the Somme, including The Battle of Pozieres, The Battle
of Flers-Courcelette and the capture of Martinpuich, The Battle of Le
Transloy and the attacks on the Butte de Warlencourt. In 1917 they
were in action in The First and Second Battle of the Scarpe, including
the capture of Guemappe during the Arras Offensive. They then moved
north to Flanders and were in action during the Battle of Pilckem and
The Battle of Langemarck.

*Thanks to the Wartime Memories Project.*

James was killed in action on the 24th April 1917.

**On that fateful day:**
I have been unable to gain access to the war diary.

***James has no known grave and is remembered on the Arras Memorial,
France along with 34,741 other servicemen.***

# ERNEST GROVES

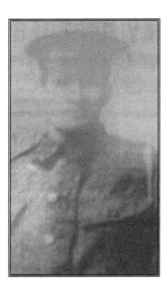

**Ernest Groves** was born in Peover, Cheshire in 1891, one of four children born to Samuel (a roadman) and Sarah Groves of Pinfold Farm, Marthall, Cheshire. Ernest was a cowman.

Ernest joined up in 1914, becoming Riflemen no. 7559 of the 1st Battalion, Kings Royal Rifle Corp. He arrived in France on the 24th March 1915.

**Brief history of the Battalion:**
1st Battalion was formed August 1914 at Aldershot. They were put under command of 6th Brigade in 2nd Division.13 August 1914. They landed at Rouen on the 13 December 1915. They transferred to 99th Brigade in same Division.

Ernest was killed in action on the 29th September 1915.

**On that fateful day:**
There is no specific entry for that day in the war diary.

*Ernest is remembered on the Loos memorial along with the names of 20.603 other servicemen.*

# GEORGE GROVES

**George Groves** was born in Over Peover, Cheshire in 1880, one of four children born to Isaac (a farm labourer) and Lydia Groves of Cinder Lane, Over Peover. George was a wagoner on a farm.

George enlisted in the army, becoming Private no. 39296 in the 8th Battalion of the Royal Welsh Fusiliers.

**Brief history of the Battalion:**

8th (Service) Battalion The Welsh Regiment was raised at Cardiff in August 1914 as part of Kitchener's Third New Army and joined 40th Brigade, 13th (Western) Division which assembled on Salisbury Plain. 40th Brigade moved to Chiseldon and Cirencester in September 1914. Near the end of February the Division concentrated at Blackdown in Hampshire, in January 1915 they became a Pioneer Battalion. They moved to the Mediterranean from the 13th of June 1915 landing at Alexandria then moving to Mudros, by the 4th of July to prepare for a landing at Gallipoli. The infantry landed on Cape Helles between the 6th and 16th of July to relieve 29th Division. They returned to Mudros at the end of the month, and the entire Division landed at ANZAC Cove between the 3rd and 5th of August. They were in action in The Battle of Sari Bair, The Battle of Russell's Top and The Battle of Hill 60, at ANZAC. Soon afterwards they transferred from ANZAC to Suvla Bay. They were evacuated from Suvla on the 19th and 20th of December 1915, and after a week's rest they moved to the Helles bridgehead. They were in action during The last Turkish attacks at Helles on the 7th of January 1916 and were evacuated from Helles on the 8th and 9th. The Division concentrated at Port Said, holding forward posts in the Suez Canal defences. On the 12th of February 1916 they moved to Mesopotamia, to join the force being assembled near Sheikh Sa'a' for the relief of the besieged garrison at Kut al Amara. They joined the Tigris Corps on the 27th of March and were in action in the unsuccessful attempts to relieve Kut. They were in action in The Battle of Kut al Amara, The capture of the Hai Salient, he capture of Dahra Bend and The passage of the Diyala, in the pursuit of the enemy towards Baghdad. Units of the Division were the first troops to enter Baghdad, when it fell on the 11 March 1917. The Division then joined "M"rshall's Column" "nd pushed north across Iraq, fighting at Delli 'A'bas, Duqma, Nahr Kalis, crossing the 'A'haim on the 18 April and fighting at Shatt al 'A'haim. Later in the year they were in action in the Second and Third Actions of Jabal Hamrin.

*Thanks to the Wartime Memories Project.*

George died from disease (pneumonia) on the 22nd December 1917.

*George is buried in Baghdad (North Gate) Cemetery, along with 4,160 other servicemen. His Grave is IV. J. 8.*

# SIDNEY GROVES

**Sidney Groves** was born in Knutsford in 1886, the son of George and Ellen Groves. He resided with his wife Marguerite Groves at 16, Towson Street, Hulme, Manchester.

He enlisted in the 71 Training Battalion (Tank Corp) in 1915 as Private no. 33538.

Sidney was invalided out of the army on the 18th July 1917 as 'sick'. He died at home from Pneumonia on the 29th November 1918.

*Sidney is buried in Knutsford cemetery*

# ALFRED HALE

**Alfred Hale** was born in Over Peover, Cheshire in 1883, one of eleven children born to Sarah Hale (a laundress) of Over Peover. Alfred was a farm labourer. He was married to Mary and they lived with his widowed mother and his grandmother.

No records exist for him but it is known he died of Pneumonia on the 7th December 1918. He died at home.

*Alfred is buried in Over Peover (St. Lawrence) Churchyard, Cheshire.*

# GEORGE HAMMAN

**George Hamman** was born in Knutsford in 1877 to John (a butcher) and Amelia Hamman of Aston, Budworth, Cheshire. He married Ann in 1911 and they set up home at 52, Mobberley Road, Knutsford.

George's service record no longer exists but we know he joined the 1st/5th Battalion of the Cheshire Regiment as Private no. 3995.

**Brief history of the Battalion:**
The 1/5th (Earl of Chester's' Battalion, Cheshire Regiment was a Territorial unit based in in Chester with Cheshire Brigade, Welsh Division, when war was declared in August 1914. They were immediately mobilised and moved to Shrewsbury and Church Stretton, by the end of August they moved to Northampton and then in December to Cambridge for final preparations. They proceeded to France on the 15th of February 1915, landing at Le Havre to join 14th Brigade, 5th Division. They were in action in The Battle of Mons and the subsequent retreat, The Battle of Le Cateau, The Battle of the Marne, The Battle of the Aisne, The Battles of La Bassee and Messines and The First Battle of Ypres. In 1915 they were in action at The Second Battle of Ypres and the Capture of Hill 60. In autumn 1915, many units were exchanged with units from

the newly arrived volunteer 32nd Division, to stiffen the inexperienced Division with regular army troops. On the 29th of November 1915 they became a Pioneer Battalion. On the 13th of February 1916 the 1/5th Chester's transferred to the newly reformed 56th (London) Division, in the Hallencourt area in February. In 1916 they were in action on The Somme taking part in the diversionary attack at Gommecourt on the 1st of July. Also The Battle of Ginchy, The Battle of Flers-Courcelette, The Battle of Morval in which the Division captured Combles and The Battle of the Transloy Ridges.

*Thanks to the Wartime Memories Project.*

George was killed in action on the 21st September 1916, when a shell burst amongst a platoon, killing several of them.

**On that fateful day:**
The war diary states:

*'21.9.16 N.W edge of BOULE AUX WOOD*
*A & B Coy with lewis gunners, sappers and signallers employed up in fire trench called RANGER TRENCH.*
*11 OR killed.'*

*George is buried in Delville Wood Cemetery, Longueval, France along with 5,523 other servicemen. He is buried in XXIV. H. 1.*

258

# HARRY HAMMOND

**Harry Hammond** was born in 1894 at Knutsford, the stepson of Frances Hammond, a widow, residing at 47, Old Market Place, Knutsford. He took employment as a gardener.

They later moved to no. 6, Old Market Street, Knutsford.

Harry's service record no longer exists but we know he joined the 5th Battalion of the Oxfordshire and Buckinghamshire Light Infantry as Private no. 11916.

He arrived in France on the 20th May 1915. He was later promoted to lance corporal.

**Brief history of the Battalion:**

5th (Service) Battalion, Oxfordshire and Buckinghamshire Light Infantry was raised at Oxford in August 1914 as part of Kitchener's'First New Army and joined 42nd Brigade, 14th (Light) Division. After training they proceeded to France, landing at Boulogne on the 21st of May 1915. They fought in the Action of Hooge, being the first division to be attacked by flamethrowers. They were in action in The Second Attack on Bellewarde.

*Thanks to the Wartime Memories Project.*

Harry died of wounds in hospital in Tottenham, Middlesex on the 3rd October 1915.

Unfortunately I have been unable to locate the exact date and place where he sustained his injuries.

*Harry is buried in Tottenham Cemetery, Middlesex, together with another 502 servicemen.*

# JACK HAMMOND

**Jack Hammond** was born in Knutsford.

He initially enlisted in the Royal Army Service Corp before transferring to the 18th Battalion of the Lancashire Fusiliers.

He went to France on the 8th July 1915.

**Brief history of the Battalion:**
The 18th Battalion, Lancashire Fusiliers was raised as a Bantam Battalion (troops who were under the normal regulation minimum height of 5 feet 3 inches) in Bury on the 13th of January 1915 by Lieut-Col. G. E. Wike and a Committee. After initial training close to home, they moved to Garswood Park, Ashton in Makerfield on the 8th of April 1915. On the 21st of June they joined 104th Brigade, 35th Division at Masham, North Yorkshire. They moved to Cholderton, Salisbury Plain for final training in August and the Battalion was formally adopted by the War Office on the 27th. They were ordered to Egypt in late 1915, but the order was soon cancelled and they proceeded to France landing at Le Havre on the 29th of January 1916, the division concentrated east of St Omer. They were in action during the Battles of the Somme at Bazentin Ridge, Arrow Head Copse, Maltz Horn Farm and Falfemont Farm. The division received new drafts of men to replace losses suffered on the Somme, but the CO. soon discovered that these new recruits were not of the same physical standard as the original Bantams, being men of small stature from the towns, rather than the miners and farm workers who had joined up in 1915. A medical inspection was carried out and 1439 men were transferred to the Labour Corps. Their places being taken by men transferred from the disbanded yeomanry regiments, who underwent a quick training course in infantry methods at a Divisional depot set up specifically for that purpose. In 1917 they were in action during the pursuit to the Hindenburg Line, at Houthulst Forest and The Second Battle of Passchendaele. In 1918 they fought in the First Battle of Bapaume, and the Final Advance in Flanders including The Battle of Courtrai and The action of Tieghem. Hey crossed the River Scheldt near Berchem on the 9th of November and by the Armistice they had entered Grammont.

*Thanks to the Wartime Memories Project.*

Jack was killed in action on the 1ˢᵗ June 1918.

## On that fateful day:
The war diary states:

*'1.6.18 HEDAUVILLE*
*Battalion takes part in the attack on AVELUY WOOD. Objectives reached but*
*Unable to be held. Capt. WS MORRIS and 2/LT THOMPSON killed in action.*
*Lieut. Ward M.C., 2/Lieuts Crowden, Grimshaw, Parry, Pritchard (died of wounds 3-6-18), Turnbull (died of wounds 4-6-18) and Gresty wounded. 2/Tt Almond wounded and missing.*
*18 O.R. killed in action.*
*5 O.R. wounded and missing*
*43 O.R. missing*
*122 O.R. wounded in action*
*17 O.R. wounded (at duty)*
*5 O.R. wounded in action and (died of wounds)*
*Battalion is relieved by the 19ᵗʰ D.L.I. and 17ᵗʰ Royal Scots.'*

*Jack is buried in Martinsart British Cemetery, France along with 488 other servicemen. His grave is I. B. 54.*

# JAMES HAMMOND

**James Hammond** was born in Knutsford in 1895, one of seven children born to Joseph (a labourer) and Martha of 50, Silk Mill Street, Knutsford, James was a bricklayer.

He enlisted in the 2nd Battalion of the Cheshire Regiment in 1914, becoming Private no. 14400.

He arrived in France on the 28th October 1915.

**Brief history of the Battalion:**

The 2nd Battalion, Cheshire Regiment was a regular unit of the British Army and was in Jubbulpore, India when war broke out in August 1914. They returned to England, landing at Devonport on the 24th of December 1914. They joined 84th Brigade, 28th Division, at Winchester and proceeded to France, embarking at Southampton and landing at Le Havre on the 17th of January 1915. 28th Division concentrated in the area between Bailleul and Hazebrouck. They saw action in the Second Battle of Ypres, where casualties were high and The Battle of Loos. In October 1915 were ordered to Egypt and sailed from Marseilles for Alexandria, then on to Salonika in January 1916. They took part in the occupation of Mazirko and the capture of Barakli Jum'a'in October 1916. In 1917 they were involved in the capture of Barakli and Kumli and in 1918 were in action in the Battle of Doiran and the pursuit to the Strumica valley. When hostilities with Bulgaria ended on the 30th of September 1918 they were in the area of Trnovo.

*Thanks to the Wartime Memories Project.*

James was hospitalised in May 1917 with malaria. He was treated and returned to his unit.

He was killed in action on the 24th January 1918.

**On that fateful day:**
There is no war diary entry for this date but we know the Battalion was resting at JAJAHLI.

*James is buried in the Dorian War Cemetery, Greece along with 1,338 other servicemen. His grave is VI. J. 24.*

# JOHN JAMES HAMMOND

**John James Hammond** was born in Knutsford but the family moved to Altrincham.

James was a regular soldier, joining the 1ˢᵗ Battalion of the Cheshire Regiment as Private no. 9011 in 1908.

His records, which still exist, show that his conduct was far from exemplary.

He arrived in France on the 21ˢᵗ July 1915.

**Brief history of the Battalion:**

The 1ˢᵗ Battalion, Cheshire Regiment was a regular unit of the British Army and was in Londonderry when war broke out in August 1914 with 15ᵗʰ Brigade in 5ᵗʰ Division. They returned to England and proceeded to France with the British Expeditionary Force, landing at Le Havre on the 16ᵗʰ of August 1914. They saw action at The Battle of Mons, The Battle of the Marne, The Battle of the Aisne, The Battles of La Bassee, at Messines and in The First Battle of Ypres. Between the 3ʳᵈ of March and 7ᵗʰ of April 1915 they were attached with 15ᵗʰ Brigade to 28ᵗʰ Division in in exchange for 83ʳᵈ Brigade in order to familiarise the newly arrived troops with the Western Front. In 1915 they were in action in The Second Battle of Ypres and the Capture of Hill 60. In March 1916 they took over a sector in the front line in the southern edge of Vimy Ridge, in front of Arras. The 5ᵗʰ Division arrived on the Somme to relieve the British units who had suffered badly in the attack on the first of July and went into action at High Wood, being withdrawn in October. The Division spent late autumn and winter near Festubert and in 1917 were in action in the Battles of Arras and the Third Battle of Ypres.

*Thanks to the Wartime Memories Project.*

He was killed in action on the 14ᵗʰ April 1917

**On that fateful day:**
The war diary states:

**'1'.4.17AVION**
*The Brigade will advance at 5am this morning. The 16ᵗʰ Warwicks as advance guard with 1ˢᵗ Cheshires in support N.E of La CEUTTE CHACES TRENCH.*

*Parties of Huns seen leaving the village of AVION – about 15 carrying machine guns taking the rad to LENS.*

*5 OR killed'.*

*John is buried in La Chaudiere Military Cemetery, Vimy along with 908 other servicemen. His grave is V. E. 4.*

# WILLIAM HAMMOND

**William Hammond** was born in 1885 and was the husband of Sarah and together they had two children. They lived at 12, Middle Walk,

Cross Town, Knutsford. He was a cooper by trade and was a very proficient ambulance man too.

He was one of the first in the town to volunteer to fight.

His service record no longer exists but we know he enlisted in 1914 and joined the 2nd Battalion of the Cheshire Regiment as Private no. 11982.

He went to France on the 6th March 1915.

**Brief history of the Battalion:**

The 2nd Battalion, Cheshire Regiment was a regular unit of the British Army and was in Jubbulpore, India when war broke out in August 1914. They returned to England, landing at Devonport on the 24th of December 1914. They joined 84th Brigade, 28th Division, at Winchester and proceeded to France, embarking at Southampton and landing at Le Havre on the 17th of January 1915. 28th Division concentrated in the area between Bailleul and Hazebrouck. They saw action in the Second Battle of Ypres, where casualties were high and The Battle of Loos.

*Thanks to the Wartime Memories Project.*

He was killed in action on the 7th May 1915.

**On that fateful day:**
The war diary states:

**'7.5.15 VERLORENHOEK**
*At 11pm no. 1 & 4 Coy took over the section of firing line held by the 15th batt Welsh regiment and no. 2 & 3 Coy occupying support trenches.*

*6 OR killed 7 wounded'.*

***William has no known grave but is remembered on the Menin Gate Memorial, Ypres, along with the names of more than 54,000 other servicemen.***

# THOMAS HENRY HARRISON

**Thomas Henry Harrison** was born in Openshaw, Lancashire in 1880 and moved with his wife Elisabeth and five children to Mount Pleasant, Earls lane, Pickmere, Cheshire, where he worked as a salt packer.

He enlisted in the 18th Battalion of the Welsh Regiment, where he rose to the rank of corporal.

**Brief history of the Battalion:**

18th (2nd Glamorgan Battalion, The Welsh Regiment was raised at Cardiff in January 1915 as a Bantam Battalion. They moved to Porthcawl and joined 43rd Division. In July they moved to Prees Heath, transferring to 119th Brigade, 40th Division. They moved to Aldershot in September. The Division proceeded to France in the first week of June 1916 and concentrated near Lillers. They went into the front line near Loos and were later in action in The Battle of the Ancre on the Somme. In 1917 they saw action during The German retreat to the Hindenburg Line, The capture of Fifteen Ravine, Villers Plouich, Beaucamp and La Vacquerie and The Cambrai Operations, including the capture of Bourlon Wood in November.

Thanks to the Wartime Memories Project.

Thomas was killed in action on the 24th November 1917.

**On that fateful day:**

The war diary states:

*24.11.17 ANNEUX CHAPELLE*

*At 9am the enemy made a counter-attack and drove back the Brigade line slightly in the NE of the wood. 'D' Company were able to hold up the attack on the left. Captain C B Percival was killed by a sniper whilst going round his front line. The remainder of 'C', 'B' and 'A' Companies under captain D G Edmonds were forced to give ground – their right flank being in the air. 2/Lt J Rogers and J H Curtis were both killed during the morning and 2/Lt H E LEESE and H S Gracie were both wounded and afterwards died of wounds. 2/Lt L G Lewis was killed later in the day. 2/Lt R D Hanson was wounded during the afternoon. The position became very uncertain just before dark. The different units in the wood had become very disorganised. Under the cover of night they were sorted out as much as possible. The different Companies then returned to approx. the same positions*

269

*as they had held on the previous night.*

*During the night 24/25 November the line held by the brigade was shortened by the taking over of the EAST side of the wood by the 2nd Scots Guards.*

This action continued the following day and then the Battalion was relieved. Their losses were reported as:
11 officers killed 3 wounded
126 OR killed or missing
136 OR wounded.

*Thomas has no known grave and is remembered on the Cambrai memorial along with the names of 7,057 other servicemen.*

# ALFRED HARROP

**Alfred Harrop** was born in 1872 and by 1911 he was a farm labourer at Fullworth Gate, Allostock, Cheshire, working for Mr and Mrs Steel.

He enlisted in the army, becoming Private no.17478 of the Cheshire Regiment. It is unclear if he was serving with the 3rd or the 9th Battalion.

He went to France on the 19th July 1915,

He died 'at home' on the 12th March 1917. As records no longer exist we don't know what the reason for his death was.

*Alfred is buried in Northwich Cemetery.*

*Note:*
*His medals were never claimed.*

# JAMES HARROP

**James Harrop** was born in Knutsford. He moved to Patricroft, Lancashire and on marrying Martha Ann and they lived at 38, Flint Street, Clayton Manchester.

He enlisted in the 19th Battalion of the Lancashire Fusiliers, becoming Private no. 17341.

### Brief history of the Battalion:

The 19th Battalion, Lancashire Fusiliers were known as The 3rd Salford Pals, the battalion was raised in Salford on the 15th of January 1915, by Mr Montague Barlow MP and the Salford Brigade Committee. They began training near home and in March they moved to Conway for training. They became part of the 96th Brigade, 32nd Division and moved on the 21st of June 1915 to Catterick in North Yorkshire, using the firing ranges at Strenshall. In August 1915 they moved for final training and firing practice at Codford on Salisbury Plain. They proceeded to France, landing at Boulogne on the 22nd of November 1915. On the 5th of January 1916 they transferred to 14th Brigade still with 32nd Division. Their first taste of action was at Thiepval Ridge on The Somme on the 1st of July 1916, the battle resulted in the Salford Pals being almost wiped out. On the 29th of July 1916 they transferred to GHQ and converted to be a Pioneer Battalion, joining 49th (West Riding) Division on the 7th of August. In 1917 they were involved in the Operations on the Flanders Coast and the Battle of Poelcapelle during the Third Battle of Ypres.

*Thanks to the Wartime Memories Project.*

James died of wounds on the 11th July 1917. Unfortunately, as his service record no longer exists, I have been unable to discover when and where he received those wounds.

*James is buried in Coxyde Military Cemetery, along with 1507 other servicemen. His grave is I. I. 14.*

# JAMES HARROP

**James Harrop** was born in Allostock, Cheshire in 1898, one of four children born to Samuel (a farmer) and Bessie Harrop of Allostock.

James enlisted in the army sometime after 1915, becoming Private no. 36585 of the 6th Battalion of the Prince of Wales Volunteers (South Lancashire Regiment).

**Brief history of the Battalion:**

The 6th (Service) Battalion, The South Lancashire Regiment was raised at Warrington in August 1914 as part of Kitchener's'First New Army and joined 38th Brigade, 13th (Western) Division; they trained at Tidworth spending the winter in billets at Winchester. Near the end of February the Division concentrated at Blackdown in Hampshire, with the 6th East Lancashire's at Alma Barracks. They sailed from Avonmouth on the 16th of June 1915 landing at Alexandria then moving to Mudros, by the 4th of July to prepare for a landing at Gallipoli. The infantry landed on Cape Helles between the 6th and 16th of July to relieve 29th Division. They returned to Mudros at the end of the month, and the entire Division landed at ANZAC Cove between the 3rd and 5th of August. They were in action in The Battle of Sari Bair, The Battle of Russell's'Top and The Battle of Hill 60, at ANZAC. Soon afterwards they transferred from ANZAC to Suvla Bay. They were evacuated from Suvla on the 19th and 20th of December 1915, and after a week's rest they moved to the Helles bridgehead. They were in action during the last Turkish attacks at Helles on the 7th of January 1916 and were evacuated from Helles on the 8th and 9[th.] The Division concentrated at Port Said, holding forward posts in the Suez Canal defences. On the 12th of February 1916 they moved to Mesopotamia, to join the force being assembled near Sheikh Sa'a' for the relief of the besieged garrison at Kut al Amara. They joined the Tigris Corps on the 27th of March and were in action in the unsuccessful attempts to relieve Kut. They were in action in The Battle of Kut al Amara, The capture of the Hai Salient, the capture of Dahra Bend and The passage of the Diyala, in the pursuit of the enemy towards Baghdad. Units of the Division were the first troops to enter Baghdad, when it fell on the 11 March 1917. The Division then joined "M"rshall's'Column" "nd pushed north across Iraq, fighting at Delli 'A'bas, Duqma, Nahr Kalis, crossing the 'A'haim on the 18 April and fighting at Shatt al 'A'haim. Later in the year they were in action in the Second and Third Actions of Jabal Hamrin

*Thanks to the Wartime Memories Project.*

James 'DIED' on the 25th May 1917.

**On that fateful day:**
James died of disease.

**Disease in the Mesopotamian Campaign:**
Like Gallipoli, conditions in Mesopotamia defy description. Extremes of temperature (120 degrees F was common); arid desert and regular flooding; flies, mosquitoes and other vermin: all led to appalling levels of sickness and death through disease. Under these incredible conditions, units fell short of officers and men, and all too often the reinforcements were half-trained and ill-equipped. Medical arrangements were quite shocking, with wounded men spending up to two weeks on boats before reaching any kind of hospital. These factors, plus of course the unexpectedly determined Turkish resistance, contributed to high casualty rates.

11012 killed
3985 died of wounds
12678 died of sickness
13492 missing and prisoners (9000 at Kut)
51836 wounded

*Data from "S"atistics of the Military Effort of the British Empire" "London: HMSO, 1920).*

*James is buried in Basra War Cemetery, Iraq, along with 2,841 other servicemen. His grave is IV. M. 12.*

# HENRY HATTON

**Henry Hatton** was born in Mobberley, Cheshire in 1878, one of thirteen children born to Henry (a retired farmer) and Hannah Hatton of Moss Lane, Mobberley. Henry took employment as a wagoner.

He enlisted in the 13th Battalion of the Cheshire Regiment in 1915, becoming private no. 27613.

**Brief history of the Battalion:**
The 13th (Service) Battalion, Cheshire Regiment was raised at Port Sunlight on 1 September 1914 by Gershom Stewart, MP. They moved to Chester and joined 74th Brigade, 25th Division in Kitchener's' Third New Army. The Division assembled in the area around Salisbury for training and the 13th Cheshires spent the winter in billets in Bournemouth. The division moved to Aldershot in May 1915 for final training. They proceeded to France on the 25th of September 1915 and concentrated in the area of Nieppe. Their first action was in defence of the German attack on Vimy Ridge in May 1916. They

then moved to The Somme and joined the Battle just after the main attack, with 75ᵗʰ Brigade making a costly attack near Thiepval on the 3ʳᵈ of July. The Division was in action at The Battle of Bazentin, The Battle of Pozieres and The Battle of the Ancre Heights.

*Thanks to the Wartime Memories Project.*

Henry was wounded in action on the 19ᵗʰ July 1916 with a severe gunshot wound to his left leg which 'shattered his femur'.

**On that fateful day:**
Henry was carried to no. 36 Field Hospital(FA), then to 38 Casualty Clearing Station (CCS) then to 13 General Hospital (GH) where his left leg was amputated. He was transferred to England on the hospital ship Cambria but he died at 9.45 p.m. on the 19ᵗʰ July 1916 at the East Suffolk and Ipswich Hospital – his death attributed to the amputation and haemorrhaging.
*(See appendix One for Casualties)*

*Henry is buried in the St Wilfred and Mary Churchyard, Mobberley.*

# PERCY HEALEY

**Percy Healey** was born in Knutsford in 1891, one of two children born to Walter Willie Healey (a postman) and Agnes Healey of Parrs bank House, Albert Street, Knutsford. . Percy worked as a compositor.

He joined the Royal Field Artillery as Driver no. 43146 of XVI Corp (HQ)

I am unable to trace exactly where he was and with which Battery at the time.

He died of disease on the 17th October 1918.

*Percy is buried in Struma Military cemetery, Greece along with 947 other servicemen. His grave is VII. J. 5.*

# HERBERT HULSE

**Herbert Hulse** was born in 1899 in Allostock, Cheshire. He was one of eight children born to William (A wheelwright) and Sarah.

Although his army records no longer exist, we know he enlisted in the army at Norwich sometime after 1915, becoming Private no. 39425 of the East Lancashire Regiment, before transferring to the 1st Battalion of the Northumberland Fusiliers as Private 65328.

**Brief history of the Battalion:**
The 1st Battalion, Northumberland Fusiliers were in Portsmouth at the outbreak of war in August 1914. They proceeded to France landing at Le Havre on the 14th of August 1914. Serving with the 9th Brigade, 3rd Division, BEF. They remained on the Western Front throughout the conflict, seeing action in most of the major battles. They saw action in The Battle of Mons and the rearguard action at Solesmes, The Battle of Le Cateau, The Battle of the Marne, The Battle of the Aisne, at La Bassee, Messines and the First Battle of Ypres. They took part in the Winter Operations of 1914-15, The First Attack on Bellewaarde and the Actions at Hooge. In 1916 they took part in The Actions of the Bluff and St Eloi Craters then moved to The Somme for The Battle of Albert, The Battle of Bazentin helping to capture Longueval, The Battle of Delville Wood and The Battle of the Ancre. In 1917 They were at Arras, seeing

action at Battles of the Scarpe and The Battle of Arleux. They moved north to the Flanders and were in action during The Battle of the Menin Road and Battle of Polygon Wood during the Third Battle of Ypres. Then moved south and were in action at The Battle of Cambrai. In 1918 they were in action on The Somme, in the Battles of the Lys, the Battles of the Hindenburg Line and the Battle of the Selle.

*Thanks to the Wartime Memories Project.*

Herbert was killed in action on the 23rd August 1918.

**On that fateful day:**
The war diary states:

***24.8.18 IN THE FIELD***
*Battalion attacked at 11am and reached its objective on Green line south of GOMIECOURT. 2 Division passed through making for ARRAS-BAPAUME Road. Battalion concentrating in Sunken Road at G 6 C owing to shelling.*

*(For report of the battle See Appendix XX)*

The diary goes on to mention all the names of the officers lost but makes no mention of 'other ranks'

*Herbert has no known grave but is remembered on the Vis-En-Artois Memorial, France along with the names of 9847 other servicemen.*

# THOMAS HOULDEN

Thomas Houlden was born in Tabley, Cheshire in 1892, the son of Joseph (a road labourer) and Elisabeth of 4, Hall Bank, Mobberley.

He enlisted in the 1/5th Battalion of the Loyal North Lancashire Regiment in 1916, arriving in France early in 1917.

**Brief History of the Battalion:**

1/5th Battalion, The Loyal North Lancashire Regiment was based in Bolton when war broke out in August 1914 with the North Lancashire Brigade, West Lancashire Division. They were mobilised and moved to Chipping Sodbury for training, then in November they moved to Sevenoaks. In February 1915 the battalion left the West Lancashire Division and preceded to France, landing at le Havre to join 16th Brigade, 6th Division. On the 11th of June 1915 the 1/5th Battalion transferred to 151st Brigade, 50th (Northumbrian) Division and saw action in the Second Battle of Ypres. On the 21st of December 1915 they transferred to 26th Brigade, 9th (Scottish) Division then on the 8th of January 1916 they transferred to the re-formed 166th Brigade, 55th (West Lancashire) Division which was concentrating in the Hallencourt area. On the 16th of February 1916 the Division relieved the French 88th Division south of Arras, they moved to The Somme in late July taking over a section of front line near the village of Guillemont. They were in action at the Battle of Guillemont, The Battle of Ginchy, The Battle of Flers-Courcelette and The Battle of Morval. The Division moved to Flanders in October 1916 and took over the front line between Wieltje and Railway Wood. In 1917 they were in action at Pilkem Ridge and Menin Road Ridge during the Third Battle of Ypres. They moved south to Cambrai where the 1/5th Loyal North Lancashire's suffered very heavily during the German Counter Attacks on the 30th of November 1917. In the Spring of 1918 having been much re-enforced, they were in action in the Battle of the Lys. On the 4th of June 1918 the battalion transferred to 170th Brigade in 57th (2nd West Lancashire) Division and absorbed the 4/5th Battalion. They were in action during the Second Battles of Arras, the Battles of the Hindenburg Line including assisting in the capture of Cambrai in October.

*Thanks to the Wartime Memories Project.*

Thomas was killed in action on the 20th August 1918.

**On that fateful day:**
There is no action recorded in the war diary for this date.

***Thomas has no known grave and is remembered on the Vis-En-Artois Memorial, along with the names of 9,847 other servicemen.***

# SIDNEY HOWARD

**Sidney Howard** was born in Manchester in 1894, the son of Albert Edward (a publican) and Catherine, who later became the licensees of the White Bear in Knutsford. Sidney stayed for a time with his uncle who ran the Rose and Crown in Knutsford.

He joined the 12th Battalion of the Manchester Regiment, becoming Private, later Lance Corporal 251776.

**Brief history of the Battalion:**

The 12th (Service) Battalion, Manchester was raised at Ashton-under-Lyne in September 1914 as part of Kitchener's Second New Army, and joined 52nd Brigade, 17th (Northern) Division. After initial training close to home, they moved to Wimborne in January 1915 they in May 1915 moved to Hursley Park, Winchester for final training. The division had been selected for Home Defence duties, but this was reversed and they proceeded to France, landing at Boulogne on the 17th of July 1915, the division concentrating near St Omer. They moved into the Southern Ypres salient for trench familiarisation and then took over the the front lines in that area. In the spring of 1916 they were in action at the Bluff, south east of Ypres on the Comines canal then moved south to The Somme seeing action during The Battle of Albert in which the Division captured Fricourt and The Battle of Delville Wood. In 1917 they moved to Arras and saw action in The First and Second Battles of the Scarpe and The Capture of Roeux. In late summer they moved to Flanders, on the 24th of September 1917 they absorbed the Headquarters troops and two squadrons of the dismounted Duke of Lancaster's Yeomanry and fought in The First and Second Battles of Passchendaele.

*Thanks to the Wartime Memories Project.*

Sidney died of wounds on the 26th October 1917.

I have been unable to trace where and when he received his wounds.

***Sidney is buried in Dozinghem Military Cemetery, along with another 3,312 other servicemen. His grave is X. D. 13.***

# SAMUEL STARKEY HOWARTH

**Samuel Starkey Howarth** was born in Knutsford in 1878, one of nine children born to Samuel (a butcher) and Mary Howarth of 91, King Street, Knutsford. Samuel assisted in his father's shop.

Samuel enlisted in the 11th Battalion of the Cheshire Regiment, becoming Private later Lance Corporal no. 16993.

The 11th (Service) Battalion, Cheshire Regiment was raised in Chester on the 17th of September 1914 as part of Kitchener's Third New Army and joined 75th Brigade, 25th Division. They trained at Codford St Mary and spent the winter in billets in Bournemouth. They moved to Aldershot for final training in May 1915 and proceeded to France on the 26th of September, the division concentrating in the area of Nieppe. On the 26th of October they transferred to 7th Brigade still with 25th Division. Their first action was in defence of the German attack on Vimy Ridge in May 1916. They then moved to The Somme and joined the Battle just after the main attack, with 75th Brigade making a costly attack near Thiepval on the 3rd of July. The Division was in action at The Battle of Bazentin, The Battle of Pozieres and The Battle of the Ancre Heights. In 1917 they were in action at The Battle of Messines attacking between the Wulverghem-Messines and Wulverghem-Wytschaete roads. In the Third battle of Ypres were in action during The Battle of Pilkem. In 1918 they were in action on The Somme, in the Battles of the Lys suffering heavy losses. On the 17th of June 1918 the battalion was reduced to cadre strength with many troops transferring to the 1/6<sup>th</sup> Cheshires. On the 23<sup>rd</sup> of June the cadre transferred to 39<sup>th</sup> Division and on the 3<sup>rd</sup> of August was disbanded in France.

*Thanks to the Wartime Memories Project.*

Samuel died of Pneumonia at home on the 26<sup>th</sup> October 1918

***Samuel is buried in Knutsford Cemetery.***

# WALTER GEORGE HOWARTH

**Walter George Howarth** was born in Knutsford in 1890, the son of Amy (a laundress) Howarth of Silk Mill Street, Knutsford. He became a domestic gardener.

By 1911 he was a boarder at 13, Chapel Street, Didsbury, plying his trade.

He enlisted in the 9th Battalion of the Lancashire Fusiliers, becoming Private no. 3624.

**Brief history of the Battalion:**
The 9th (Service) Battalion was formed at Bury on 31 August 1914 as part of K1 and came under orders of 34th Brigade, 11th (Northern) Division. They moved to Belton Park near Grantham. In April 1915 moved to Witley Camp near Godalming in Surrey. The Battalion sailed from Liverpool on 5 July 1915, going via Mudros to Suvla Bay, disembarking on 6 August 1915. In January 1916 they moved to Egypt., then went on to France in July 1916.

*Thanks to The Long, Long Trail.*

Walter was killed in action on the 21st August 1915.

**On that fateful day:**
The war diary for that date makes no reference to this date whatsoever.

*Walter is remembered on the Helles Memorial, Turkey, along with the names of 20,885 other servicemen.*

# GEORGE WILKINSON HULME

**George Wilkinson Hulme** was born in High Legh, Cheshire in 1895 and by 1911 he was working as a wagoner for a Mr Peter Wilkinson at Mere Heys Farm, Winterbottom, Nr. Knutsford.

He enlisted in the army, becoming Private no. 277258 in the 2/7th Battalion of the Manchester Regiment.

**Brief history of the Battalion:**

The 2/7th Battalion were formed in August 1914 in Burlington Street, Manchester. It was part of Manchester Brigade, East Lancashire Division. On the 25 September 1914 they landed at Alexandria in Egypt. On the 6th May 1915 the Battalion landed on Gallipoli. On the 26 May 1915 the formation became 127th Brigade, 42nd (East Lancashire) Division. On the 8th December 1915 they were evacuated from Gallipoli, landed on Mudros and preceded to Egypt. Then on the 2nd March 1917 they landed Marseilles and proceeded to the Western Front.

*Thanks to the Long, Long Trail.*

George was killed in action on the 2nd August 1917.

**On that fateful day:**

There is no entry in the war records for this day.

*George is remembered on the Nieuport Memorial, Belgium along with the names of 566 other servicemen.*

# JOHN HULSE

**John Hulse** was born on the 2nd June 1898 in Lower Peover, Cheshire. He was the son of John, a brewer's carter, working for The Bells of

Peover, and Lydia Hulse. He was a single man who lived with his parents and four siblings at Free Green, Over Peover, Cheshire.

He was a quiet, sensitive boy who wrote poetry (see Appendix nine). He enlisted shortly after his 18th birthday and joined the Cheshire Regiment, service number 243692. Shortly after reaching the front he was drafted into the Machine Gun Company, given the new service number of 142980. This company only came into existence in April 1917. He remained within the 25th Brigade as did his former regiment.

**Brief history of the Battalion:**

The 25th Machine Gun Company was formed from the Machine Gun Sections of 25th Brigade, 8th Division on the 10th of January 1916. They were in action at the Battle of The Somme. In 1917 they fought in The German retreat to the Hindenburg Line and then moved to Flanders and were in action in The Battle of Pilkem and The Battle of Langemarck. On the 20th January 1918 they joined with the other Machine Gun Companies of the Division to form the 8th Machine Gun Battalion.

John was killed in action on the 12th April 1918.

*John's 'Death Plaque' – one of 1.1 Million sent to grieving families.*

## On that fateful day:
No records exist for the day he died but we know it was during that failed German offensive John Hulse was killed. He has no known grave. He is just one of 62,049 machine gunners who were killed out of a total of 170,500 drafted into the company.

*John is remembered on the Ploegstreert Memorial, Belgium, along with the names of 11,386 other servicemen.*

*John's memorial in Lower Peover Churchyard (You can see Sydney Leicester's in the right background).*

# ARTHUR HULSTON

**Arthur Hurlston** was born in Crewe in 1891, the son of John and Ann Hurlston of 21, Wood Street, Crewe.

He enlisted in the army at Northwich, becoming Sapper no. 51025 of the Lines of Communication Company, Royal Engineers.

**Brief history of the R.E Company:**

When the British government declared war on Germany, the War Office issued orders for mobilisation of the British Expeditionary Force in accordance with the existing plan. The 13 Field Companies then at home on a peacetime establishment were reorganised to create twelve Field Companies, two for each of the six Divisions of the BEF. Men required to bring these Companies up to war establishment units came from the RE Training Depot at Aldershot (mounted men) and the RE Reserve Battalion and Depot Companies at Chatham (dismounted men).

Orders were soon given to recall regular units that were on garrison duty overseas (often once they had been replaced by an outgoing Territorial unit). As they arrived in England, these units were formed into new regular Divisions.

In September 1914 an urgent recommendation was received from GHQ in France that the needs of war required a third Field Company per Division. This had been recommended in 1912 but not implemented. Arrangements were made for eight Territorial Field Companies to fill these places in the first eight Divisions. The Companies were given numbers in February 1917.

*Thanks to The Long, Long Trail.*

Arthur 'died' in Italy on the 28th September 1918. His service records no longer exist so we do not know when or from what he died.

*Arthur is buried in Staglieno Cemetery, Genoa, along with 352 other servicemen. His grave is I. C. 3.*

# JAMES HURDSFIELD

**James Hurdsfield** lived at 3, Green Street, Knutsford with his wife, Drusilla (Kent) and this three children. He was a painter.

He enlisted in the 2<sup>nd</sup> Battalion of the Cheshire Regiment as private no. 12874, later transferring the Royal Defence Corp as Private no. 414879.

He suffered from Myalgia, contracted whilst at the front, and was invalided out of the service.

He died at home on the 13<sup>th</sup> January 1918.

*James is buried in Knutsford Cemetery.*

# HARRY ILLIDGE

**Harry Illidge** was born in Wolverhampton and enlisted in Knutsford in the 8<sup>th</sup> Battalion of the Cheshire Regiment, becoming Private no. 16098.

**Brief history of the Battalion:**

The 8th (Service) Battalion, Cheshire Regiment was raised in Chester on the 12th of August 1914 as part of Kitchener's First New Army and joined 40th Brigade, 13th (Western) Division which assembled on Salisbury Plain. 40th Brigade moved to Chiseldon and Cirencester in September 1914. Near the end of February the Division concentrated at Blackdown in Hampshire. They moved to the Mediterranean from the 13th of June 1915 landing at Alexandria then moving to Mudros, by the 4th of July to prepare for a landing at Gallipoli. The infantry landed on Cape Helles between the 6th and 16th of July to relieve 29th Division. They returned to Mudros at the end of the month, and the entire Division landed at ANZAC Cove between the 3rd and 5th of August. They were in action in The Battle of Sari Bair, The Battle of Russell's Top and The Battle of Hill 60, at ANZAC. Soon afterwards they transferred from ANZAC to Suvla Bay. They were evacuated from Suvla on the 19th and 20th of December 1915, and after a week's rest they moved to the Helles bridgehead. They were in action during The last Turkish attacks at Helles on the 7th of January 1916 and were evacuated from Helles on the 8th and 9th. The Division concentrated at Port Said, holding forward posts in the Suez Canal defences. On the 12th of February 1916 they moved to Mesopotamia, to join the force being assembled near Sheikh Sa'ad for the relief of the besieged garrison at Kut al Amara. They joined the Tigris Corps on the 27th of March and were in action in the pprox.sful attempts to relieve Kut. They were in action in The Battle of Kut al Amara, The capture of the Hai Salient, the capture of Dahra Bend and The passage of the Diyala, in the pursuit of the enemy towards Baghdad. Units of the Division were the first troops to enter Baghdad, when it fell on the 11 March 1917.

*Thanks to the Wartime Memories Project.*

Harry was killed in action on the 20th February 1917.

## On that fateful day:
The war diary states:

*20.2.17 In the field.*
*Turks are digging in all along the bund. Opposite my sector and with a few mwn moving about but goog execution with the machine gun. Our no 5 piquet had to move back owing to a sudden rise in the river. A salvage party managed to recover 80 rifles this evening. '*

*Harry is remembered on the Basra memorial along with the names of 40,682 other servicemen.*

# PETER JACKSON

**Peter Jackson** was born in Plumley, Cheshire in 1882 and by 1910 he married Mary Beatrice and went to live at 12, Longford Road, Birkdale in Lancashire. He was a traveller in groceries.

He enlisted in the Kings Liverpool Regiment as Private no. 58999 before transferring to the 5ᵗʰ Battalion of the Royal Welsh Fusiliers becoming Private no. 66206.

**Brief history of the Battalion:**

1/5ᵗʰ (Flintshire) Battalion, The Royal Welch Fusiliers were a Territorial unit based in Flint serving with North Wales Brigade, Welsh Division when war broke out in August 1914, they had just set out for their for annual summer camp, they were at once recalled and were mobilised for war, taking up position at Conway. At the end of August they went to Northampton to join the rest of the Division and to prepare for deployment to overseas. On the 18ᵗʰ of November orders were received to prepare for a move to India, but this was withdrawn. They moved to Cambridge in December and to Bedford in May 1915, when the formation was renamed 158ᵗʰ Brigade, 53ʳᵈ (Welsh) Division. On the

2nd of July orders arrived to re-equip for service in the Mediterranean. Leaving the artillery and train behind, the rest of the Division left 14-19 July and they embarked at Devonport on the 19th of July to Imbros. The Division made a landing at Suvla Bay, Gallipoli on the 9th of August 1915 and were involved in operations in the Suvla Bay area suffering heavy losses. By the time they were evacuated to Mudros on the 11th of December the Division stood at just 162 officers and 2428 men (pprox.. 15%). From Mudros they went on to Alexandria and to Wardan, where the divisional artillery re-joined between the 11th and 22nd of February 1916. They were in action at The Battle of Romani in the Palestine campaign and in 1917 158th Brigade fought at The First Battle of Gaza and the whole Division were in action during The Second Battle of Gaza, The Third Battle of Gaza when they were involved in capture of Beersheba, Tell Khuweilfe, and The Capture of Jerusalem. In December they were in action in The Defence of Jerusalem.

*Thanks to the Wartime Memories Project.*

Peter died at sea on the 4th May 1917, when the transport ship 'Transylvania' that was on its way to Salonika with reinforcements was torpedoed of Cape Vado a few miles south of Savona and sank with the loss of over 400 men.

***Peter is remembered on the Savona memorial, Italy along with the names of 274 other servicemen.***

# THOMAS JACKSON

**Thomas Jackson** was born in Lower Peover, Cheshire in 1892, one of two children born to W. George (a blacksmith) and Mary (a laundress) of Lower Peover.

Thomas' service record no longer exists but we know he enlisted in the army sometime in 1916 and became Private no. 35733 in the Cheshire Regiment but whilst in France he was transferred to the 8th Battalion of the Border Regiment with the service no. 33287.

**Brief history of the Battalion:**

The 8th (Service) Battalion, The Border Regiment was raised in Carlisle in September 1914 as part of Kitchener's Third New Army. They joined 75th Brigade, 25th Division and moved to Codford for training in November 1914, being billeted in Boscombe. The Battalion moved to Romsey in May 1915 and then to Aldershot following in June. They proceeded to France on the 27th of September 1915, landing at Boulogne. The 25th Division concentrated around Nieppe and saw action in 1916 on Vimy Ridge. The Division then moved to The Somme in late June 1916 and saw action in the Battle of Albert with 75th Brigade suffering heavily on the 3rd of July near Martinsart and again in mid-July in the Ovillers area. Between the 23rd of July and 10th of August 1916, the 25th Division held a sector of the line north of the River Ancre and in late September and October they were in action during the Battle of the Ancre Heights. At the end of October the Division moved to Flanders and took over the Ploegstreet sector where they would spend the first quarter of 1917. The Battalion was in action in the <u>Battle of Messines</u> and the Third Battle of Ypres. In 1918 they were in action at the Battle of St Quentin and The First Battle of Bapaume, before returning to Flanders. The 25th Division was in the front line at Ploegstreet when the enemy launched the Spring Offensive on the 12th of April and the 75th Brigade suffered heavily around the area of Hill 63 before withdrawing to Kemmel and then to Bailleul taking part in heavy fighting throughout the Battles of the Lys.

*Thanks to the Wartime Memories Project.*

Thomas died of wounds on the 3rd August 1917. He is believed to have received those wounds on the 31st July or 1st August 1917.

**On that fateful day:**
The war diary states:

*31.7.17 BELGIAN CHATEAU AREA*
*Fine. Battalion moved from assembly area at 7.40am to positions of readiness. During the night we took over the line gained by the 2nd West Yorks Regt – the 8th Division having attacked during the morning. Casualties 9 wounded including Lt King wounded on duty.*

*1.8.17*
*At 1.30am Battalion was ordered from Wind Lane to take up position in close support of the 23rd Bde who were holding BALLEWARDE RIDGE. At 4am the Bn was in position between BELLEWARDE LAKE and YPRES-ROULERS RAILWAY. 'C' Coy (Capt. King) and 'D' Coy (Capt. Duggan) RIGHT and LEFT FRONT RESPECTIVELY. 'A' Coy (Capt. Smith) and 'B' Coy (Leiut. Binnie) in support – Battalion H.Q.*

*and Aid Post at BELLEWARDE FARM. Rained heavily all day. Men suffered from exposure and cold. Enemy shelled the position fairly continuously. Two parties 50 men each sent forward at night to assist dig Support trenches on West Slope of WESTHOEK RIDGE.*

***Thomas is buried in Brandhoek New Military Cemetery, Leper, Belgium, along with 558 other servicemen. He is in Grave IV. B. 2.***

# SYDNEY JACKSON

**Sydney Jackson** was born in Lower Peover.

He enlisted in the Cheshire Regiment before transferring to the 14th Battalion of the Royal Welsh Fusiliers as Private no. 75894.

**Brief history of the Battalion:**
14th (Service) Battalion, The Royal Welch Fusiliers was raised at Llandudno on the 2nd of November 1914 by the Welsh National Executive Committee. Later in the month they joined 128th Brigade, 43rd Division at Llandudno, which was renamed 113th Brigade, 38th (Welsh) Division on the 28th of April 1915. They moved to Winchester for final training in August 1915 and proceeded to France in December 1915. In July 1916 they were in action at Mametz Wood on The Somme, suffering severe casualties. The Division did not return to major action for more than a 12 months. In 1917 they were in action in the Third Battles of Ypres, in 1918 they were in action on The Somme, in the Battles of the Hindenburg Line and the Final Advance in Picardy.

*Thanks to the Wartime Memories Project.*

The remaining records show Sydney 'died' whist serving.

*Sydney is buried in Valenciennes (St Roch) Communal Cemetery, France along with 885 other servicemen. His grave is V. C. 10.*

# JOSEPH JERVIS

**Joseph Jervis** was born in Knutsford in 1896, one of ten children (only two survived), born to Henry (a bricklayer) and Hannah Jervis of 13, Canute Place, Knutsford.

His service records no longer exist but we know he enlisted in the army at Knutsford on the 2nd November 1916, becoming S/4/090750 in the Royal Army Service Corp (Special Battalion) Royal Engineers, later transferring to the Royal Engineers 1st Special Battalion.

He embarked for France on the 7th September 1915.

**Brief history of the Company:**

No Special Companies existed in 1914. They were a war time invention. The Great War was the first in which chemical weapons were deployed. There was great moral shock and outrage at the first use of Chlorine, released by the Germans against defenceless French troops in the Ypres Salient. The Special Companies of the Royal Engineers were formed to develop the British response. By 1918, gas was used both offensively and defensively, delivered by a range of sophisticated techniques.

As early as 3 May 1915 the British Secretary of State for War, Lord Kitchener, authorised the preparation of measures to retaliate against the German use of poison gas. Experimental research work was carried out at Porton, and a laboratory established at Helfaut, near St Omer in

France. The Kestner-Kellner Alkali Company, being the only firm in Britain capable of manufacturing Chlorine gases in quantity, supervised trials with the final large-scale one taking place at Runcorn on 4 June. The method – as used by the Germans – was to form a continuous cloud by discharging compressed gas from cylinders to the atmosphere, and allowing the wind to move it over the enemy positions.

Special Companies of technically skilled men, under Major C.H. Foulkes of the Royal Engineers, were formed with a Depot at Helfaut, to deal with the new weapon. No's *186 and 187 Special Companies* were formed first, in July 1915, followed by *188 and 189 Companies* in August. All of the men were given the rank of Chemist Corporal. On 4 September 1915 the first two Companies, totalling 34 Sections of 28 men, were assigned to First Army for forthcoming operations.

The P (Phenate) gas helmet with glass eyepieces was introduced in November 1915. It did not protect adequately against Phosgene, and was replaced by the PH (Phenate-Hexamine) helmet from January 1916. From August 1916, the PH was replaced by the small box respirator, which although an unwieldy design gave protection against the different gases in use.

### The Special Brigade is formed:

Despite the limited results achieved by the cloud gas discharge at Loos, it was believed sufficiently successful to warrant further development. One of the first acts of Sir Douglas Haig on his appointment as Commander-in-Chief was to request that the War Office expand the four Special Companies of the RE into a more substantial force, viz.

Four Special Battalions, each of four Companies, to handle gas discharge from cylinders and smoke from candles;

Four Special Companies to handle gas shells fired from 4-inch Stokes mortars. Each Company to have 48 such weapons;

Four Special Sections to handle flame projectors (throwers); plus a Headquarters and Depot, making all an establishment of 208 officers and 5306 men.

This request was approved and the Brigade built up by adding volunteers from units already in France to the four original Companies. Later, drafts from England would join. The force was designated the *Special Brigade*. It was placed under the command of Col. Foulkes, RE, who was appointed Assistant Director of Gas Services; he reported to Brigadier-General H.Thuillier, RE, Director of Gas Services. Lt-Col. Cummins, RAMC acted as Director of Anti-GasMeasures.

By the end of May 1916, No 1 Special Battalion and No 2 (less a Company) were allocated to Fourth Army; No 3 (less a Company) to Second Army; No 4 (also less a Company) to Third Army. No 4A Battalion was provisionally formed from the three detached Companies, and was attached to First Army. No 5 Battalion was the Stokes mortar unit, and had 3 Companies attached to Fourth Army and 1 to Third Army. The Flame Projector Sections arrived in France 26 June 1916.

*Thanks to the Long, Long Trail.*

Joseph was killed in action on the 2nd November 1916.

**On that fateful day:**
I have been unable to gain access to the war diary.

*Joseph is buried in Hebuterne Military Cemetery, France along with another 750 other servicemen. His grave is SEP. Mem. 7.*

# ARTHUR JOHNSON
*(Brother of Harry)*

**Arthur Johnson** was born in Mobberley in 1889, one of six children born to Samuel (a drainer on an estate?) and Pricilla Johnson of Town Lane, Mobberley. He worked as a cowman on a farm and later a locomotive fireman.

He enlisted in the 4th Battalion of the Grenadier Guards as Guardsman no. 22594.

**Brief history of the Battalion:**
The 4th Battalion, Grenadier Guards was formed at Marlow. They proceeded to France on the 14th of July 1915 and joined 3rd Guards Brigade, Guards Division on the 19th of August. They were in action in The Battle of Loos. In 1916 they fought on The Somme in The Battle of Flers-Courcelette and The Battle of Morval, capturing Lesboeufs.

Harry died of wounds on the 27th June 1916.

**On that fateful day:**
The war diary has no specific entry for this date.

*Arthur is remembered on the Thiepval Memorial along with the names of 72,208 other servicemen.*

# FRED JOHNSON

**Fred Johnson** was born in Ollerton, Cheshire in 1896, one of seven children born to Emma Johnson, a widow of Beech Cottage, Ollerton. He worked as a gardener.

His service records exist, so we know he attested on the 20ᵗʰ November 1915 and became Private no. 33199 of the 14ᵗʰ Battalion of the Cheshire Regiment.

Fred was mobilised on the 27ᵗʰ January 1916 and started his training during which he contracted scarlet fever.

He died on the 11ᵗʰ May 1916 at Prees Heath Military Hospital.

*Fred is buried in Marthall (All Saints) Cemetery*

# HARRY JOHNSON
*(Brother of Arthur)*

**Harry Johnson** was born in Mobberley in 1894, the son of Samuel (a drainer on an estate?) and Pricilla Johnson of Town Lane, Mobberley.

He was a groom/gardener.

He enlisted in the 32nd Ammunition Column of the Royal Field Artillery as Gunner 24372, later transferring to the 31st Column.

**Brief history of the Column:**

31st Divisional Ammunition Column, Royal Field Artillery joined 31st Division on the 30th of December 1915 at Fovant on Salisbury Plain. They transferred to 32nd Division and proceeded to France, re-joining 31st Division when they returned from Egypt in March. They were in action during the attack on Serre in on the 1st of July during The Battle the Somme. They were also in action during The Battle of the Ancre.

*Thanks to the Wartime Memories Project.*

Harry died of wounds on the 27th June 1916. I have been unable to discover when and where he received those wounds.

*Harry is buried in Bertrancourt Military Cemetery along with 416 other servicemen. His grave is 1. E. 8.*

# WILLIAM JOHNSON

**William Johnson** was born in Knutsford in 1896, one of eight children born to Thomas (a labouring Plaster) and Hannah (A charwoman) who lived at 14, Swinton Square, Knutsford. William was a stable boy.

He joined the army sometime after 1915, becoming Private no. 40510 of the 20th Battalion of the Manchester Regiment. He was formerly Private no. 1826 of the Cheshire Yeomanry.

He achieved the rank of Sergeant.

**Brief history of the Battalion:**

The 20th (5th City) Battalion, Manchester Regiment was raised in in Manchester on the 8th of November 1914 by the Lord Mayor and City. They moved to Morecambe for training and in April 1915 moved to Grantham to join 91st Brigade, 30th Division. In September 1915 they moved to Larkhill, Salisbury Plain for final training and proceeded to France in November 1915, landing at Boulogne. On the 20th of December 1915, 91st Brigade transferred to 7th Division the 20th Manchesters then transferred to 22$^{nd}$ Brigade still with 7$^{th}$ Division. In 1916 they were in action during the Battles of the Somme, including the capture Mametz, The Battle of Bazentin, the attacks on High Wood, The Battle of Delville Wood, The Battle of Guillemont and the Operations on the Ancre. In 1917 They fought during The German retreat to the Hindenburg Line and the flanking operations round Bullecourt during The Arras Offensive, before moving to Flanders for the Third Battle of Ypres, seeing action in The Battle of Polygon Wood, The Battle of Broodseinde, The Battle of Poelcapelle and The Second Battle of Passchendaele. In late 1917 7$^{th}$ Division was selected to move to Italy. They took up position in the line along the River Piave, in late January 1918.

*Thanks to the Wartime Memories Project.*

William was killed in action on the 9$^{th}$ August 1918.

**On that fateful day:**
The war diary states:

*9.8.18*
*At 6pm on the 8$^{th}$ 'A' and 'C' Companies left the camp and marched to the front line (Canove di Sotto, Gordon Trench etc.). The general onset began at midnight. The Manchesters share of the raid was very successful – 2 Austrian Officers and 49 men being taken prisoner besides 3 machine guns and plenty of stores. The raiders withdrew at 2am on the 9$^{th}$. Many of the enemy were killed but our casualties were light.*
*1 officer wounded*
*3 O.R. killed*
*2 O.R. wounded and missing*
*11 O.R. wounded.*

*After the raid the two companies marched back to Carriola Camp and rested for the remainder of the day.*

*William has no known grave but is remembered on the Giavera Memorial, Italy together with 417 other servicemen.*

# CLARENCE WILLIAM JONES

**Clarence William Jones** was born on Lostock Garlem in 1891, the son of John (an engine driver) of 4, Hall Lane, Lostock.

He originally joined the East Lancashire Regiment before becoming Private 49394 of the 19th Battalion of the Lancashire Fusiliers.

He arrived in France on the 6th November 1915.

**Brief history of the Battalion:**
The 19th Battalion, Lancashire Fusiliers were known as The 3rd Salford

Pals, the battalion was raised in Salford on the 15ᵗʰ of January 1915, by Mr Montague Barlow MP and the Salford Brigade Committee. They began training near home and in March they moved to Conway for training. They became part of the 96ᵗʰ Brigade, 32ⁿᵈ Division and moved on the 21ˢᵗ of June 1915 to Catterick in North Yorkshire, using the firing ranges at Strenshall. In August 1915 they moved for final training and firing practice at Codford on Salisbury Plain. They proceeded to France, landing at Boulogne on the 22ⁿᵈ of November 1915. On the 5ᵗʰ of January 1916 they transferred to 14ᵗʰ Brigade still with 32ⁿᵈ Division. Their first taste of action was at Thiepval Ridge on The Somme on the 1ˢᵗ of July 1916, the battle resulted in the Salford Pals being almost wiped out. On the 29ᵗʰ of July 1916 they transferred to GHQ and converted to be a Pioneer Battalion, joining 49ᵗʰ (West Riding) Division on the 7ᵗʰ of August. In 1917 they were involved in the Operations on the Flanders Coast and the Battle of Poelcapelle during the Third Battle of Ypres. In 1918 they were in action during the Battles of the Lys, The pursuit to the Selle and the Final Advance in Picardy.

*Thanks to the Wartime Memories Project.*

He was killed in action on the 13ᵗʰ October 1918.

**On that fateful day:**
The war diary for this date no longer exists but the history of the written Battalion for that date says:

*'The 19ᵗʰ Battalion was taken away from its pioneer work and on the 13ᵗʰ, detailed 'A' and 'C' and half of 'B' Companies to attack and take SAULZOIR and the line of the railway beyond the River Selle to the east of it and as the first objective with the high ground beyond it as the second. Leiut. R.B. Norman earned his Military Cross in this fight by the way in which he led his platoon through very heavy machine-gun fire and, even after he had been wounded in the head, he went on*

*directing the fire of his platoon until he was again hit. This time his wound was so severe he had to go back to battalion Headquarters where, nevertheless, he gave a full and clear and most valuable report on the situation. Men of the battalion penetrated into SAULZOIR and got as far as the Selle; but a counter-attack. Supported by tanks, prevented the objectives being reached anywhere on the divisional front.'*

*Clarence is buried in York Cemetery, Haspres, France along with 137 other servicemen. His grave is D. 30.*

# HORACE WILLIAM JONES

**Horace William Jones** was born in Barrow, Cheshire in 1896, one of six children born to Robert (a railway porter/signalman) and Sarah Ellen Jones of Spring Bank, Mobberley. He was a gardener.

He enlisted in the 10<sup>th</sup> Battalion of the Cheshire Regiment as private no. 16041and arrived in France on the 25<sup>th</sup> September 1915.

**Brief history of the Battalion:**

The 10th (Service) Battalion, Cheshire Regiment was raised in Chester on the 10th of September 1914 as part of Kitchener's Third New Army and joined 75th Brigade, 25th Division. They trained at Codford St Mary and spent the winter in billets in Bournemouth. They moved to Aldershot for final training in May 1915 and proceeded to France on the 26th of September, the division concentrating in the area of Nieppe. On the 26th of October they transferred to 7th Brigade still with 25th Division. Their first action was in defence of the German attack on Vimy Ridge in May 1916. They then moved to The Somme and joined the Battle just after the main attack, with 75th Brigade making a costly attack near Thiepval on the 3rd of July. The Division was in action at The Battle of Bazentin, The Battle of Pozieres and The Battle of the Ancre Heights. In 1917 they were in action at The Battle of Messines attacking between the Wulverghem-Messines and Wulverghem-Wytschaete roads. In the Third battle of Ypres were in action during The Battle of Pilkem. In 1918 they were in action on The Somme, in the Battles of the Lys suffering heavy losses. On the 21st of June 1918 the battalion was reduced to cadre strength with many troops transferring to the 9th Cheshires.

*Thanks to the Wartime Memories Project.*

Horace's service record no longer exists but we know he was a prisoner of war when he died on the 24th April 1918.

***Horace is buried in Cologne Southern Cemetery along with over 2,500 other servicemen. His Grave is XI. E. 15.***

# GEORGE KENNERLEY

**George Kennerley** was born in 1892, one of seven children born to John (a postmen) and Alice Kennerley of 23, Tatton Street, Knutsford – they later moved to number 37.

George enlisted in the 'B' Company 8th Battalion of the Cheshire Regiment, becoming Private no. 34972

.

**Brief history of the Battalion:**
The 8th (Service) Battalion, Cheshire Regiment was raised in Chester on the 12th of August 1914 as part of Kitchener's First New Army and joined 40th Brigade, 13th (Western) Division which assembled on Salisbury Plain. 40th Brigade moved to Chiseldon and Cirencester in September 1914. Near the end of February the Division concentrated at Blackdown in Hampshire. They moved to the Mediterranean from the 13th of June 1915 landing at Alexandria then moving to Mudros, by the 4th of July to prepare for a landing at Gallipoli. The infantry landed on Cape Helles between the 6th and 16th of July to relieve 29th Division. They returned to Mudros at the end of the month, and the entire Division landed at ANZAC Cove between the 3rd and 5th of August. They were in action in The Battle of Sari Bair, The Battle of Russell's Top and The Battle of Hill 60, at ANZAC. Soon afterwards they transferred from ANZAC to Suvla Bay. They were evacuated from Suvla on the 19th and 20th of December 1915, and after a week's rest they moved to the Helles bridgehead. They

were in action during the last Turkish attacks at Helles on the 7th of January 1916 and were evacuated from Helles on the 8th and 9th. The Division concentrated at Port Said, holding forward posts in the Suez Canal defences. On the 12th of February 1916 they moved to Mesopotamia, to join the force being assembled near Sheikh Sa'ad for the relief of the besieged garrison at Kut al Amara. They joined the Tigris Corps on the 27th of March and were in action in the unsuccessful attempts to relieve Kut. They were in action in The Battle of Kut al Amara, The capture of the Hai Salient, the capture of Dahra Bend and The passage of the Diyala, in the pursuit of the enemy towards Baghdad. Units of the Division were the first troops to enter Baghdad, when it fell on the 11 March 1917. The Division then joined "Marshall's Column" and pushed north across Iraq, fighting at Delli 'Abbas, Duqma, Nahr Kalis, crossing the 'Adhaim on the 18 April and fighting at Shatt al 'Adhaim.

*Thanks to the Wartime Memories Project.*

George 'died' on the 6th April 1918 – it can be assumed he died as a result of disease and not fighting.

*George is remembered on the Basra memorial, Iraq along with the names of 40,682 other servicemen.*

317

# JAMES FREDERIC KEENS

**James Frederic Keens** was born in Knutsford in 1896, one of three children born to John Frederic (a domestic gardener) and Margurite Alice Keens of 11, Stanley Road, Knutsford. James was a Grocery assistant. The family later moved to 7, Freeholders Terrace, Stanley Road, Knutsford. James belonged to the Methodist Church in Knutsford where he went to Sunday School and was a member of the choir.

His service record no longer exists but we know he enlisted in 1914, becoming Private no. 25236 in the 1st Battalion of the Cheshire Regiment.

**Brief history of the Battalion:**
The 1st Battalion, Cheshire Regiment was a regular unit of the British Army and was in Londonderry when war broke out in August 1914 with 15th Brigade in 5th Division. They returned to England and proceeded to France with the British Expeditionary Force, landing at Le Havre on the 16th of August 1914. They saw action at The Battle of Mons, The Battle of the Marne, The Battle of the Aisne, The Battles

of La Bassee, at Messines and in The First Battle of Ypres. Between the 3$^{rd}$ of March and 7$^{th}$ of April 1915 they were attached with 15$^{th}$ Brigade to 28$^{th}$ Division in in exchange for 83$^{rd}$ Brigade in order to familiarise the newly arrived troops with the Western Front. In 1915 they were in action in The Second Battle of Ypres and the Capture of Hill 60.

*Thanks to the Wartime Memories Project.*

Frederic died of wounds on the 17$^{th}$ May 1915.

*Memorial inside the Methodist Church in Knutsford.*

**On that fateful day:**
Unfortunately I have been unable to identify where and when he received his wounds.

*Frederick is buried in Dickbusch New Military Cemetery, West-Vlaanderen, Belgium, together with 624 other servicemen.*

# HARRY KENT

**Harry Kent** was born in Plumley in 1893, one of thirteen children born to Henry William (a general labourer) and Sarah Ann Kent of Patmos Cottage, Plumley, Cheshire.

Harry's service record no longer exists but we know he enlisted first in the Cheshire Yeomanry as Private no. 1363 and then transferring into the Prince of Wales Volunteers (South Lancashire regiment) as Private 31520.

**Brief history of the Battalion:**

2nd Battalion, The South Lancashire Regiment was based at Tidworth with 7th Brigade, 3rd Division when war was declared in August 1914. They proceeded to France with the BEF and landed at Le Havre on the 14th of August 1914. They saw action in The Battle of Mons and the rear-guard action at Solesmes, The Battle of Le Cateau, The Battle of the Marne, The Battle of the Aisne, at La Bassee, Messines and the First Battle of Ypres. They took part in the Winter Operations of 1914-15, The First Attack on Bellewaarde and the Actions at Hooge. On the 18th of October 1915 they transferred with 7th Brigade to 25th Division and on the 26th they transferred to 75th Brigade, 25th Division. They were in action in defence of the German attack on Vimy Ridge in May 1916. On the 21st of June 1916 they transferred to 64th Brigade in 21st Division and were in action in the Battles of The Somme, including The Battle of Morval in which the Division captured Gueudecourt.

*Thanks to the Wartime Memories Project.*

Harry died of wounds on the 21st October 1916.

**On that fateful day:**

Unfortunately I have been unable to discover when and where he received his wounds.

*Harry is buried in the Warloy-Baillon Communal Cemetery Extension,*
*Somme, France, together with 1331 other servicemen. His grave is IV. C. 20.*

# ALBERT KETTLE

**Albert Kettle** was born in Northwich in 1891, one of three children born to Charles (a brick-layer) and Alice Kettle of 6, Leicester Street, Northwich. The 1911 census also shows that two of Albert's cousins lived at the address too. On leaving school he went to work for his father as a labourer, but left to go to work as a farm labourer on Tabley Estate, just outside Knutsford, and took up residence in a tithe house known as Yew Tree Cottage, Pickmere.

At the outbreak of the war, Albert enlisted in the 10th Battalion of the Cheshire Regiment, becoming Private no. 24209.

**Brief history of the Battalion:**
The 10th (Service) Battalion, Cheshire Regiment was raised in Chester on the 10th of September 1914 as part of Kitchener's Third New Army and joined 75th Brigade, 25th Division. They trained at Codford St Mary and spent the winter in billets in Bournemouth. They moved to Aldershot for final training in May 1915 and proceeded to France on the 26th of September, the division concentrating in the area of Nieppe. On the 26th of October they transferred to 7th Brigade still with 25th Division. Their first action was in defence of the German attack on Vimy Ridge in May 1916. They then moved to The Somme and joined the Battle just after the main attack, with 75th Brigade making a costly attack near Thiepval on the 3rd of July. The Division was in action at The Battle of Bazentin, The Battle of Pozieres and The Battle of the Ancre Heights. In 1917 they were in action at The Battle of Messines attacking between the Wulverghem-Messines and Wulverghem-Wytschaete roads. In the Third battle of Ypres were in action during The Battle of Pilkem.

Albert arrived in the Balkans in January 1915.

In January 1916 he was invalided home. There are no records to say why this happened, so we don't know if he was wounded or succumbed to the numerous diseases that were easy to contract in that theatre of the war. He eventually returned to his unit in November 1916. They were now fighting on the Western Front.

Albert was killed in action on the 17th February 1917.

**On that fateful day:**
The History of the Cheshire Regiment – Arthur Crookenden (2005) takes up the story:

*'17<sup>th</sup> Feb.*

*Up early to find it not raining ( ground had been frozen, but unluckily it had begun to thaw on the 16<sup>th</sup>). The raiders arrived in good time, drew their bombs and assembled in the front trenches – according to plan, without a hitch, about 20 minutes before zero. So they did not have long to hang about before the attack, which was always a trying time. Was in the front trenches myself to wish them luck, after which I took post in the front line between the two parties, with one of the Battalion snipers so that if we saw any German snipers, or machine guns we could pick them off.*

*10.40 a.m.*

*Our hurricane bombardment began on the front to be attacked. Howitzers and heavy guns turned on to known machine gun positions, and strong points, other heavy guns fired on other German batteries while 60 pounders and machine guns swept all the German communication trenches which they would be likely to use. The barrage under which we went to form up was not as thick or as accurate as it should have been. It was a bit behind instead of on top of the German trench. However it kept the enemy's heads down and our fellows were able to climb out of our trenches, get through our wire and form up in three waves without being troubled.*

*They went across quite well..... I saw the left party reach the German trench, and the right party get to the German wire. Thinking all was well I made my way back to Battalion Battle H.Q., where I was supposed to be. On arrival there I heard that the right party had failed to get in owing to the wire being uncut. Apparently it had been much knocked about, but not properly destroyed as erroneously reported. The right party held on for three or four minutes in the hope that the left party might be able to help them. They got badly knocked about by machine gun fire, till a very gallant lewis-gunner, standing up in the wire, emptied the whole of the magazine into the loophole and knocked the German machine gun out. The German trench was found to be packed. Our fellows bombed them and undoubtedly knocked a good many over. As it was impossible to get through the wire, the right party withdrew. On the left we got into the German front line. Killed 35, apart from those in nine dugouts, full of Germans who refused to come out, and who had to be bombed with fumite bombs. 'C' Company, for the support trench went over in splendid style. They reached the support trench, which they found very much battered by our artillery and badly pinched, and suffered a lot of casualties from machine guns on both flanks. The withdrawal was carried out very well, but our artillery was disappointing and did not keep the German machine guns down and those cost us a lot of casualties.*

*The raid was a failure owing to the wire reported cut on the right. Our losses were 40 killed and 60 wounded. We accounted for over 100 Germans exclusive to those killed by artillery fire, but it was a pity that the men who were so keen and who behaved so well did not have a better chance.'*

Albert Kettle was killed in this action.

On the Tabley War Memorial, situated within the small chapel on the estate Albert is remembered mistakenly as Arthur Kettle.

*Albert is buried in Berks Cemetery Extension, Belgium, along with 876 other servicemen. His grave is I. O. 17.*

# DONALD CURRIE KINGSLEY

**Donald Currie Kingsley** was born in Chorlton-Cum-Hardy in 1893, the only son of Charles (a cotton manufacturer) and Ethel Kingsley of 'Oakdene', Mobberley. Donald was a book-keeper in his father's business.

He emigrated to New Zealand and became a fisherman. He married Ethel Rosamund Hawkin at Wellington on the 8th November 1915.

At the outbreak of the war he joined the 8th Reinforcements of the 1st Battalion of the Canterbury Regiment of the New Zealand Expeditionary Force as Private no. 6/3374.

They embarked on the 13th November 1915, just 5 days after his wedding. He fought in Gallipoli and on the Western Front.

**Brief history of the Battalion:**
The Canterbury Battalion was formed on the outbreak of war recruited from the four existing Territorial Regiments in the province: 1st (Canterbury), 2nd (South Canterbury), 12th (Nelson) and 13th (North Canterbury and Westland). The four companies in the battalion were numbered and named after the four regiments, a system unique to the NZEF, which explains why they were numbered 1st, 2nd, 12th and

13th. When the 2nd and 3rd Battalions were formed the same company numbering was used. The battalion arrived in Egypt with the New Zealand Infantry Brigade in December 1914. The Turks attacked the Suez Canal at the beginning of February 1915 and part of the battalion was in action, suffering only one man wounded. On 25th April 1915 the battalion landed on Gallipoli with the New Zealand Brigade and there it fought throughout the campaign till taken off in December 1915 and transported back to Egypt. On 1st March 1916 the 2nd NZ Infantry Brigade was formed and one of the battalions created for it was the 2nd Canterbury; in April 1916 the NZ Division arrived in France where it served until the armistice and then took part in the march to Germany.

He was killed in action on the 8th June 1917.

*Donald is remembered on the Messines Ridge (New Zealand) Memorial along with the names of 1,531 other servicemen.*

# LEOPOLD FREDERICK KIRK

**Leopold Frederick Kirk** was born in Hale, Cheshire in 1894, the son of Frederick and Emma (a widow) of Burnham Cottage, Pavement Lane, Mobberley. Frederick lived in Bowden, Cheshire. He was a sheet metal fitter and also assisted his grandmother to run a boarding house.

He enlisted in the 10th Battalion of the Cheshire Regiment as Private no. 14705. He attested in Altrincham on the 4th September 1914 and arrived in France on the 26th September 1915.

**Brief history of the Battalion:**
The 10th (Service) Battalion, Cheshire Regiment was raised in Chester on the 10th of September 1914 as part of Kitchener's Third New Army and joined 75th Brigade, 25th Division. They trained at Codford St Mary and spent the winter in billets in Bournemouth. They moved to Aldershot for final training in May 1915 and proceeded to France on the 26th of September, the division concentrating in the area of Nieppe. On the 26th of October they transferred to 7th Brigade still with 25th Division. Their first action was in defence of the German attack on Vimy Ridge in May 1916. They then moved to The Somme and joined the Battle just after the main attack, with 75th Brigade making a costly attack near Thiepval on the 3rd of July. The Division was in action at The Battle of Bazentin, The Battle of Pozieres and The Battle of the Ancre Heights. In 1917 they were in action at The Battle of Messines attacking between

the Wulverghem-Messines and Wulverghem-Wytschaete roads. In the Third battle of Ypres were in action during The Battle of Pilkem.

*Thanks to the Wartime Memories Project.*

Fred received a gunshot wound to the face on the 12th July 1916 – he was treated and returned to the Battalion.

He was killed in action on the 7th June 1917 during the battle of Messines Ridge.

**On that fateful day:**
The war diary states:

*'7.6.17 – MARTIN TRENCH*
*At 2.15 am tea and rum issued.*
*3.10am Batt left the trenches and advanced to the attack. They got away very well – the arrangements made with the RE (Royal Engineers) for paths etc. being excellent. The men kept close up to our barrage and our objective – OCCUR TRENCH was taken without much opposition. The rest of the day was spent in consolidation.*
   *Killed 1 officer 26 OR*
   *Wounded 26 officers 141 OR*
   *Missing 7 OR.'*

**Fred is buried in St Quentin Cabaret Military Cemetery, along with 460 other servicemen. His grave is II. P. 2.**

# FRANK KNOWLES

**Frank Knowles** was born in Knutsford in 1896, one of eight children born to Rickard (a farmer) and Elizabeth of Shaw Heath, Knutsford. Frank worked with his father on the farm.

His service record no longer exists but we know he enlisted sometime after 1915, becoming Rifleman no. 4920 in the 16th Battalion of the London Regiment.

**Brief history of the Battalion:**
16th (2nd Queen's Westminster Rifles) Battalion, The London Regiment, was a second line Territorial unit formed at Somerset House, London in September 1914, from the troops of the 16th (1st Queen's Westminster Rifles) Battalion who had not volunteered for service overseas. They joined 2/4th London Brigade, 2/2nd London Division at White City, later retitled 179th Brigade, 60th (2/2nd London) Division. They moved to Maidstone in January 1915 then to Watford in April, to Saffron Walden in June and to Sutton Veny in January 1916 to prepare for service overseas. Due to the Irish rebellion, plans to embark for France were withdrawn and on the 28th of April the 2nd London Scottish landed at

Cork for security duties in Ireland, based at Ballincollig and moving to Macroom. On the 14th of May they returned to England, sailing from Rosslare to Fishguard and returned to Sutton Veny to continue training. They proceeded to France on the 22nd of June, landing at Le Havre.

*Thanks to the Wartime Memories Project.*

Frank was killed in action on the 10th September 1916.

**On that fateful day:**
The Battalion went into action on the 9th September 1916, attacking from their trenches 500 yards N.E. of Faviere Wood, going N. and E of Leuze Wood and N. into Bouleaux Wood.

**The war diary takes up the story:**

*'10.9.16*
*1am*
*Orders were received from Brigade that the enemy trench on the S.E. side of the wood must be taken by dawn.*
*The night was very dark and the enemy were pouring heavy shells into the wood without cessation and the position from which to attack this trench as well as the exact bearing of the trench and its distance from the wood was unknown – the maps being known not to be accurate. The was also no communication except by Runner, which took over an hour each way, with Brigade, and it was impossible to arrange an earlier hour that (sic) 7am for the attack.*
*'D' Company closed on its left and 'C' Company was formed on the right of 'D', each attacking in ways of platoons in line. 'D' Company's leading platoon was ordered to swing to its left to attack the sunken road trench on the N. side of COMBNES – LEUZE WOOD road and half the H.Q. Bombers were given to O.C. 'D' Company for the purpose of helping*

in the attack on this trench. 2/Lt Johnson and a patrol from 'C' Company reconnoitred the direction of the attack for 'C' Company's attack.

The casualties during the night were heavy 2/Lt Apergis and Johnson being killed or wounded and some 40 O.R. of 'C' and 'D'; being killed or wounded.

I received at 6.50 am a message from Brigade that the artillery barrage had been arranged. A thick mist had come on since 3 am which was still on at 7 am, so that you could not see more than 40 or 50 yards, and all promised well but telephone communication from the brigade to the artillery had broken down and the right part of the barrage was never given, in fact there was hardly any at all.

### 7. am

The two companies went across and got nearly to their objectives – they were held up principally by rifle and M.G. fire from the trench they were attacking & M.G. from the sunken road on the north. The trench was found to be strongly held and Capt.'s Green and Griselle were obliged to withdraw the remnants of their companies – some 25 all ranks of each company – 'B' Company pushing a platoon up to the sap leading from the centre of the wood to the S.E. to guard that flank in case of counter attack.

### 12.30 pm

In the middle of the day, the Brigadier came up to the road and ordered a bombing attack on this sap to be made in the last effort to take the enemy's trench. For this purpose 'A' Company 2nd London's, who were also on the east side of the wood, was put under my command, as well as the two Stokes-Mortars.

### 3 pm

The bombing attack started – the 2nd London's, who were already in our end of this sap being ordered to clear this sap and its junction with the enemy trench, which was the main objective, from which point the Westminster's were to carry on with the capture of the main trench – the attack being made by the remaining men of the H.Q.

*bombers supported by 'B' and 'A' Companies – an artillery barrage working up and along the trench at the rate of 30 yards a minute, was arranged and was given, but it was not successful in keeping the enemy's rifle fire down.*

*The 2ⁿᵈ London pretty well made their objective when Capt. Long was killed and the rest came back bringing our men with them and Lieut. Webb was unable tyo stop the retirement. The losses in 'B' Company were heavy both in the attack and in the retirement and our casualties during the night of the 9ᵗʰ/10ᵗʰ and during this day were:*

*Officers 4 killed, 4 wounded.*

*O.R. 52 killed 166 wounded 80 missing.*

*From start to finish we had, as it turned out, no chance. Ordered to attack from a wood we had never been in before on a black dark night and on to a position were unable to properly locate and then owing to the breakdown in communication, launched in the morning to the attack without the artillery barrage. And again after some 14 hours exceedingly heavy shelling being sent to it again to bomb up a trench, which as a trench, hardly existed, with hardly any trained bombers to lead the attack, it is no wonder that both the attacks failed, especially as we know, as we learnt later the strength of the sunken road trench from which the enemy were able to bring so heavy a cross machine gun fire on both out attacks.*

*The remains of 'B', 'C; and 'D' were re-organised and lined the eastern edge of the wood till the evening when the brigade was relieved by the 5ᵗʰ Division and the battalion returned to the CITADEL.'*

**Frank is buried in Combles Communal Cemetery Extension, Somme, France together with over 1,500 other servicemen. His grave is VII. B. 10.**

# TOM LEA

**Tom Lea** was born in Knutsford in 1896, one of eight children born to Thomas (a railway porter) and Mary Ann Lea of 16, Princes Street, Knutsford. Tom was employed as a carter.

He enlisted in the 4th Reserve Battalion of the Cheshire Regiment as private no. 78854 but he never got the chance to serve.

He died on the 17th October 1918 from Pneumonia.

*Tom is buried in Knutsford Cemetery.*

# PATRICK LEECH

Patrick Leech was born in Hulme, but he moved to 41, Old Market Place, Knutsford with his wife, Elizabeth and five children.

He enlisted in the 1st Battalion of the Cheshire Regiment in 1914, becoming Private no. 11678 and arrived in France on the 26th January 1915.

**Brief history of the Battalion:**

The 1st Battalion, Cheshire Regiment was a regular unit of the British Army and was in Londonderry when war broke out in August 1914 with 15th Brigade in 5th Division. They returned to England and proceeded to France with the British Expeditionary Force, landing at Le Havre on the 16th of August 1914. They saw action at The Battle of Mons, The Battle of the Marne, The Battle of the Aisne, The Battles of La Bassee, at Messines and in The First Battle of Ypres. Between the 3rd of March and 7th of April 1915 they were attached with 15th Brigade to 28th Division in in exchange for 83rd

Brigade in order to familiarise the newly arrived troops with the Western Front.

*Thanks to the Wartime Memories Project.*

He was killed in action on the 9th April 1916.

**On that fateful day:**
The war diary has no entry for this day.

*Patrick is buried in Faubourg D'Amiens Cemetery, Arras along with 2,647 other servicemen. His grave is I. A. 17.*

*Note:*
*His name is written as 'LEACH' on his army medal card and in the Commonwealth Graves commission records.*

# WILLIAM LEECH

**William Leech** was born on Tremlow, Cheshire in 1892, the son of William (a farmer) and Agnes (a farmer) of Cranage, Cheshire. William also worked on the farm.

He enlisted in the 9th Battalion of the Cheshire Regiment, becoming Private no. 5083, later re-numbered to 50218.

**Brief history of the Battalion:**

The 9th (Service) Battalion, Cheshire Regiment was raised in Chester on the 13th of September 1914 as part of Kitchener's Second New Army and joined 58th Brigade, 19th (Western) Division. They moved to Salisbury Plain for training and went into billets in Basingstoke in December 1914 for the winter, returning to Salisbury Plain in March 1915. They proceeded to France on the 19th of July 1915, landing at Boulogne, the division concentrated near St Omer. Their first action was at Pietre, in a diversionary action supporting the Battle of Loos. In 1916 they were in action during the Battle of the Somme, capturing La Boisselle and being involved in The attacks on High Wood, The Battles of Pozieres Ridge, the Ancre Heights and the Ancre. In 1917 they were in action in The Battle of Messines and the Third Battles of Ypres. On the 7th of February 1918 they transferred to 56th Brigade in same Division. In 1918 they fought on The Somme during The Battle of St Quentin and The Battle of Bapaume and in the Battles of the Lys at Messines, Bailleul and The First Battle of Kemmel Ridge. They fought in The Battle of the Aisne and during the Final Advance in Picardy they were in action in The Battle of the Selle, The Battle of the Sambre and the passage of the Grand Honelle.

*Thanks to the Wartime Memories Project.*

William died of wounds on the 19th August 1918 – I have been unable to discover when and where he received those wounds.

*William is buried in Pernes British Cemetery along with 1099 other servicemen. His grave is IV. A. 38.*

# FREDERICK GEORGE LEECH

**Frederick George Leech** was born in Knutsford in 1895, one of seven children born to William (a carter) and Sarah Leech who moved to 33, Albion Street, Sale, Cheshire. Frederick worked as a chauffeur.

338

Frederick enlisted in the 9ᵗʰ Battalion of the Cheshire Regiment, becoming Private no. 15381.

**Brief history of the Battalion:**
The 9ᵗʰ (Service) Battalion, Cheshire Regiment was raised in Chester on the 13ᵗʰ of September 1914 as part of Kitchener's Second New Army and joined 58ᵗʰ Brigade, 19ᵗʰ (Western) Division. They moved to Salisbury Plain for training and went into billets in Basingstoke in December 1914 for the winter, returning to Salisbury Plain in March 1915. They proceeded to France on the 19ᵗʰ of July 1915, landing at Boulogne, the division concentrated near St Omer. Their first action was at Pietre, in a diversionary action supporting the Battle of Loos. In 1916 they were in action during the Battle of the Somme, capturing La Boisselle and being involved in the attacks on High Wood, The Battles of Pozieres Ridge, the Ancre Heights and the Ancre.

*Thanks to the Wartime Memories Project.*

He was killed in action on the 3ʳᵈ November 1917.

**On that fateful day:**
The war diary has no entry for this day.

*Frederick is remembered on the Thiepval memorial along with 72,208 other servicemen who have no known graves.*

# SYDNEY LEICESTER

**Photograph courtesy of** *The Knutsford Guardian*

**Sydney Leicester** was born in Tabley in 1891. In 1911 he was a horseman on a farm and lived with his parents William, a farmer, and Ann and his sister Meriel in Green Lane, Tabley, Cheshire. The small terrace of three 'two up – two down' cottages no longer stand; a modern scout hut now occupies the same profile at the end of the lane.

He was a well-known character in the area, attending Tabley school and being a member of the Tabley Chapel choir.

In 1913 Sydney secured employment with the Cheshire Lines Railway Company in Trafford Park, Manchester.

He enlisted in the 12th Battalion of the Manchester Regiment (a Pals Battalion), becoming Private no. 13835.

**Brief history of the Battalion:**

The 12<sup>th</sup> (Service) Battalion, Manchester was raised at Ashton-under-Lyne in September 1914 as part of Kitchener's Second New Army, and joined 52<sup>nd</sup> Brigade, 17<sup>th</sup> (Northern) Division. After initial training close to home, they moved to Wimborne in January 1915, then in May 1915 moved to Hursley Park, Winchester for final training. The division had been selected for Home Defence duties, but this was reversed and they proceeded to France, landing at Boulogne on the 17<sup>th</sup> of July 1915, the division concentrating near St Omer. They moved into the Southern Ypres salient for trench familiarisation and then took over the front lines in that area. In the spring of 1916 they were in action at the Bluff, south east of Ypres on the Comines canal then moved south to The Somme seeing action during The Battle of Albert in which the Division captured Fricourt and The Battle of Delville Wood.

*Thanks to the Wartime Memories Project.*

Sydney became a 'sniper'.
He was killed in action on the 7th July 1916.

**On that fateful day:**
The war diary states:

*7/7/1916*
*Battalion arrived at Railway Copse at 6.30am and were distributed in trenches on ridge under hedge 800yards N of Copse which they reached under heavy fire and with some loss. 7.25am Lieut. N.G. Crawhall arrived with orders that we were to assault Quadrangle Support at 8.0am, the 9<sup>th</sup> Northumberland Fus and 9<sup>th</sup> West Riding Regt having failed. There being no time to issue written orders, the C.O. (Lieut. Col E.G. Harrison) and Adjutant (Capt. B. DuVal) went up to hedge to organise attack. Attack launched at 7.50am*

*from Ridge to go over 9ᵗʰ Bn Northumberland Fus in Quadrangle Trench. Organisation D and B Coy leading, C Coy support, A Coy Reserve, Battn Bombers held by H.Q. About 10.0am news came of complete failure of attack under barrage and enfilade M.G. Fire. At 2.30pm the C.O. was ordered to go up and organise attack with all available troops in Quadrangle Trench and was wounded on his way up. The Adjutant sent orders to O.C. 9ᵗʰ North. Fus and advised 52ⁿᵈ Brigade. Battalion relieved by 51ˢᵗ Bde at 7.30pm. The following casualties occurred. Lieut. Col. E.G. Harrison CB DSO Wounded. Major G.S.W. Rusbridger wounded. Major H.F. Browell wounded. Capt. H. McKean killed. Capt. E.R. Thompson wounded. Capt. J.H. Betts killed. Lieut. H. Bate wounded & missing. Lieut. N.G. Crawhall wounded & missing. 2ⁿᵈ Lt. E. Kingsley wounded & missing BK. 2ⁿᵈ Lt. F. Latimer killed. 2ⁿᵈ Lt. J. Adams wounded. 2ⁿᵈ Lt. J.S. Greenwood killed. 2ⁿᵈ Lt. A.B. King killed. 2ⁿᵈ Lt. C.J. Alderton killed. 2ⁿᵈ Lt E.F. Smith killed, and 539 O.R.*

*Night 7/8ᵗʰ Battn returned to Meaulte.*

**Sydney is remembered on the Thiepval Memorial along with the names of 72,203 other servicemen.**

***Sydney is also remembered in Lower Peover churchyard.***

*Note:*

In a letter home shortly before he was killed he wrote:

*'Last Wednesday one of the Germans tried to pinch my testament out of my pocket but he did not quite manage it. The bullet went through the top corner of my tunic pocket taking with it part of my pocket book, a tidy corner of my prayer book and a part of my pocket, and then went through my sleeve without putting a scratch on me. I could not think what was the matter for a few minutes but I fancied myself rather lucky.'*

# WILLIAM LEIGH

**William Leigh** was born in Knutsford in 1891 and was the adopted son of George (a barrister and J.P.) and Annie Jane Leigh (a J.P.) of Underwood, Glebelands Road Knutsford. He was a superintendent registrars clerk.

He joined the army in 1914, becoming Private no. 1490 of the 1$^{st}$/6$^{th}$ Battalion of the Manchester Regiment.

**Brief history of the battalion:**

The 1/6$^{th}$ Battalion, Manchester were a Territorial unit, when war broke out in August 1914 they were based in Stretford Road, Hulme as part of the Manchester Brigade, East Lancashire Division. They were mobilized and moved to Rochdale to prepare for service overseas. They proceeded to Egypt arriving at Alexandria on the 25$^{th}$ of September to defend the Suez Canal from the Turkish forces in Palestine. They were in action in the Turkish attack on the Suez Canal on the 3$^{rd}$ of February 1915.

In the first week of May the division embarked from Alexandria, landing at Cape Helles, Gallipoli, where they saw action in the attempts to capture the heights of Krithia and the Battle of Krithia Vineyard which was a diversionary attack for the British Landing at Suvla Bay.

*Thanks to the Wartime Memories Project.*

William was killed in action on the 5ᵗʰ May 1915.

## On that fateful day:

There is no entry in the war diary for this date but I have found a letter, sent home by an anonymous Stockport soldier, who writes about this day:

*'Our tug couldn't get to the landing stage and so we lay from 6 o'clock until 9 o'clock in the bay waiting for a chance to land. (Once) landed they kept us on the cliff for another 2 hours and by that time we had begun to feel cold. The order to advance came just as I had unrolled my great coat and we marched about three miles along those cliffs with all our equipment in our hands. Then we made shallow dug-outs but sleep was impossible – we were so cold.'*

**William has no known grave but is remembered on the Hellas Memorial, Turkey, along with the names of 20,885 other servicemen.**

# JOHN LEONARD

**John Leonard** was born in Knutsford in 1881. He was employed as a carter. He married Mabel and they set up home in Swinton Square, Knutsford. Together they had three children, John, Agnes and James.

The family later moved to 28, King Street, Knutsford.

John's army records no longer exist but it was more than likely conscripted into the army, becoming Private 240952 in the 17th Battalion of the Royal Welsh Fusiliers, and went to France at the end of 1916.

**Brief history of the Battalion:**

The 17th (2nd North Wales) Battalion, The Royal Welch Fusiliers was raised at Llandudno at Llandudno on the 2nd of February 1915. They trained in Llandudno, joining 113th Brigade, 38th (Welsh) Division on the 28th of April 1915. They moved to Winchester for final training in August 1915 and proceeded to France in December 1915. In July 1916 they were in action at Mametz Wood on The Somme, suffering severe casualties. The Division did not return to major action for more than 12 months. In 1917 they were in action in the Third Battles of Ypres, a battle better known as 'Passchendaele'.

346

*Thanks to the Wartime Memories Project.*

John was killed in action on the 4th August 1917.

**On that fateful day:**
The war diaries for the R.W.F. were unavailable at the time of writing.

*John has no known grave so is remembered at the Menin Gate Memorial, Ypres, along with the names of 54,406 other servicemen who likewise have no know grave.*

# HARRY LIGHT

**Harry Light** was born in Blackheath, Kent in 1888. He and his wife Frances and their one child came to live at 10, Moordale Road, Knutsford. Harry was a grocery shop assistant.

He enlisted in the 3rd Battalion of the South Wales Borderers as Private no 29583 but there is no record of him having served. He died on the 20th February 1917.

*He is buried in Knutsford Cemetery.*

# MERVYN LLOYD

**Mervyn Lloyd** was born in 1884 in Reigate, Surrey, one of four children born to Richard B. (a bank director) and Katherine Lloyd of 'Silkwood', Reigate. He was the estate manager at Mere Country House, Cheshire.

He joined the Northumberland Fusiliers, rising to the rank of Captain in the 3rd Battalion but at the time he was wounded he was attached to the 1st Battalion.

**Brief History of the Battalions:**
The 1st Battalion, Northumberland Fusiliers were in Portsmouth at the outbreak of war in August 1914. They proceeded to France landing at Le Havre on the 14th of August 1914. Serving with the 9th Brigade, 3rd Division, BEF. They remained on the Western Front throughout the conflict, seeing action in most of the major battles. They saw action in The Battle of Mons and the rear-guard action at Solesmes, The Battle of Le Cateau, The Battle of the Marne, The Battle of the Aisne, at La Bassee, Messines and the First Battle of Ypres. They took part in the Winter Operations of 1914-15, The First Attack on Bellewaarde and the Actions at Hooge.

*Thanks to the Wartime Memories Project.*

He was wounded in the leg France, a wound that was not thought to be serious. He was invalided back to England and died on the 15th March 1915.

His commanding officer stated that 'he was popular with all classes'.

*Mervyn is buried in Farnham Civil Cemetery.*

*Note:*
*He set up the Boy Scout movement in Mere.*

# WILLIAM HARRISON LOMAS

**William Harrison Lomas** was born in Manchester in 1895, the son of Percy and Mary Elisabeth Lomas of Over Peover, Cheshire. He enlisted in the army in 1914 becoming Private no. 1210 in the Cheshire Yeomanry, later transferring to the Prince of Wales (South Lancashire Regiment) as Private no. 31592.

**Brief history of the Regiment:**
The 1/1st Battalion Cheshire Yeomanry were based in Chester in August 1914 when war broke out, serving with the Welsh Border Mounted Brigade in the Mounted Division. In November 1915 they converted to a dismounted unit and on the 3rd March 1916 they proceeded to Egypt, leaving from Devonport on His Majesty's Transport "Haverford", landing at Alexandria became part of the 4th Dismounted Brigade at to Beni Salama Camp. On the 18th of April 1916 the Cheshire Yeomanry entrained at Wardar and moved to Minia Lower Camp. From the 1st of June 1916 one Troop was posted to canal transport guard duties at Samalita and the remaining Troops manned this position in rotation until the regiment moved to El Alamein on the 14th of November 1916. In March 1917 the regiment merged with 1/1st Shropshire Yeomanry

to form the 10th (Shropshire and Cheshire Yeomanry) Battalion, King's Shropshire Light Infantry transferring to 231st Brigade, 74th (Yeomanry) Division. They moved to France in May 1918, landing at Marseilles and entraining for the north. After training, the Division took over a sector of the front line near Merville on the 14th of July 1917. In 1918 they were in action in The Second Battles of the Somme, The Battles of the Hindenburg Line and The Final Advance in Artois and Flanders. At the Armistice they were at Ath and then moved to Frasnes-les-Buissenal where they were engaged in repairing the Tournai-Leuze railway.

*Thanks to the Wartime Memories Project.*

William was 'died' on the 27th August 1917. Unfortunately I have been unable to discover how.

*Thomas is buried in Lijssenthoek Military Cemetery, Belgium, together with 9901 other servicemen. His grave is XVII. G. 14.*

# CHARLES ASGILL LOVER

**Charles Asgill Lover** was born in 1886. He was the stepson of George (a farmer) an Louisa Lord of Over Peover, Cheshire.

Charles enlisted in the army in 1915 and went to France on the 14th November 1915 as Private no. PS/7098 of the Royal Fusiliers. He was commissioned on the 25th September 1916 and transferred as a Lieutenant to the North Staffordshire Regiment.

Charles was on attachment to the York and Lancashire Regiment when he died on the 1st September 1918. He died at home.

*Charles is buried in St. Lawrence Churchyard, Over Peover.*

# JOSEPH LOWE

**Joseph Lowe** was born in Knutsford in 1878. He and his wife Kate and their five children lived in Old Market Place, Knutsford. Joseph worked for the local council as a scavenger.

He enlisted in the 1ˢᵗ Battalion of the South Wales Borderers as Private no. 19157.

He arrived in France on the 8ᵗʰ May 1915.

**Brief history of the Battalion:**
1ˢᵗ Battalion, The South Wales Borderers were in Bordon serving with 3ʳᵈ Brigade, 1ˢᵗ Division when war was declared in August 1914. They proceeded to France, landing at Le Havre on the 13ᵗʰ of August 1914 and fought on the Western Front throughout the war, taking part in most of the major actions. In 1914 they were involved in The Battle of Mons and the subsequent retreat, including the recapture Gheluvelt at the height of the crisis on 31ˢᵗ of October, alongside the 2ⁿᵈ Worcester's. They were in action at The Battle of the Marne, The Battle of the Aisne, the First Battle of Ypres and the Winter Operations of 1914-15. In 1915 they were in action during The Battle of Aubers and The Battle of Loos. In 1916 they were in action in the Battles of the Somme.

*Thanks to the Wartime Memories Project.*

Joseph died of wounds on the 2$^{nd}$ July 1916 and although his records no longer exist it is a safe bet to say he received his wounds the previous day – the first day of the battle of the Somme when the British army lost over 59,000 servicemen, killed, wounded or missing. The worst day the army had ever had.

*Joseph is buried in Barlin Communal Cemetery Extension, along with 1,291 other servicemen. His grave is I. J. 28.*

# GEORGE LUCAS

**George Lucas** was born in Knutsford in 1896, one of six children born to George (a joiner) and Elizabeth Lucas of 41, Tatton Street, Knutsford. On leaving school George became a labourer.

George enlisted in the army in 1916, becoming Private no. 33129 of the 3rd Battalion of the Cheshire Regiment.

George died on the 9th June 1916 in training at Bidston Training Camp, when a detonator accidentally went off, killing him instantly.

*George is buried in Knutsford Graveyard.*

# ROWLAND FRANCIS KEITH MACDONALD

**Rowland Francis Keith Macdonald** was born in 1892 in Newport, Tipperary, He was the son of A. Le Clare and Kathleen Macdonald. He became a clerk.

He married Mary Wildgoose and set up home at 'Hartford', Garden Road, Knutsford.

He enlisted in the 28th (Artists) Battalion of the London Regiment as Private no. 767182. However, prior to this he was with another Regiment and although his service records still exist I find it impossible to make out what Regiment that was.

**Brief history of the Battalion:**

The Artists Rifles originated in May 1860 as a corps of rifle volunteers, formed by an art student, Edward Sterling, from members of the artistic professions. When the Territorial Force was created in 1908 it became the 28th (County of London) Battalion, London Regiment. Shortly after the outbreak of the Great War second line and third line battalions were formed, the 2nd/28th an 3rd/28th. The 1st/28th arrived in France at the end of October 1914 and became an Officers Training Corps (OTC) at Bailleul and in April 1915 it moved to St Omer. In November the 1st/28th and 2nd/28th were merged and the battalion was sent to the front at the end of June 1917, allocated to the 190th Brigade, 63rd (RN) Division.

*Thanks to the Wartime Memories Project.*

He was wounded by a gunshot to the abdomen whilst fighting in Gallipoli in 1915. I have been unable to discover exactly when he received those wounds. He died of wounds at home on the 25th December 1917.

***Rowland is buried in Knutsford Cemetery.***

# FRANCIS PATRICK McGOWAN

**Francis Patrick McGowan** was born in Knutsford in 1888, one of nine children born to John (a tailor) and Jean McGowan of 21, Queens Street, Knutsford. On leaving school Francis took up the trade of joiner.

He attested on September 4th 1914 at Manchester and became Rifleman No. Z1230 in the 4th Battalion of the Rifle Brigade (Prince Consorts Own).

**Brief history of the Regiment:**

The Rifle Brigade fielded 28 battalions during the First World War, from its original complement of 4 regular and 2 reserve, seeing service primarily on the Western Front, but also in Macedonia. The regiment lost 11,575 killed during the course of the war. They were awarded 52 battle honours, 10 Victoria Crosses and numerous other decorations.

The 8th Battalion of the Rifle Brigade (together with the 7th & 9th battalions) was part of the 41st Brigade of the 14th (Light) Division of XV Corps. They were mainly made up of volunteers from the outbreak of World War I. The battalion saw action including at the Ypres Salient and the Somme. Notably the action they were in at Hooge, Belgium (30–31 July 1915) saw the first use of flamethrowers

357

by the Germans, Sidney Clayton Woodroffe was awarded the VC for his actions in this battle.

Alfred George Drake, a corporal in the 8th Battalion, was posthumously awarded the VC for his actions on 23 November 1915, near La Brique, Belgium.

They also participated in the Battle of Flers-Courcelette (15 September 1916) during the Somme Offensive which saw the first ever deployment of the tank in battle.

Patrick was killed in action on the 8th May 1915.

**On that fateful day:**
The war diary states:

*8.5.15*
*Marched 12.15pm arrived VLAMERTINGHE CHATAEU 1.30pm*
*Marched 8.30pm (arrived no. 2 Pontoon Bridge at midnight) and involved in dug outs on east bank of the canal.*
There is no report of any casualties.

***Francis has no known grave and is remembered on the Menin gate memorial, along with the names of 54,406 other servicemen.***

# ROBERT MELROSE

**Robert Melrose** was born in High Legh, Cheshire in 1899, one of five children born to Job (a gamekeeper) and Minnie Melrose of High Legh.

Robert enlisted but was too young to be sent to the war but he did join the 3rd Battalion of the Cheshire Regiment. There is no record of him receiving any medals so it would seem he never went abroad.

He died on the 30th September 1918.

*Robert is buried in Rostherne, Cheshire (St. Mary) Churchyard.*

# GORDON HOLLAND MERRIMAN

**Gordon Holland Merriman** was born in Knutsford in 1885, one of five children born to Frank (a branch insurance manager) and Margarita Merriman of Hollingford House, Knutsford.

He was educated at Winchester and Woolwich and proved to be a fine athlete.

He was 'gazetted' as an officer in 1907 in the Royal Field Artillery, and served in India.

He went to France at the outbreak of the war with the Royal Horse Artillery but reverted back to the Royal Field Artillery on promotion to Captain, serving with the 95th Battery.

**Brief history of the Battery:**

XCV Brigade, Royal Field Artillery, served with 21st Division. 21st Division was established in September 1914, as part Kitchener's Third New Army. The Division concentrated in the Tring area, training at Halton Park before winter necessitated a move into local billets, with the artillery at High Wycombe and Berkhamsted. In

May 1915 they moved to Aston Clinton with one brigade staying at Berkhamsted. On the 9th of August they moved to Witley Camp for final training. They proceeded to France during the first week of September and marched across France to going into the reserve for the British assault at Loos on the 26th of September suffering heavy casualties.

*Thanks to the Wartime Memories Project.*

Gordon was killed in action on the 12th May 1915

**On that fateful day:**
During heavy shelling, he saw two men get hit, he ran from his dugout and saw to their removal to safety, then seeing the ammo was on fire he ordered everyone to cover – then he was struck by shrapnel, dying instantaneously.

*Gordon is buried in Perth Cemetery (China Wall), Belgium along with 2,791 other servicemen. His grave is II. B. 1.*

# FRED MILNER

**Fred Milner** was born in Pudsey, Leeds in 1876. He married Mary Ellen and lived at 11, Middle Walk, Knutsford and together they had 2 children. He was a boot maker.

He enlisted in the Kings Liverpool Regiment, becoming Private no. 66163. He was placed with the Labour Battalion.

There is no record of Fred having received any medals so it appears that he was never sent abroad. He died at home on the 23$^{rd}$ February 1917 – he was 41 years old.

*Fred is buried in Knutsford Cemetery.*

# WILLIAM SIDNEY MOORE

**William Sidney Moore** was born in Sale, Cheshire in 1892, one of five children born to William Clark (a registrar) and Nancy Moore of Manor Cottage, Mobberley Road, Knutsford. William Jr was a clerk.

William joined 'B' Battery of the 169th Brigade of the Royal Field Artillery as Gunner no. 245331.

William was killed in action on the 19th July 1918.

**On that fateful day:**

I have been unable to locate the war diary.

*William is buried in Crucifix Corner Military Cemetery, Villers-Bretonneux, France along with 660 other servicemen. His grave is III. E. 12.*

363

# FRED MOSS

**Fred Moss** was born in Chelford in1894 but from an early age went to live with his Auntie Sarah at 125, Water Street, Radcliffe. He was a plasterer.

He enlisted at Bury, Lancashire in the Royal Welsh Fusiliers before transferring to 2/5th Battalion of The Lancashire Fusiliers as Private no. 1798.

## Brief history of the Battalion:

The 2/5th Battalion, Lancashire Fusiliers was a Second Line Territorial unit, formed at Bury on the 9th of September 1914 from the troops of the 5th Battalion who had not volunteered for service overseas and new recruits. They moved to Mossborough and spent the winter in billets in Southport. On the 8th of February 1915 they joined 197th Brigade, 66th (2nd East Lancashire) Division. On the 17th of April they transferred to 3rd Highland Brigade, Highland Division, at Bedford. They proceeded to France, landing at Boulogne on the 4th of May, the brigade soon being retitled 154th Brigade, 51st (Highland) Division. The Division concentrated in the area of Lillers, Busnes and Robecq and were rushed to the defence of Ypres, being in action until the 19th of May when they moved to Estaires on the River Lys. They were in action in the Battle of Festubert and The Second Action of Givenchy before moving south to The Somme taking over the line near Hamel. On the 7th of January 1916 they transferred to 164th Brigade, still with

51st (Highland) Division they were in action in the Battles of the Somme, including the attacks on High Wood and The Battle of the Ancre, capturing Beaumont Hamel, taking more than 2000 prisoners.

*Thanks to the Wartime Memories Project.*

Fred died of wounds on the 8th August 1916. I have been unable to discover where and when he received those wounds as his service records no longer exist.

*Fred is buried in Abbeville Communal Cemetery, along with 774 other servicemen. His grave is VI. L. 11.*

# EDWARD MOSTON

**Edward Moston** was born in Knutsford in 1895, the son of Thomas (a joiner) and Annie Moston of 32, Mobberley Road, Knutsford. He was an errand boy in 1911.

He enlisted in the army at a London Recruiting office and became Private no. m/2/018473 of the Army Service Corp before transferring to become Private no. 33896 of the 16th Battalion Royal Warwick Regiment.

**Brief History of the Battalions:**

The Royal Army Service Corps (RASC) was the unit responsible for keeping the British Army supplied with all its provisions barring weaponry, military equipment and ammunition, which were under the remit of the Royal Army Ordnance Corps.

16th (Service) Battalion (3rd Birmingham) was Formed at Birmingham in September 1914 by the Lord Mayor and a local committee. On the 26 June 1915 it came under command of 95th Brigade, 32nd Division. The Battalion Landed at Boulogne 21 November 1915. On 26 December 1915 it transferred to 15th Brigade, 5th Division. They moved to Italy with the Division in November 1917 but returned to France April 1918. On the 4 October 1918 the Battalion transferred to 13th Brigade in same Division.

Edward was killed in action on the 29th June 1918.

**On that fateful day:**

The war diary states:

*29.6.18*

*15th Infty.Bde O.O.* (Operational Order) *received saying that Bn will relieve the 1st NORFOLK REGT in the LE SART section of the front on the night June 30th/July 1st.*

There is no mention of any casualties.

*Edward is buried in Tannay British Cemetery, France along with 378 other servicemen. His grave is C. 3. 7.*

# LEONARD MOSTON

**Leonard Moston** was born in Crewe in 1888, the son of John (a farm labourer) and Mary Moston of Manor House, Warford, Cheshire. Leonard was also a farm labourer.

He attested for the army on 4th September 1916 and in November 1915 joined the Cheshire Regiment as Private no. 15904. He was later transferred to XV Battalion of the Army Cycle Corp as Private no. 6670.

**Brief history of the Corp:**
The Army Cycle Corp was part of the Royal Army Service Corp.

## *The organization of the ASC*

The ASC was organized into Companies, each fulfilling a specific role. Some were under orders of or attached to the Divisions of the army; the rest were under direct orders of the higher formations of Corps, Army or the GHQ of the army in each theatre of war.

### *Base Depots*

Horse Transport Companies (including Companies in Divisional Trains, Reserve Parks and Small Arms Ammunition (SAA) Trains and Cycle Corp).

Mechanical Transport Companies (including Companies in Divisional Supply Columns and Ammunition Parks, Companies attached to the heavy artillery, Omnibus Companies, Motor Ambulance Convoys, Bridging and Pontoon units and Workshops)

The Army Remounts Service (Companies involved in the provision of horses)

### *The ASC Labour Companies*

Leonard died in hospital in Malta on the 29th September 1918.

### On that fateful day:

Whilst fighting in Salonika, Leonard scraped his leg on some barbed wire – after a few days he fell ill and was rushed to hospital and eventually evacuated to Malta, where he died from septicemia.

*Leonard is buried in Pieta Military Cemetery, Malta along with 1303 other servicemen. His grave is A. XIX. 7.*

> *NOTE:*
> *His parents received a telegram a few days before he died telling*
> *them he was 'out of danger'.*

# WILLIAM MURPHY

**William Murphy** was born in Mobberley in 1899, one of five children born to Frank (a gardener) and Mary Murphy of Sprout Lane, Mobberley. William became a labourer.

He enlisted in the army, becoming Private no. 32603 of the 15th Battalion in the Cheshire Regiment.

**Brief history of the Battalion:**
The 15th (1st Birkenhead) Battalion, Cheshire Regiment was raised at Birkenhead as a Bantam Battalion on the 18th of November 1914 by Alfred Bigland MP. Bantam Battalions were those which admitted troops who were under the normal regulation minimum height of 5 feet 3 inches. After initial training close to home, they moved to Hoylake. In June 1915 they joined 105th Brigade, 35th Division at Masham, North Yorkshire. The Battalion was adopted by the War Office on the 15th of August 1915 and they moved to Salisbury Plain for final training. They were ordered to Egypt in late 1915, but the order was soon cancelled and they proceeded to France in the last week of January 1916, landing

at Le Havre and the division concentrated east of St Omer. They were in action during the Battles of the Somme at Bazentin Ridge, Arrow Head Copse, Maltz Horn Farm and Falfemont Farm. The division received new drafts of men to replace losses suffered on the Somme, but the CO. soon discovered that these new recruits were not of the same physical standard as the original Bantams, being men of small stature from the towns, rather than the miners and farm workers who had joined up in 1915. A medical inspection was carried out and 1439 men were transferred to the Labour Corps. Their places being taken by men transferred from the disbanded yeomanry regiments, who underwent a quick training course in infantry methods at a Divisional depot set up specifically for that purpose. In 1917 they were in action during the pursuit to the Hindenburg Line, at Houthulst Forest and The Second Battle of Passchendaele. In 1918 they fought in the First Battle of Bapaume, and the Final Advance in Flanders including The Battle of Courtrai and The action of Tieghem.

*(See Appendix Six for further information on the 'Bantam Battalions').*

William was killed in action on the 25th May 1918.

**On that fateful day:**

The war diary has no entry for this day.

*William is buried in Varennes Military Cemetery, France along with another 1219 servicemen. His grave is III. B. 10.*

# PETER MURPHY

**Peter Murphy** was born in Knutsford, Cheshire in 1896, the son of John (a platelayer) and Sarah of 8, Market Place, Knutsford. On leaving school Peter took up the trade of domestic gardener.

He married Mabel and moved to 5, Edgerton Terrace, Manchester Road, Knutsford.

On the outbreak of war, Peter enlisted in the army, attesting at Chester Recruiting Office on the 14th July 1814, becoming Driver no. 36828 of the Royal Field Artillery.

He went to France on the 14th July 1915 with 'B' Battery, 50th (L) Bde.

He was hospitalised on the 20th September 1916 with wounds, but although his records still exist, it is not stated how or where he was wounded.

He was killed in action on the 1st October 1917.

**Brief history of the Brigade:**
L Brigade, Royal Field Artillery, served with 9th Scottish Division. 9th (Scottish) Division was formed in late August 1914, part of Kitchener's First New Army. Following training in Scotland, they moved to Salisbury in late August and to Bordon in September. They proceeded to France between the 9th and 12th of May 1915 and went into action in the Battle of Loos. In 1916 they were in action in the Battle of the

Somme, including the capture of Longueval, The Battle of Delville Wood and The Battle of Le Transloy. In 1917 they fought in the First and Second Battles of the Scarpe during the Arras Offensive, The First Battle of Passchendaele and The action of Welsh Ridge.

Thanks to the Wartime Memories Project.

**On that fateful day:**
I have been unable to locate the war diary for this date.

*Peter is buried in Ypres Reservoir Cemetery, together with 2613 other servicemen. His grave is I. D. 91.*

# JAMES HIGGINSON NORBURY

**James Higginson Norbury** was born in Knutsford in 1888, one of nine children born to John (a butcher) and Sarah (a butcher)

Norbury of Queen Street, Knutsford. When he left school he became a bank clerk.

James joined the army and became Private no. 5372 in the 20th Battalion of the Royal Fusiliers (City of London Regiment).

He arrived in France on the 15th November 1915.

He was promoted to Lance Corporal.

**Brief history of the Battalion:**

20th (3rd Public Schools) Battalion, The Royal Fusiliers (City of London Regiment) was raised in at Epsom on the 11th of September 1914 by the Public Schools and University Men's Force. Following initial training near home, on the 26th of June 1915 they joined 98th Brigade, 33rd Division. The Division concentrated at Clipstone camp near Mansfield in Nottinghamshire in July 1915. In August they moved to Salisbury Plain for final training and firing practice. They proceeded France in November and by the 21st, 33rd Division had concentrated near Morbecque, being strengthened by the exchange of 98th Brigade for the experienced 19th Brigade from 2nd Division and the on the 27th of November, the 3rd Public Schools Battalion transferred to 19th Brigade. On the 26 of February 1916 the battalion transferred to GHQ and was disbanded on the 24th of April 1916 with many of the men being commissioned.

*Thanks to the Wartime Memories Project.*

James was killed in action on the 20th July 1916.

**On that fateful day:**

The Battalion war diary for this dates state:

*'20.7.16 HIGH WOOD – Map reference MARTINPUCH AREA 19th Brigade attack at 3.25 am on HIGH WOOD. Attack by 1st Cameronians and 5th Scots Rifles and 20th Royal Fusiliers in support –*

*2nd Royal Welsh Fusiliers in reserve, North corner and North West corner of wood not taken.*

*2nd Royal Welsh Fusiliers came up about 12 noon. The front and support line set across wood from east to west, with a strongpoint about S4 in support line.*

*Held on to this position until relieved by 100th Brigade at midnight then withdrew to* (unintelligible) *ground MAMETZ WOOD*

*Casualties:*

*Officers 4 killed   8 wounded  3 missing*

*O.R. 375 killed, wounded or missing. '*

***James has no known grave and id remembered on the Thiepval Memorial, Somme, France along with the names of 72,203 other servicemen.***

# REGINALD NORBURY

**Reginald Norbury** was born in Knutsford in 1897, the son of Edward (a blacksmith) of Toft Smithy, Toft, Knutsford. His father was a widower and was living with his brother.

In 1911 Reginald was employed as a Grocer's errand-boy.

Unfortunately, his service records no longer exist, but we know that sometime in 1916, on becoming 19 years of age, he enlisted in the army. Becoming Private no. 34586 in the Cheshire Regiment, but on arriving in France he was transferred to the 14th Battalion of the Royal Welsh Fusiliers, becoming Private no. 56395.

**Brief history of the Battalion.**

The 14th (Service) Battalion, The Royal Welch Fusiliers was raised at Llandudno on the 2nd of November 1914 by the Welsh National Executive Committee. Later in the month they joined 128th Brigade, 43rd Division at Llandudno, which was renamed 113th Brigade, 38th (Welsh) Division on the 28th of April 1915. They moved to Winchester for final training in August 1915 and proceeded to France in December 1915. In July 1916 they were in action at Mametz Wood on The Somme, suffering severe casualties. The Division did not return to major action for more than a 12 months. In 1917 they were in action in the Third Battles of Ypres, in 1918 they were in action on The Somme, in the Battles of the Hindenburg Line and the Final Advance in Picardy.

*Thanks to the Wartime Memories Project.*

Reginald was killed in action on the 8th January 1918.

**On that fateful day:**

The war diaries for the R.W.F. were not available at the time of writing.

*Reginald is buried at Ration Farm Cemetery, La Chappelle-D'Armentiers, France, together with 1331 other servicemen. His grave is IV. B. 7.*

# ROBERT NORBURY
*(Brother of Samuel)*

Robert Norbury was born in Mobberley in 1888, one of seven children born to Patsy Norbury of Dairy Farm, Mobberley, Robert was a farm labourer.

He enlisted in the Army in May 1917, first as Private no. 4185 of the Cheshire Regiment before transferring to the Royal Garrison Artillery, becoming Gunner no. 92043 in 111th Heavy Brigade.

## Brief history of the Brigade:

Heavy Batteries RGA were equipped with heavy guns, sending large calibre high explosive shells in fairly flat trajectory fire. The usual armaments were 60 pounder (5 inch) guns, although some had obsolescent 5 inch howitzers. As British artillery tactics developed, the Heavy Batteries were most often employed in destroying or neutralising the enemy artillery, as well as putting destructive fire down on strongpoints, dumps, store, roads and railways behind enemy lines.

Robert was wounded when a bomb dropped by an enemy aircraft exploded nearby. He died of wounds on the 14th July 1918.

*Robert is buried in Ypres Reservoir Cemetery with 2613 other servicemen. His grave I. F. 17.*

# SAMUEL NORBURY
*(Brother of Robert)*

**Samuel Norbury** was born in Mobberley in 1888, one of seven children born to Patsy Norbury of Dairy Farm, Mobberley, Samuel was an assistant to a jeweller.

He enlisted in the Cheshire Regiment as Private no. 4185 before transferring to the 6th battalion of the Kings (Shropshire Light Infantry) as Private no. 205109.

### Brief history of the Battalion:
A war-raised Service Battalion, formed in Shrewsbury in September 1914, posted to the 60th Brigade of the 20th Division. It landed at Boulogne on 22nd July 1915 and then served entirely on the Western Front.

The 6th fought at Loos in September 1915, around Ypres in 1916 (where it relieved the 1st Battalion) and then on the Somme, including the capture of Guillemont.

It fought at Langemarck (3rd Ypres) in August 1917 and on the Menin Road, Ypres, in September. They served against the Hindenburg Line near Cambrai at the end of the year and throughout the German Spring Offensive in 1918, seeing severe fighting at St. Quentin.

Samuel was killed in action on the 14th July 1918.

**On that fateful day:**
The war diary for the Battalion states that they were 'resting and training' near Lens. There was no action reported on that day but mention was made of shelling. It would appear that Samuel was a victim of it.

*Samuel is buried in Sucrerie Cemetery along with almost 400 other servicemen. His grave is V. D. 9.*

# WILLIAM ERNEST OAKES

**William Ernest Oakes** was born in Oakmere, Cheshire in 1889, one of ten children born to William (a carter) and Eunice of 15, Cranford Avenue, Knutsford.

On leaving school he became a chauffeur and lived at 43, Stockwell Street, Leek, Staffordshire.

He enlisted in the army sometime after 1915 and became Private no. 38536 of the 21st Battalion of the Northumberland Fusiliers (Tyneside Scottish).

**Brief history of the Battalion:**

21st (2nd Tyneside Scottish) Battalion, Royal Northumberland Fusiliers was raised on the 26th of October 1914 in Newcastle mainly from men of Scottish decent from the North East. Initially training in Newcastle City centre the 2nd Tyneside Scottish moved to Alnwick camp, in the grounds of Alnwick castle on the 29th of January 1915. They joined 102nd Brigade, 34th Division at Ripon in June 1915. In late August they moved to Salisbury Plain to begin final training. They proceeded to France in January 1916 and concentrated at La Crosse, east of St Omer. They were in action during the Battles of the Somme, including the capture of Scots and Sausage Redoubts, attacking just north of the village of La Boisselle, not far from Albert. At 7.28 am on 1st July 1916 two great mines were detonated beneath the German positions, one to the north of the village and one to the south. At 7.30 am the whistles sounded and the attack began. The 2nd Tyneside Scottish had 500 yards to cover, under heavy machine gun fire, before reaching the German lines, and many men of the battalion lost their lives. In 1917 they fought in the First and Second Battles of the Scarpe and the Battle of Arleux during the Arras Offensive. In August they were involved in the fighting at Havrincourt and in October they took part in The Third Battles of Ypres at the Broenbeek.

*Thanks to the Wartime Memories Project.*

William was killed in action on the 9th April 1917.

## On that fateful day:

### *9.4.17 ROCLINCOURT*

**2.30am**
*'B' Coy conducted thorough examination of the enemy wire and reported that for the most part this was non-existent in the front of us.*

**5.30am**
*Zero Hour The battalion advanced on the 2ⁿᵈ coy front with 'A' Coy on the right and 'B' Coy on the left with 'C' and 'D' coy in support. The 101ˢᵗ Brigade was on our right and we had the 22ⁿᵈ NF (3ʳᵈ Tyneside Scottish) on our left. The first objective was the BLACK LINE, a system of German trenches comprising 4 distinct lines. NO MAN'S LAND was about 70 yards across but the Battalion had formed up close to the remains of Boshe wire at pprox.. 4.40am and when the barrage lifted the troops rushed forward to attack. The capture of the first objective was accomplished in about an hour. A message time 6.30am was received from Capt H.W.Waller O.C. 'A' Coy to the effect that KACHEN WERG, a trench beyond the BLACK LINE had been captured by his company.*

### *ROCLINCOURT*
*The capture was accomplished with small loss. O.C. No. 3 Platoon 2ⁿᵈ Lt R.A. Macneill was killed in the second line of German trenches and 2ⁿᵈ Lts Corlett, Donaghy and Woodcock were wounded before reaching the 1ˢᵗ objective. These latter officers were in command of nos. 1, 2 and 5 Platoons. The 2ⁿᵈ objective named the BLUE LINE distant about 1200 yards was attacked about 7.45am and its capture completed about 11am. Again, casualties in the other ranks were comparatively few but at this time the toll of officers was severe. O.C. commanding 14 Platoon, 2ⁿᵈ Lt TE Bainbridge was killed, together with his Platoon Sergeant while at work establishing a bombing*

*post near the railway cutting. Hostile snipers gave a great deal of trouble at this point, but prompt action was taken to route them out. O.C. 'A' Coy with a small party captured a light field gun. A machine gun and machine gunner were also captured in an emplacement. Battalion H.Q. moved up to the BLACK LINE and was established. After the consolidation of the BLUE LINE, Headquarters moved again. The night passed fairly quietly but the weather was extremely cold.*

**Personal note:**

My thoughts are with the wounded and dying me out in no man's land that night in that 'extreme cold'.

***William has no know grave but is remembered on the Arras Memorial along with the names of 34,791 other servicemen.***

# ERIC WILLIAM OGDEN

**Eric William Ogden** was born in Wilmslow, Cheshire in 1898, one of five children born to William (a clog and boot maker) and Emily Ogden of 76, King Street, Knutsford.

He enlisted in the army in 1915, joining the Cheshire Regiment as private no.16097, later transferring to the 6th Battalion of the Royal Inniskillings Fusiliers becoming Private no. 48736.

**Brief history of the Battalion:**

The 6th Battalion, The Royal Inniskilling Fusiliers was raised at Omagh in August 1914, part of Kitchener's First New Army. They joined 31st Brigade, 10th (Irish) Division and moved to Dublin for training then on to Kildare by early 1915. In April 1915, they moved to Basingstoke, England for final training. They departed from Liverpool on the 9th of July for Lemnos and landed at Sulva Bay on the 7th of August 1915 and made an attack on Chocolate Hill on the 7th and 8th. They were withdrawn from Gallipoli on the 29th of September 1915 to Mudros, moving to Salonika, landing between the 6th and 10th of October. On the 7th and 8th of December they were in action at Kosturino, in the retreat from Serbia. Some units of the Division were in action at the Karajakois and Yenikoi in late September and early October. They sailed from Salonika to Egypt in early September 1917, concentrating near Rafa to prepare for the Palestine Campaign. Between April and

June 1918, many British units of the Division were replaced by Indian units, and the 6th Inniskillings were sent to France on the 2nd of May. On the 7th of June they joined 43rd Brigade, 14th (Light) Division, then on the 18th transferred to 103rd Brigade, 34th Division. On the 29th they transferred to Lines of Communication and on the 16th of July joined 151st Brigade, 50th (Northumbrian) Division. Went back into action in October in the Battles of the Hindenburg Line, The pursuit to the Selle and the Final Advance in Picardy.

*Thanks to the Wartime Memories Project.*

Eric was killed in action on the 8th November 1918 – just 3 days before the armistice was signed.

## On that fateful day:

*8.11.18 DOURLERS*
*07.30*
*Advanced resumed to final objective – MAUBEUGE-AVESNES ROAD. And final objective captured at 08.05. Very considerable hostile artillery & M.G. all morning.*
*Enemy counter-attacked from 11.00 to 14.00 but failed to reach our advance posts at any point.*

*15.30*
*149th Bde (3rd Royal Fus.) passed through front line to continue the advance.*

*16.00*
*Battalion marched back to billets at ST. REMY CHAUSSEE.*

This action had commenced the previous day. The diary makes no mention of the number of casualties.

*Eric is buried in Dourlers Communal Cemetery Extension, France, along with 161 other servicemen. His grave is I. C. 7.*

# WILLIAM OLLIER

**William Ollier** was born in 1896 in Barnton, Cheshire and in 1911 he was living with his mother and step-father at Moor-side, Knutsford and he was an apprentice cabinet maker.

He joined the 8th Battalion of the Cheshire Regiment as Private no. 33490.

**Brief history of the Battalion:**

The 8th (Service) Battalion, Cheshire Regiment was raised in Chester on the 12th of August 1914 as part of Kitchener's First New Army and joined 40th Brigade, 13th (Western) Division which assembled on Salisbury Plain. 40th Brigade moved to Chiseldon and Cirencester in September 1914. Near the end of February the Division concentrated at Blackdown in Hampshire. They moved to the Mediterranean from the 13th of June 1915 landing at Alexandria then moving to Mudros, by the 4th of July to prepare for a landing at Gallipoli. The infantry landed on Cape Helles between the 6th and 16th of July to relieve 29th Division. They returned to Mudros at the end of the month, and the entire Division landed at ANZAC Cove between the 3rd and 5th of August. They were in action in The Battle of Sari Bair, The Battle of Russell's Top and The Battle of Hill 60, at ANZAC. Soon afterwards they transferred from ANZAC to Suvla Bay. They were evacuated from Suvla on the 19th and 20th of December 1915, and after a week's rest they moved to the Helles bridgehead. They were in action during the last Turkish attacks at Helles on the 7th of January 1916 and were evacuated from Helles on the 8th and 9th. The Division concentrated at Port Said, holding forward posts in the Suez Canal defences. On the 12th of February 1916 they moved to Mesopotamia, to join the force being assembled near Sheikh Sa'ad for the relief of the besieged garrison at Kut al Amara. They joined the Tigris Corps on the 27th of March and were in action in the unsuccessful attempts to relieve Kut. They were in action in The Battle of Kut al Amara, The capture of the Hai Salient, the capture of Dahra Bend and The passage of the Diyala, in the pursuit of the enemy towards Baghdad. Units of the Division were the first troops to enter Baghdad, when it fell on the 11 March 1917. The Division then joined "Marshall's Column" and pushed north across Iraq, fighting at Delli 'Abbas, Duqma, Nahr Kalis, crossing the 'Adhaim on the 18 April and fighting at Shatt al 'Adhaim. Later in the year they were in action in the Second and Third Actions of Jabal Hamrin and fought at Tuz Khurmatli the following April.

*Thanks to the Wartime Memories Project.*

William 'died' on the 17ᵗʰ October 1917 and as his service records no longer exist we can only speculate that he died from disease.

*William is buried in Baghdad North Gate Cemetery, along with 4,160 other servicemen.*

# FRED PADMORE

**Fred Padmore** was born in Melton Mowbray.
He enlisted in the 6ᵗʰ Battalion of the Kings Own (Royal Lancaster Regiment) as Private no. 16079.
He arrived in Mesopotamia on the 13ᵗʰ June 1915.

## Brief history of the Battalion:

6th (Service) Battalion, The King's Own (Royal Lancaster Regiment) was raised at Lancaster in August 1914 as part of Kitchener's First New Army and joined 38th Brigade, 13th (Western) Division and trained on Salisbury Plain. Near the end of February the Division concentrated at Blackdown in Hampshire. They moved to the Mediterranean from the 13th of June 1915 landing at Alexandria then moving to Mudros, by the 4th of July to prepare for a landing at Gallipoli. The infantry landed on Cape Helles between the 6th and 16th of July to relieve 29th Division. They returned to Mudros at the end of the month, and the entire Division landed at ANZAC Cove between the 3rd and 5th of August. They were in action in The Battle of Sari Bair, The Battle of Russell's Top and The Battle of Hill 60, at ANZAC. Soon afterwards they transferred from ANZAC to Suvla Bay. They were evacuated from Suvla on the 19th and 20th of December 1915, and after a week's rest they moved to the Helles bridgehead. They were in action during the last Turkish attacks at Helles on the 7th of January 1916 and were evacuated from Helles on the 8th and 9th. The Division concentrated at Port Said, holding forward posts in the Suez Canal defences. On the 12th of February 1916 they moved to Mesopotamia, to join the force being assembled near Sheikh Sa'ad for the relief of the besieged garrison at Kut al Amara. They joined the Tigris Corps on the 27th of March and were in action in the unsuccessful attempts to relieve Kut. They were in action in The Battle of Kut al Amara, The capture of the Hai Salient, the capture of Dahra Bend and The passage of the Diyala, in the pursuit of the enemy towards Baghdad. Units of the Division were the first troops to enter Baghdad, when it fell on the 11 March 1917. The Division then joined "Marshall's Column" and pushed north across Iraq, fighting at Delli 'Abbas, Duqma, Nahr Kalis, crossing the 'Adhaim on the 18 April and fighting at Shatt al 'Adhaim. Later in the year they were in action in the Second and Third Actions of Jabal Hamrin and fought at Tuz Khurmatli the following April.

*Thanks to the Wartime Memories Project.*

Fred died of disease on the 27th October 1917.

*Fred is buried in Baghdad (North Gate) Cemetery, Iraq along with 4,455 other servicemen. His grave is XX. A. 4.*

# FRED PARMENTER

**Fred Parmenter** was born in Knutsford, one of seven children born to William (a groom/coachman) and Elizabeth Parmenter of Silk Mill Street, Knutsford.

389

John took up the trade of Domestic gardener.

He married Sarah in 1907 and moved to Tong Village, just outside Bradford, where together they had one child.

His service records no longer exist but we know he enlisted at Bradford in the East Yorkshire Regiment, becoming Private no. 6664 sometime in 1916, before transferring into the 2nd Battalion of the Durham Light Infantry as Private no. 79107.

**Brief history of the Battalion:**

The 2nd Battalion, Durham Light Infantry was at Lichfield with 18th Brigade in 6th Division, when war broke out in August 1914. They moved to Dunfermline then by the 13th August were at Cambridge engaged in training. They proceeded to France on the 10th of September 1914, landing at St Nazaire and at once moving to reinforce the hard-pressed BEF on the Aisne. They then moved north to Flanders and in 1915 saw action at Hooge. In 1916 they were on The Somme and in 1917 at Hill 70 and Cambrai. In 1918 they were again on the Somme then moved to Flanders in the spring taking part in the fighting retreat as the German's advanced through Bailleul to Kemmel. The 2nd DLI were in action during the Allied Advance in Flanders later that year and returned to the Cambrai area during Battles of the Hindenburg Line.

*Thanks to the Wartime Memories Project.*

Fred was killed in action on the 18th September 1918.

**On that fateful day:**

The war diary tells us that the battalion was stationed as Reserve at Monchy-La-Gashe, France. There is no record of any action on the 18th September 1918.

*Fred has no known grave but is remembered on the Vis-En-Artois Memorial, France along with the names of 9847 other servicemen.*

# SAMUEL EDWARD PARROTT

**Samuel Edward Parrott** was born in Harphurhey, Manchester in 1897, one of eight children born to Tom (a labourer) and Clara Theresa

Parrott of 4, White Bear Yard, Heathside, later moving to 5, County Terrace, Stanley Road, Knutsford. When he left school he became a farm labourer.

Samuel joined the army sometime after 1915, becoming Private no. 5408 in the 5th Battalion of the Gordon Highlanders.

**Brief history of the Battalion:**

The 5th Battalion was formed in August 1914 at Peterhead. Part of Gordon Brigade in the Highland Division. It then moved to Bedford.3 May 1915. It landed at Boulogne. On the 12th May 1915 formation retitled to 153rd Brigade in 51st (Highland) Division.

**51st Highland Division:**

Warned for France on 13 April 1915 the Division moved via Southampton and Folkestone and was complete in France by 5 May. At that point, on 11 May 1915, 1/1 Highland Division was renamed 51st Highland Division. At the same time the brigades were renumbered 152nd (Seaforth and Camerons), 153rd (Gordon Battalions) and 154th (Lancashire Battalions). The Brigade numbers, but not the names in brackets) would be retained by the Division thereafter.

**The Brigades were composed of the following:**

**152nd infantry Brigade** – 5th and 6th Seaforths, 6th and 8th Argyll and Sutherland Highlanders.

**153rd infantry Brigade** – 5th and 7th Gordons and 6th and 7th Black Watch.

**154th infantry Brigade** – 1/4th Royal Lancaster Regiment,1/4th Royal North Lancashire Lancaster Regiment, 1/8th Liverpool Irish Regiment and 2/5th Lancashire Fusiliers.

At the end of May to 2/5th Lancashire Fusiliers were relieved by 6th Scottish Rifles who remained with the division when the second fifth returned.

On 19 May the Division relieved the 2nd Division, part of 1st Corps, which had advanced to the Le Quinque Rue-Bethune road and were consolidating their position. This was the Division's first experience of digging into the Flanders mud where one could not dig down sufficiently because of the water and had also to build up breastworks to provide protection. On 30 May the Division was reassigned to the Ivth Corps. Plans were made for the Corps to attack the German positions from Chapelle St Rochalong the Rue d'Ouvert.

The Division fought at Festubert in May and Givenchy in June.

In September Major General G M Harper took command of the Division and remained as GOC until March 1918.

At the end of the year the four English battalions of 154 Brigade left to go to the 55th Division. The 6th Scottish Rifles were reduced to cadre strength and sent back to their base which left 154 Brigade to be reconstituted with 4th Seaforth, 4th and 5th Black Watch and 4th Camerons.

## 1916

Further organisational changes as a result of losses and reduce strength saw 4th Camerons and 4th and 5th Black Watch being replaced by 4th Gordons, 7th Argyll and Sutherland Highlanders and 9th Royal Scots to the new Brigade consisted of 4th Seaforth, 4th Gordons, 7th Argyll and Sutherland Highlanders and 9th Royal Scots

In March the Division went into the line from Neuville St. Vaast to Roclincourt. During this period, assailed by mines and follow on attacks the 1/6th Argylls had to be withdrawn from the Division because of devastating casualties.

*Thanks to the 51st Highland Division Museum.*

Samuel was killed in action on the 13th November 1916.

## On that fateful day:
There is no entry in the war diary for this date.

*Samuel is buried in Mailly Wood Cemetery, France, along with 702 other servicemen. His grave is I. D. 21.*

# GEORGE PEERS

**George Peers** was born in Knutsford in 1880. He was a postman living at Beechwood Terrace, Tatton Street, Knutsford with his wife, Mary Elisabeth and his son George.

He enlisted in the army in Londonderry, in the Royal Army Medical Corp as Private no.25418.

**Brief history of the Corp;**

The RAMC operated the army's medical units and provided medical detachments for the units of infantry, artillery and other arms. The Corps was assisted in its work by voluntary help from the British Red Cross, St John's Ambulance, the Friends Ambulance Unit, the Voluntary Aid Detachments and hundreds of private and charitable ventures.

George died 'at home' in Londonderry on the 29th June 1915 and buried in the cemetery there.

# SAMUEL LAST PEERS

**Samuel Last Peers** was born in Knutsford in 1892, the son of John (a house painter) and Mary Ann Peers of 6, Church View, Knutsford before moving to 39, Tatton Street, Knutsford. Samuel was an assistant grocer.

He joined the army, joining the Cheshire Regiment in September 1916 as Private no. 45863, later transferring to the 195th Company of the Machine Gun Corp as Private 64000.

**Brief history of the Company:**
The 195th Machine Gun Company joined 25th Division on the 16th of December 1916. In 1917 they were in action at The Battle of Messines attacking between the Wulverghem-Messines and Wulverghem-Wytschaete roads. In the Third battle of Ypres were in action during The Battle of Pilkem. On the 1st of April 1918 the Company joined with the other MGC's of the Division to become No 25 Battalion, Machine Gun Corps.
Samuel was killed in action on the 11th August 1917.

**On that fateful day:**
To-date I have been unable to locate the war diary for the infantry brigade.

*Samuel has no known grave and is remembered on the Menin Gate Memorial along with the names of 54,406 other servicemen.*

# MAYSON PENN

**Mayson Penn** was born in Gosport in 1892, the son of Mayson Penn (an insurance agent) and Christina Agnew Penn of Stanley Road, Knutsford. Mayson Jr became an insurance clerk.

Mayson Jr emigrated to Australia on the 13th September 1912 aboard the S.S. Otway, bound for Sydney, where he became an orchardist..

On the outbreak of war he, like so many other young Australians, joined the army, becoming Private no P744 of the 19th Battalion of the A.I.F.

**Brief history of the Battalion:**
The 19th Battalion was raised at Liverpool in New South Wales in March 1915 as part of the 5th Brigade. Some of the 19th's original recruits had already served with the Australian Naval and Military Expeditionary Force (AN&MEF) in the operations to capture German New Guinea in 1914. The 19th left Australia in late June, trained in Egypt from late July until mid-August, and on 21 August landed at ANZAC Cove.

At Gallipoli the Battalion participated in the last action of the August Offensive – the attack on Hill 60 – before settling into defensive routine in the trenches.

Mayson was killed in action on the 25th August 1915.

**On that fateful day:**
The war diaries were not available at the time of writing.

His service records state:

*Buried Isolated Graves foot of W Slope of DAMAKJELIK BAIR near DAMAKJELIK KURYN 2 5/8 miles SE of LALA BABA, Gallipoli.*

He was buried along with three other Australian soldiers – their graves never found.

*Mayson is remembered on the Lone Pine Memorial, Turkey along with 4,923 other servicemen.*

# WILLIAM THOMPSON PENNINGTON

**William Thompson Pennington** was born in Mobberley in 1883, one of twelve children born to Peter (a road labourer) and Elizabeth

Hannah Partington of 3, Hall Brook, Mobberley. He was a domestic gardener.

He joined the 1ˢᵗ Battalion of the Cheshire Regiment on the 4ᵗʰ April 1918 as Private no. 66575.

**Brief history of the Battalion:**

The 1ˢᵗ Battalion, Cheshire Regiment was a regular unit of the British Army and was in Londonderry when war broke out in August 1914 with 15ᵗʰ Brigade in 5ᵗʰ Division. They returned to England and proceeded to France with the British Expeditionary Force, landing at Le Havre on the 16ᵗʰ of August 1914. They saw action at The Battle of Mons, The Battle of the Marne, The Battle of the Aisne, The Battles of La Bassee, at Messines and in The First Battle of Ypres. Between the 3ʳᵈ of March and 7ᵗʰ of April 1915 they were attached with 15ᵗʰ Brigade to 28ᵗʰ Division in in exchange for 83ʳᵈ Brigade in order to familiarise the newly arrived troops with the Western Front. In 1915 they were in action in The Second Battle of Ypres and the Capture of Hill 60. In March 1916 they took over a sector in the front line in the southern edge of Vimy Ridge, in front of Arras. The 5ᵗʰ Division arrived on the Somme to relieve the British units who had suffered badly in the attack on the first of July and went into action at High Wood, being withdrawn in October. The Division spent late Autumn and winter near Festubert and in 1917 were in action in the Battles of Arras and the Third Battle of Ypres. In 1918 they took part in the Battle of Hazebrouck, with the 1ˢᵗ Cheshires fighting in the Defence of Nieppe Forest. In August after a short period of rest they returned to the Somme and the 5ᵗʰ Division was in more or less continuous action until the end of October 1918, seeing action in the Battles of the Hindenburg Line and the Final Advance in Picardy.

William died of the wounds he received at the 13ᵗʰ Field Hospital on the 23ʳᵈ October 1918 – just 19 days before the armistice was signed.

***William is buried in Bethencourt Communal Cemetery, France along with over 80 other servicemen. His grave is D. 11.***

# CHARLES LEIGH PICKERING

**Charles Leigh Pickering** was born in Altrincham, one of three children born to John (an importer) and Sarah. Robert was a buyer in his father's business. He moved and lived in 'Bramley', Knutsford.

He enlisted in the 2ⁿᵈ Battalion of the Cheshire Regiment as a 2/ Lieutenant before transferring to the Royal Flying Corp.

**History of 30ᵗʰ Squadron – Royal Flying Corp:**
No 30 Squadron was formed for service in Egypt in October 1914 at Farnborough, but was not allocated the squadron number 30 until 24 March 1915. Initially a single flight of BE2s at Ismailia Airfield.

However, the first aircrews from the squadron to see action were a separate flight, provided by the Australian Flying Corps (AFC). In early 1915, the Australian Government received a request for assistance for air support from the British Government of India. The AFC was still in its infancy and could only provide enough aircrews and ground staff for half a flight. All aircraft were to be provided by the Indian Government. Captain Henry Petre was appointed commander, before the half-flight sailed for Bombay. The Australians were augmented by personnel from the Indian Army and New Zealand.

On 20 April, the half-flight left India for Mesopotamia (Iraq) to provide air support to Indian and British troops during the Mesopotamian campaign against the Ottoman Empire (Turkey). The unit was commonly known in Australia as the "Mesopotamian Half Flight" (or "Australian Half-Flight").

Upon its arrival in Basra on 26 May, the half-flight took delivery of two Maurice Farman Shorthorns and a Maurice Farman Longhorn. These three biplanes were of a "pusher" design, so-called because the propeller faced backwards, behind the cockpit and were already obsolete. In particular, they were not suitable for desert conditions: their top speed was only 50 mph (80 km/h), while the wind (known locally as the *shamal*) often reached 80 mph (129 km/h). Secondly, the warmer air reduced aerodynamic lift, rendering the Farmans unable to take off on some occasions. In addition, the Longhorn was a second-hand aircraft with persistent mechanical problems, meaning that it spent many hours undergoing maintenance.

Nevertheless, the half-flight was immediately put to use on reconnaissance missions. Shortly afterwards, the Indian Army captured the town of Amarah, and the half-flight moved there on 9 June.

On 4 July, the half-flight's equipment was augmented with two Caudron G.3 aircraft, which were still not up-to-date, but generally preferred to the Farmans. On 30 July, one of the Caudrons was forced to land in enemy territory due to mechanical problems. It was later reported that the crew — Lieutenants George Pinnock Merz and W.

W. A. Burn (a New Zealander) — were killed by armed civilians in a running gun battle, over several miles. They were Australia's first military aviation casualties.

On 24 August, the half-flight was formally attached to No. 30 Squadron RFC, which referred to it as "B" Flight. The rest of 30 Sqn relocated to Iraq in April 1916. In April the squadron carried out one of the earliest air supply mission when it air-dropped food and other supplies to the garrison at Kut which was besieged by the Turks.

After breaking out, Allied forces met with stiff opposition outside Baghdad, and were forced back to Kut on 4 December, where they were again besieged. Ottoman forces eventually broke through and nine AFC ground staff became prisoners of war. Like the rest of the Allied POWs, they endured a punishing forced march to Turkey and only four of them survived captivity.

By 7 December, Petre was the last remaining AFC airman in Mesopotamia. He was transferred from 30 Squadron RFC to Mo. 1 Squadron AFC, based in Egypt. Petre flew the only remaining Shorthorn to 1 Sqn's base in Egypt.

The rest of 30 Sqn carried out bombing and reconnaissance missions until the end of the war with a variety of aircraft including SPADs, DH-4s and RE.8s.

Robert was killed in action on the 15th April 1917.

*Picture of a B.E.2C*

## On that fateful day:

Robert's casualty record states that whilst piloting a B.E.2 C. aircraft he was engaged in aerial combat in the Basra area when he was shot down. The other occupant of the aircraft Lt. H.W. Craig, a 27 year old Irishman was also killed. His grave is XIV. L. 14.

*Robert is buried in Baghdad War cemetery along with 4455 other servicemen. His grave is XIV. K. 14, right next to Craig. There is also a memorial to him in Knutsford Cemetery.*

# WILLIAM ARTHUR PIERCE

**William Arthur Pierce** was born in Welshpool in 1891 and came to live and work with his uncle and aunt, James (a publican) and Rachel Plant at The Old Church House, Lower Peover.

He enlisted in the 2ⁿᵈ Battalion of the Border Regiment in 1914, becoming Private no. 6066.

He arrived in France on the 18ᵗʰ January 1915. He was promoted to Acting Corporal.

**Brief history of the Battalion:**

The 2ⁿᵈ Battalion, The Border Regiment were based at Pembroke Dock when war broke out in August 1914. On the 5ᵗʰ of September they moved to Lyndhurst to join 20ᵗʰ Brigade in 7ᵗʰ Division. They landed at Zeebrugge on the 6ᵗʰ of October 1914 ready for action on the Western Front. They saw action in The First Battle of Ypres at the end of 1914 and in 1915 were in action at: The Battle of Neuve Chappelle, The Battle of Aubers, The Battle of Festubert, The second action of Givenchy, and The Battle of Loos.

*Thanks to the Wartime Memories Project.*

William was killed in action on the 16ᵗʰ May 1915.

**On that fateful day:**

The Battalion war diary states:

*16.5.15 FESTUBERT*

*The Brigade was allotted the task of breaking the line at two points. The Border Regiment from P5 to PRINCES ROAD, roughly 150 yards and the 2ⁿᵈ Scots Guards from PRINCES ROAD to 150 yards to the right.*

*At 3.15 am two platoons of 'A' Company made the assault but was stopped by two of our own heavy howitzer shells which dropped after the bombardment should have stopped.*

*They advanced a second time after heavy loss and gained the German trench. They were at once supported by the remaining two platoons of 'A' Company.*

*An attempt was made to progress further but the advance was stopped by a ditch full of water and by heavy machine gun fire which enfiladed from the left.*

*The whole of 'B' Company was then pushed over and occupied the German front line trench with orders to hold P% at all costs. 80 Brigade Bombers were attached to the Company for this purpose. Attempts were made to bomb down the trench to the left – which was still in the hands of the Germans. About 200 yards was gained but on each occasion the ground had to be given up owing to the shortage of bombs. These parties came under fire from a trench mortar during each attempt and suffered very heavy losses but despite their losses P5 was held until the Battalion was relieved.*

*About this time the communication trench P5 P4 which was our objective was made good.*

*The machine gunners with two guns were then sent up to a point about midway between P5 and P4 to strengthen the line.*

*'C' and 'D' Companies pushed on into the German trench and prolonged the line to the right.*

*During these operations the Battalion suffered very heavily. Lieut. WOOD was wounded midway between the British and the German trenches and was brought in by Sgt Maj. Davenport and Corporal Coleman but he died as soon as he reached the British trench.*

*Major ASW Moffatt was in command of the two leading companies but was hit in the head in the German communication trench and died shortly afterwards.*

The diary goes on to list the names of 9 officers that had been killed and 4 wounded.

*During the night the Battalion was relieved by the 1ˢᵗ Grenadier Guards and on account of the serious losses it had sustained + returned to the old British line where it was re-organised.*

*The total casualties during these operations were:*
*Officers 11 killed  5 wounded*
*Other Ranks 110 killed  240 wounded  35 missing.*

*William is remembered on the Le Touret Memorial, France along with the names of 13,394 other servicemen.*

# HAROLD WILLIAM PIERPOINT

**Harold William Pierpoint** was born in Poulton in 1894, one of ten children born to Arnold Hugh (a gamekeeper) and Alice Pierpoint of mere, Knutsford. Harold worked as a mechanic.

He enlisted in the 1/6th Battalion of the Manchester Regiment, becoming Private no. 251047.

**Brief history of the Battalion:**
The 1/6th Battalion, Manchester were a Territorial unit, when war broke out in August 1914 they were based in Stretford Road, Hulme as part of the Manchester Brigade, East Lancashire Division. They were mobilized and moved to Rochdale to prepare for service overseas. They proceeded to Egypt arriving at Alexandria on the 25th of September to defend the Suez Canal from the Turkish forces in Palestine. They were in action in the Turkish attack on the Suez Canal on the 3rd of February 1915. In the first week of May the division embarked from Alexandria, landing at Cape Helles, Gallipoli, where they saw action in the attempts to capture the heights of Krithia and the Battle of Krithia Vineyard which was a diversionary attack for the British Landing at Suvla Bay. The much depleted division were evacuated from Gallipoli in the first week of January 1916, returning to Alexandria via Mudros. They returned to duty on the Suez Canal and were in action in the Battle of Romani in August. In early 1917 they were ordered to the Western Front, departing from Alexandria in February. They went into the front line at Ephey, moved to Havrincourt then were withdrawn to Albert for rest and training during July and August. In September they moved north to Flanders and were in action during the Third Battle of Ypres at Iberian, Borry Farm, Beck House Farm and Sans Souci. At the end of the month they moved to the coast at Nieuport until November when they moved to La Bassee Canal at Givenchy.

*Thanks to the Wartime Memories Project.*

Harold was killed in action on the 5th September 1917, when he was hit by a shell while working with a ration party, bringing food up to the front-line trenches

**On that fateful day:**
There is no mention in the war diary of any action on this day –

however a diary entry from Robert Darbyshire goes some way to say what was happening:

### 5ᵗʰ September 1917

*Nothing much doing until about noon when Jerry started to put a barrage on our trench – most awful. Dick Griffiths with his section, 9 altogether, got a 5.9 shell to themselves and out of the 9 only 2 were living when we were able to get to them and one of them had both his legs blown off. The other was wounded in 40 places. Every bone in Carl Ashley's body was broken. Nick carter had a hole in his stomach as big as a dinner plate. Dick had the left half of his face, and left shoulder and arm blown clean off and was unrecognisable except for the two stripes on his arm. A more ghastly sight I never saw and don't waqnt to see again. This happened about 1pm and Jerry was still dropping shells into our trench however the shelling slackened off until about 9pm when he opened out again for 15 minutes.*

*So up to our report going in at midnight we had 1 officer, 2 N.C.O.'s and 30 men killed or wounded.*

***Harold is remembered on the Tyne Cot Memorial, Belgium, along with the names of 34,952 other servicemen.***

# GUY KENYON PIERSON

**Guy Kenyon Pierson** was born in Knutsford, one of five children born to Charles (a land agent) and Betsy Pierson who moved to The Mount, Altrincham. On marrying Edith Alice he moved to 'Ingleside', Mobberley.

He enlisted in the 9th Battalion of the Royal Fusiliers as private no SPTS/4228.

**Brief history of the Battalion:**

9th Battalion, The Royal Fusiliers (City of London Regiment) was raised at Hounslow on 21 August 1914 as part of Kitchener's First New Army and joined 36th Brigade, 12th (Eastern) Division. 36th Brigade underwent training at Colchester then final training was undertaken near Aldershot from the 20th of February 1915, with the cavalry, motor machine gun battery, sanitary and veterinary sections joining. The Division proceeded to France between the 29th of May and 1st of June 1915 landing at Boulogne, they concentrated near St Omer and by 6th of June were in the Meteren-Steenwerck area with Divisional HQ being established at Nieppe. They underwent instruction from the more experienced 49th (South Midland) Division and took over a section of the front line at

Ploegsteert Wood on the 23rd of June 1915. They were in action in The Battle of Loos from the 30th of September, taking over the sector from Gun Trench to Hulluch Quarries consolidating the position, under heavy artillery fire. On the 9th they repelled a heavy German infantry attack and on the 13th took part in the Action of the Hohenzollern Redoubt, capturing Gun Trench and the south western face of the Hulluch Quarries. During this period at Loos, 117 officers and 3237 men of the Division were killed or wounded. By the 21st they moved to Fouquieres-les-Bethune for a short rest then returned to the front line at the Hohenzollern Redoubt until the 15th of November, when they went into reserve at Lillers. On the 9th of December, 9th Royal Fusiliers assisted in a round-up of spies and other suspicious characters in the streets of Bethune. On the 10th the Division took over the front line north of La Bassee canal at Givenchy. On the 19th of January they began a period of training in Open Warfare at Busnes, then moved back into the front line at Loos on the 12th of February 1916. In June they moved to Flesselles and carried out a training exercise. They moved to Baizieux on the 30th June and went into the reserve at Hencourt and Millencourt by mid-morning on the 1st of July. They relieved the 9th Division at Ovillers-la-Boisselle that night and attacked at 3.15 the following morning with mixed success. On the 7th they attacked again and despite suffering heavy casualties in the area of Mash Valley, they succeeded in capturing and holding the first and second lines close to Ovillers. They were withdrawn to Contay on the 9th July.

*Thanks to the Wartime Memories Project.*

Guy was killed in action on the 7th July 1916.

**On that fateful day:**
The war diary for the above date states:

## '7.7.16 IN FRONT OVILLERS

### 4.30 am

*Our bombardment commenced and became intense at 5.30 am at which time the Company took up its position in the front line ready for the assault. 'A' Coy on the left – 'D' on the right were to form the first line and to be followed immediately by 'B' + 'C' Coys respectively. The enemy retaliated almost immediately as soon as our bombardment commenced + our trenches were shelled by guns of big calibre. There were no dug-outs available and our casualties were very heavy. 'C' Coy suffered most heavily, being reduced to about 40. It was then decided that 'C' Coy should go over with 'D'. At 8.30 am, the time for the assault 'A' and 'D' with the remnants of 'C' left our trenches.*

*'A' Coy was decimated by M.G. fire and the same fate met 2 platoons of 'B' which followed. The remaining platoon of 'B' were ordered to remain in the trench as it was seen to be useless to send them across at the same place. 'D' + 'C' on the left were more successful + although greatly weakened managed to reach the German trench which they carried by assault.*

*The Enemy's fire and support trenches were captured and consolidated. Two M.G. were put out of action + 50 prisoners were captured.*

*Continual bombing attacks were beaten off with loss to the Enemy.*

*About 5.30 pm the remaining platoons of 'B' Coy managed to get across and brought with them a large supply of bombs. It was raining heavily during the day. In the morning we bombed along the trench on our left flank and gained about 90 yards. We handed this over to the 9th Essex (35th Bde) which had arrived.*

*During the day the Enemy shelled us rather heavily.*

### 7 pm

*Trench taken over by 2nd Batt Manchester Regiment. The Batt was met by cookers at CRUCIFIX CORNER where they had tea.'*

The war diary makes no mention of the number of casualties but as you can see from the above diary extract – they must have been considerable.

This action, we now know as The Battle of the Somme, continued throughout on until November.

*Guy is remembered on the Thiepval Memorial along with the names of 72,203 other servicemen who have no known grave.*

# JAMES MILLS PRESTON

**James Mills Preston** was born in Heaton Moor, Stockport in 1889, one of three children born to Joseph (a domestic gardener) and Mary Preston. His father became a gardener on the Tabley Estate.

By May 1910 James was working for the Duke of Devonshire at Chatsworth House in Derbyshire, earing £3.15s a month as a gardener. He left there in December 1911 and moved to Newbury in Berkshire and continued his profession as a jobbing domestic gardener.

He enlisted at the Newbury recruiting office in 1916, joining the 15th (Service) Battalion of the Hampshire Regiment becoming Private no. 22782.

In April 1917 James was hospitalised (there is no receord as to why), but it was serious enough to warrant him the be returned to England. He was admitted to the County of Middlesex War Hospital, Napsbury, St. Albans.

**Brief history of the Battalion:**

15th (2nd Portsmouth) Battalion, Hampshire Regiment was raised at Portsmouth on the 5th of April 1915 by the Mayor and local Committee and was adopted by The War Office on the 30th of May 1915. After initial training close to home they joined 122nd Brigade, 41st Division at Aldershot in October. In February 1916 they moved to the Marlborough Lines, Aldershot for final training and proceeded to France in early May, the division concentrating between Hazebrouck and Bailleul. In 1916 they were in action at The Battle of Flers-Courcelette and The Battle of the Transloy Ridges on the Somme. In 1917 they fought during The Battle of Messines, The Battle of Pilkem Ridge, and The Battle of the Menin Road and took part in the Operations on the Flanders coast.

James was killed in action on the 5th August 1917.

**The war diary states:**

*5th August 1917*
**Iron Bridge Tunnels**
*At 4am in a heavy mist the enemy attempted to re-take HOLLEBEKE. He succeeded in getting into FORRET FARM and tried to take*

HOLLEBEKE, *working round the village from the rear as well as round the front. On this occurring Capt J P FOWLER slightly withdrew his company from HOLLEBEKE and cut off a small party who had got behind him. The left 'with the exception of one post of one officer and 15 men' held firm; the whole of this post were taken prisoner except one sergeant who returned and one man who was afterwards seen dead.*

*Very little information reaching Batt: HQ Major G D Amery and 2nd Lt S Lazenby went forward to clear up the situation; on further information the 2 companies who had previously been in reserve, were sent forward in support to OPAL RESERVE. the CO proceeding to OPTIC TRENCH. At that moment a message arrived from Capt J P FOWLER giving his dispositions; an immediate counter-attack under cover of the mist was ordered, Major G D Amery having become a casualty. Capt C C OXBORROW's Coy advanced with some men of the 12th East Surrey Regt and eventually assisted to re-capture HOLLEBEKE. One platoon from the reserve company was detailed to attack FORRET FARM with the assistance of some men of the 12th East Surreys. In addition a Company were ordered to do the same thing, but came up on East side. The village and FORRET FARM were cleared and 17 prisoners taken; in the meantime while the above orders were being put into effect by means of Major R Pennell personally delivering the orders given, the CO returned to 12th E Surrey Regts HQ and asked for a slow rate of fire for ¼ hour then rapid for same period, followed again by a further period of slow fire which was carried out and which fortunately coincided with the attack on HOLLEBEKE. On arrival of one platoon of the 15th Bn Hants Regt near FORRET FARM a Stafford officer was re-organising some of the E Surrey Regt. He handed over the command to 2nd Lt P E Shields, and the Hants and Surreys re-took Forret Farm taking 13 prisoners. ½ company of the Staffords were brought up at 2nd Lt P E Shields request and 'stood by' in support, 200 yards in rear, but were not required.*

*Our forward positions were reinforced by Y Coy.*
*Enemy were observed massing for another attack and at 9.30pm they*
*commenced crawling towards our lines, but were completely dispersed*
*by MG fire and a well-timed barrage, our lines remaining intact.*

*James has no known grave and is remembered on the Menin Gate, along with*
*the names of 54.415 other servicemen.*

# JOHN JOSEPH PRICE

**John Joseph Price** was born in Knutsford in 1892, one of four
children born to Robert (a general labourer) and Lucy Price of 21,
Stanley Road, Knutsford. John was a plumber's apprentice.

He enlisted in the 18th Battalion of the Manchester Regiment, becoming Private no. 10987.

**Brief history of the Battalion:**

The 18th (3rd City) Battalion, Manchester Regiment was raised in Manchester on the 28th of August 1914 by the Lord Mayor and City. Initially they trained at Heaton Park but moved in April 1915 to Belton Park, where they joined 90th Brigade, 30th Division. They to Larkhill in September 1915 for final training and proceeded to France on the 6th of November 1915. Concentrating near Amiens. In 1916 they were in action during the Battle of the Somme, in which the Division captured Montauban. In 1917 they took part in the pursuit of the German retreat to the Hindenburg Line, the Arras Offensive and The Battle of Pilkem Ridge.

John died of wounds on the 24th April 1917. I have been unable to discover when and where he received those wounds.

*John is buried in Abbeyville Cemetery Extension with 2102 other servicemen.*
*His grave is II. F. 7.*

# THOMAS RAYNER

**Thomas Rayner** was born in Davenham, Cheshire in 1893, one of seven children born to Thomas (a house painter) and Mary Elisabeth of 7, Market Square Knutsford. On marrying Lillian he went to live at 6, Grosvenor Road, Altrincham. He took up the occupation of gardener.

He enlisted in the army becoming Private, later Lance Corporal 307388 of the 11th Battalion of the Lancashire Fusiliers.

**Brief history of the Battalion:**
The 11th (Service) Battalion, Lancashire Fusiliers was raised at Codford in October 1914 as part of Kitchener's Third New Army, and joined 74th Brigade, 25th Division. The Division assembled for training in the area around Salisbury. They proceeded to France on the 25th of September 1915, landing at Boulogne and the division concentrated in the area of Nieppe. Their first action was in defence of the German attack on Vimy Ridge in May 1916. They then moved to The Somme and joined the Battle just after the main attack, with 75th Brigade making a costly attack near Thiepval on the 3rd of July. The Division was in action at The Battle of Bazentin, The Battle of Pozieres and The Battle of the Ancre Heights. In 1917 they were in action at The Battle of Messines attacking between the Wulverghem-Messines and Wulverghem-Wytschaete roads. In the Third battle of Ypres were in action during The Battle of Pilkem.

*Thanks to the Wartime Memories Project.*

Thomas was killed in action on the 11th August 1917.

**On that fateful day:**
There is no specific entry for this date in the war diary.

*Thomas has no know grave and is remembered on the Menin Gate, Ypres along with the names of 54,406 other servicemen.*

# CHARLES RICHARDSON

**Charles Richardson** was born in 1882 in Knutsford, and in 1911 was living with his mother Caroline, sister and his step-father William (a baker) at 43, Tatton Street, Knutsford. He was a plumber.

He married Alice Richardson Lansloot of 45, Dyk Straat, Malines, Belgium.

Charles enlisted in the army, becoming Private no. 12273 of the 1st Battalion of the Cheshire Regiment.

He arrived in France on the 6th March 1915.

**Brief history of the regiment:**

The 1st Battalion, Cheshire Regiment was a regular unit of the British Army and was in Londonderry when war broke out in August 1914 with 15th Brigade in 5th Division. They returned to England and proceeded to France with the British Expeditionary Force, landing at Le Havre on the 16th of August 1914. They saw action at The Battle of Mons, The Battle of the Marne, The Battle of the Aisne, The Battles of La Bassee, at Messines and in The First Battle of Ypres. Between the 3rd of March and 7th of April 1915 they were attached with 15th Brigade to 28th Division in in exchange for 83rd Brigade in order to familiarise the newly arrived troops with the Western Front. In 1915 they were in action in The Second Battle of Ypres and the Capture of Hill 60.

*Thanks to the Wartime Memories Project.*

Charles was killed in action on the 16th January 1916.

**On that fateful day:**

The war diary states:

*'16.1.16*

**Batt in billets.**

*The Germans fired three shells into BRAY but only one exploded.'*

It gave no indication of any casualties but it seems that this shell killed Charles.

***Charles is buried in Citadel New Military Cemetery, Fricourt, together with 379 other servicemen.***

# PETER EDWARD RICHARDSON
*(Brother of William Richardson)*

**Peter Edward Richardson** was born in 1891 in Knutsford, one of ten children born to Peter (a house painter) and Annie Richardson of 9, Gannon Square, Knutsford. On leaving school Peter became a domestic gardener.

He enlisted in the army, becoming Private no. 4448 in 'C' Company, 8th Battalion of the Northumberland Fusiliers.

He arrived in the Balkans on the 10th July 1915.

He was promoted to Lance Corporal.

**Brief history of the Battalion:**
The 8th (Service) Battalion, Northumberland Fusiliers, was raised at Newcastle in August 1914 as part of Kitchener's First New Army. After initial training close to home, they moved to Belton Park, Grantham. On the 4th of April 1915 the Division assembled at Witley and Frensham for final training. They served with 34th Brigade, 11th (Northern) Division proceeding to Gallipoli in July 1915 sailing from Liverpool to Murdos, landing near Lala Baba at Suvla Bay on the 6th of August 1915.

*Thanks to the Wartime Memories Project.*

Peter was killed in action on the 7th August 1915. (see pageXX)

**On that fateful day:**
There is no entry in the war diary for this date.

*Peter is remembered on the Hellas Memorial, Turkey, along with the names of 20,885 other servicemen.*

# WILLIAM RICHARDSON
*(Brother of Peter Edward Richardson)*

**William Richardson** was born in 1896 in Knutsford, one of ten children born to Peter (a house painter) and Annie Richardson of 9, Gannon Square, Knutsford. On leaving school William became a labourer.

William enlisted in the army becoming Private no. 15567 of the 8th Battalion Northumberland Fusiliers.

### Brief history of the Battalion:

The 8th (Service) Battalion, Northumberland Fusiliers, was raised at Newcastle in August 1914 as part of Kitchener's First New Army. After initial training close to home, they moved to Belton Park, Grantham. On the 4th of April 1915 the Division assembled at Witley and Frensham for final training. They served with 34th Brigade, 11th (Northern) Division proceeding to Gallipoli in July 1915 sailing from Liverpool to Murdos, landing near Lala Baba at Suvla Bay on the 6th of August 1915. On the 20th December 1915 the Division was withdrawn from Gallipoli to Imbros and then to Egypt in January

1916 where they took over defence of a section of the Suez canal. They were recalled to France in June, embarking from Alexandria on 3rd of July, arriving as reinforcements to the battle of The Somme.

*Thanks to the Wartime Memories Project.*

William was killed in action on the 26th September 1916.

**On that fateful day:**
The war diary states:

**26.9.16 IN THE FIELD**
*Battalion marched out and relieved the 6th York & Lancaster Regt during the night in front line trenches.*
*Battalion engaged in an attack in ZOLLERN REDOUBT and STUFF REDOUBT. Copy of report on operations attached (See Appendix XX)*
*Casualties 19 officers 430 OR*

***William has no known grave and is remembered on the Thiepval Memorial, Somme, France along with the names of 72,203 other servicemen.***

# CHARLES RIDGWAY

**Charles Ridgway** was born in 1890 in Rostherne, Cheshire, one of seven children born to Edwin and Sarah Ridgway of Rostherne. The family later moved to Brookside farm, Mobberley. Charles worked as a furniture Draughtsman.

On the 1st September 1914 he attested on the in the army in Bristol, becoming Private no. 18194 in the 9th Reserve Cavalry.

On arriving in France he had transferred to the 1st Battalion of the East Surrey Regiment, becoming Private no. 10599.

**Brief history of the Battalion:**
1st Battalion, The East Surrey Regiment was in Dublin with 14th Brigade, 5th Division when war broke out in August 1914. They proceeded to France, landing at Le Havre on the 15th of August 1914. They were in action in The Battle of Mons and the subsequent retreat, The Battle of Le Cateau, The Battle of the Marne, The Battle of the Aisne, The Battles of La Bassee and Messines and The First Battle of Ypres. In 1915 they were in action at The Second Battle of Ypres and the Capture of Hill 60.

In autumn 1915, many units were exchanged with units from the newly arrived volunteer 32$^{nd}$ Division, to stiffen the inexperienced Division with regular army troops. On the 12$^{th}$ of January 1916 transferred to 95$^{th}$ Brigade with 5$^{th}$ Division. In March 1916, 5$^{th}$ Division took over a section of front line between St Laurent Blangy and the southern edge of Vimy Ridge, near Arras. They moved south in July to reinforce The Somme and were in action at, High Wood, The Battle of Guillemont, The Battle of Flers-Courcelette, The Battle of Morval and The Battle of Le Transloy. In October they moved to Festubert and remained there until March 1917 when they moved in preparation for the Battles of Arras. On 7 September 1917 the 5$^{th}$ Division moved out of the line for a period of rest before, being sent to Flanders where they were in action during the Third Battle of Ypres.

*Thanks to the Wartime Memories Project.*

Charles was killed in action on the 29$^{th}$ July 1916.

**On that fateful day:**
The war diary states:

*29.7.16 LONGUEVAL*
*Heavy shelling on both sides with the enemy's shelling through LONGUEVAL making communication well-nigh impossible.*

*Many wounded of several days were occupying shell holes in and around the village – it was impossible to get them away or even provide them with water which they cry for as one passes. Water is a great difficulty. Many attempts were made to get the water up through the barrage but much more was actually needed than received.. At about 2pm orders were received to attack 2 enemy posts NW of the village – the attack was carried out at 3.30pm by no's 2 and 4 coy. No 2 on the right. A previous bombardment by our heavies was to have put out of action the enemy machine guns in the posts. This however* was not apparently accomplished as our attack was met by heavy machine gun fire and the few who got forward pluckily were unable to push forward or backwards from the indifferent cover they reached and finally had to withdraw to their original position after dusk.

Our losses were heavy from Noon 27$^{th}$ inst. to noon 29$^{th}$ inst. we lost 12 officers and 308 OR.

The loss of the OR between these dates containing the names of many old stagers who will be hard to replace.

**Charles has no known grave and is remembered on the Thiepval Memorial, Somme, France along with the names of 72,203 other servicemen.**

# DOUGLAS MARSHALL RIGBY

**Douglas Marshall Rigby** was born in Altrincham in 1892, the son of Marshall (a solicitor) and Grace Rigby of White Knowle, Buxton.

Douglas later moved to The Gorse, Knutsford. He was a clerk.

He enlisted in the army as a 2/Lieutenant in the 1/6th Cheshire Regiment.

**Brief history of the Battalion:**

The 1/6th Battalion, Cheshire Regiment was a Territorial unit based in Stockport with Cheshire Brigade, Welsh Division when war broke out in August 1914. They proceeded to France on the 10th of November 1914 joining 15th Brigade, 5th Division on the 17 December 1914. On the 1st of March 1915 they transferred to GHQ and took over guard and other duties at Rouen, Abbeville and Dieppe. On the 9th of January 1916 they transferred to 20th Brigade, 7th Division then on the 29th of February 1916 to 118th Brigade, in the newly arrived 39th Division to replace units who had remained in England to complete their training. On the 30th June 1916 they were in action in an attack near Richebourg l'Avoue with the Sussex battalions suffered heavy casualties. They were in action during the Battles of the Somme, including, the fighting on the Ancre, The Battle of Thiepval Ridge, The Battle of the Ancre heights and the capture of Schwaben Reddoubt and Stuff Trench as well as The Battle of the Ancre. In 1917 they fought in The Battle of Pilkem Ridge, The Battle of Langemarck, The Battle of the Menin Road Ridge, The Battle of Polygon Wood and The Second Battle of Passchendaele. In 1918 they were in action at The Battle of St Quentin, The actions at the Somme crossings, The Battle of Bapaume and The Battle of Rosieres before moving to Flanders. They took part n The fighting on Wytschaete Ridge, The First and Second Battle of Kemmel and The Battle of the Scherpenberg. On the 28th of May 1918 they transferred to 75th Brigade, 25th Division and were in action at The Battle of the Aisne, on the 17th of June the battalion absorbed men of the 11th Cheshires, which was reduced to cadre. On the 8th of July 1918 they transferred to 21st Brigade, 30th Division. They were in action during the Advance in Flanders and by the Armistice had crossed the River Scheldt with advanced units reaching the line between Ghoy and la Livarde, North West of Lessines.

*Thanks to the Wartime Memories Project.*

Douglas arrived in France on the 22nd February 1915.

He was killed in action on the 4th September 1918.

**On that fateful day:**
The war diary has no entry for this date.

*Douglas is buried in the Wulverghem-Lindenhoek Road Military Cemetery along with 1010 other servicemen. His grave is II. A. 22.*

# CHARLES FREDERICK RILEY

**Charles Frederick Riley** was born in Tabley, Cheshire in 1886, one of three children born to Thomas (a farm teamsman) and Harriet Alice Louisa Riley of Tabley. Charles too was a farm labourer. He married Alice and moved to Tabley Hill, Cheshire.

He enlisted in the Cheshire Yeomanry in 1912 but in 1915 he was discharged as being physically unfit to serve.

---

# GEORGE RILEY

**George Riley** was born in Daresbury, Cheshire in 1888, one of three children born to Thomas (a horseman on a farm) and Mary Ann Riley of 80, Budworth Road, Tabley, Cheshire. He was a general labourer by trade, and married Hannah Eliza Smith in 1908 and set up home at 25, School Lane, Lostock Gralam, Cheshire, where they had four children.

George enlisted in July 1915 in the Cheshire Regiment, becoming Private no. 27379 in the 13th (Service) Battalion. He was called to service on the 21st February 1917. He was later transferred to the 16th Battalion.

**Brief history of the Battalion:**

The 16th (2nd Birkenhead) Battalion, Cheshire Regiment was raised at Birkenhead as a Bantam Battalion on the 18th of November 1914 by Alfred Bigland MP. Bantam Battalions were those which admitted troops who were under the normal regulation minimum height of 5 feet 3 inches After initial training close to home, they moved to Hoylake. In June 1915 they joined 105th Brigade, 35th Division at Masham, North Yorkshire. The Battalion was adopted by the War Office on the 15th of August 1915 and they moved to Salisbury Plain for final training. They were ordered to Egypt in late 1915, but the order was soon cancelled and they proceeded to France in the last week of January 1916, landing at Le Havre and the division concentrated east of St Omer. They were in action during the Battles of the Somme at Bazentin Ridge, Arrow Head Copse, Maltz Horn Farm and Falfemont Farm. The division received new drafts of men to replace losses suffered on the Somme, but the CO. soon discovered that these new recruits were not of the same physical standard as the original Bantams, being men of small stature from the towns, rather than the miners and farm workers who had joined up in 1915. A medical inspection was carried out and 1439 men were transferred to the Labour Corps. Their places being taken by men transferred from the disbanded yeomanry regiments, who underwent a quick training course in infantry methods at a Divisional depot set up specifically for that purpose. In 1917 they were in action during the pursuit to the Hindenburg Line, at Houthulst Forest and The Second Battle of Passchendaele.

*Thanks to the Wartime Memories Project.*

George was reported missing in action on the 22nd October 1917 and it was later discovered that he had been seriously wounded in the thigh and arm and had been taken prisoner by the Germans. He subsequently died of his wounds on the 25th November 1917 at Kreigslag German Military Hospital in Ghent.

His wife received a weekly pension of 33/9 (£1.68 approx) for herself and her four children.

*George is buried in Ghent City Cemetery, Belgium, along with 194 other servicemen. His grave is B.2. He also has a memorial in Knutsford cemetery.*

# ARTHUR PARRY ROBERTS

**Arthur Parry Roberts** was born in Old Colwyn, Denbighshire in 1897, the son of Cornelius (a domestic gardener) and Margaret Roberts of 12, Cranford Avenue, Knutsford.

Arthur enlisted in the Cheshire Regiment as Private no. 27986, before transferring to the 3ʳᵈ Company of the Machine Gun Corp (Infantry) as Private no. 6697.

**Brief history of the Company:**
The 3ʳᵈ Machine Gun Company was formed from the Machine Gun Sections of the 3ʳᵈ Brigade, 1ˢᵗ Division on the 26ᵗʰ of January 1916 they were in action in the Battles of the Somme. In 1917 they saw action in The German retreat to the Hindenburg Line and the Third Battle of Ypres.

*Thanks to the Wartime Memories Project.*

Arthur died of wounds on the 15ᵗʰ April 1917. Unfortunately his service records no longer exist so I have been unable to discover where and when he received his wounds.

*Arthur is buried in Barlin Communal Cemetery Extension along with 1,171 other servicemen. His Grave is I.A.4*

# HENRY ROYLE

**Harry Royle** was born in Lower Peover, Cheshire in 1893, one of three children born to Henry (a railway lorryman) and Martha Royle of 4, Canute Place, Knutsford. Henry was a groom.

He joined the 8th Battalion of the Kings (Shropshire Light Infantry) as Private no. 23909.

**Brief history of the Battalion:**
The 8th (Service) Battalion was a war-raised Service Battalion, formed in Shrewsbury in September 1914 under Lt. Col. C. H. Sisted. Joined the 66th Brigade of the 22nd Division and landed in France on 28th October 1915, heading for Amiens.

After only a few weeks on the Western Front, the Battalion was sent to Macedonia, arriving on November 6th 1915. It spent the remainder of the war on the Salonika front around Doiran, suffering severely from malaria as well as from its encounters with the enemy. Periods of routine trench work, in reserve, along the Struma or in the defences of Salonika were interspersed with some severe fighting, as at "Pip Ridge", near Lake Doiran, in February 1917 and again in September 1918.

Henry was killed in action on the 25th April 1917.
**On that fateful day:**

## The war diary states:

*24.4.17*
*01.00 hrs.*
*The Liaison Officer from 11ᵗʰ Worcester's Regt. On right of 'B' Company reported that Batt had encountered very serious opposition & required urgent support. Orders were sent to the two platoons in support in Green Ravine to proceed without delay in accordance with the pre-arranged plan to reinforce the left flank of the 11ᵗʰ Worcester Regt. Under difficulties & (a) message was dispatched to the 66ᵗʰ Infantry Bde requesting 2 additional platoons to support 'B' Company on Hill 380.*

*01.38 hrs*
*'B' Company (right) estimated its casualties at about 20 including Capt. L. Profit killed.*

*02.45 hrs*
*A Bulgarian prisoner was brought in from 'D' Coy (centre) & reports received that number of enemy wounded were lying on MAMELON WORKS*

*02.53 hrs.*
*Heavy rifle fire was reported on PETIT COURONNE.*

*04.00 hrs*
*A Bulgarian prisoner was brought in. M.O. Captain BOWELL proceeded to JACKSON Ravine in front of MAMELON*

*04.05 hrs*
*One platoon South Lancs arrived from Bde Reserve & another platoon was also sent from Bde Reserve to Green Ravine.*

**04.45 hrs**
*2/Lt Austin reported that 11ᵗʰ Worcester's owing to very heavy losses had withdrawn to their original trench line and for that reason the right flank of HILL 380 was exposed.*

**05.00 hrs**
*Three Bulgarian prisoners were brought in.*

**05.30 hrs**
*'C' Coy (left) reported that enemy counter attack launched about 05.00 hrs and had been repulsed.*

**09.25 hrs**
*Another Bulgarian prisoner brought in. From this time forward with the exception of intermittent shelling of our trenches by the enemy no incident occurred worthy of record.*

**20.00 hrs**
*Red and green lights were sent up on PETIT COURONNE & at 20.40 hrs the centre Coy 'D' reported that the enemy were advancing to the attack. The barrage signal was accordingly sent up from Bn. H. Qrs and from the left Coy 'C', simultaneously with this a report was received that HILL 380 was being heavily shelled. Our barrage opened and at the same time that of the enemy was directed against out trench line. Two platoons under 2/Lt Fairer ('A' Coy) were ordered to reinforce the centre company.*

**21.00 hrs**
*Our barrage with that of the enemy died down & enemy counter-attack was easily driven off, only a few of their attacking party reaching our new wire. 'D' Coy (Centre) detailed a bombing party which was sent forward and succeeded in driving the enemy out of a ravine in front of JACKSON Ravine.*

## 21.35 hrs

*Lt Lloyd who was wounded reported at H. Qrs & brought information concerning the recent enemy counter-attack*

## 21.45 hrs

*Two platoons from Bde reserve were detailed in Reserve.*

## 23.35 hrs

*Searchlights were operating on HILL 380.*

The diary makes no mention of casualties but the attacks by the enemy continued throughout the following day. He died during the same action as Sidney Burgess.

**Henry is buried in Dorian Military Cemetery with 1,338 other servicemen.**

# JACK RUSHTON

**Jack Rushton** was born in Knutsford in 1897, one of nine children born to John (a basket and umbrella maker) and Elizabeth Rushton of 16, King Street, Knutsford. Jack worked as a grocers assistant.

He enlisted in the army in 1914, becoming Private no. 18621 of the 2$^{nd}$ Battalion of the Cheshire Regiment.

Jack arrived in France on the 6$^{th}$ March 1915.

**Brief history of the Battalion:**
The 2$^{nd}$ Battalion, Cheshire Regiment was a regular unit of the British Army and was in Jubbulpore, India when war broke out in August 1914. They returned to England, landing at Devonport on the 24$^{th}$ of December 1914. They joined 84$^{th}$ Brigade, 28$^{th}$ Division, at Winchester and proceeded to France, embarking at Southampton and landing at Le Havre on the 17$^{th}$ of January 1915. 28$^{th}$ Division concentrated in the area between Bailleul and Hazebrouck. They saw action in the Second Battle of Ypres, where casualties were high and The Battle of Loos.

*Thanks to the Wartime Memories Project.*

Jack was killed in action on the 8$^{th}$ May 1915 – just 59 days after arriving.

## On that fateful day:
The war diary states:


*'8.5.15*
*A heavy bombardment of the trench was commenced by the enemy about daybreak and was carried on incessantly until the line was broken by a fierce infantry attack made with overwhelming numbers. Asphyxiating gas was used freely by the enemy. The positions occupied by the Batt HQ and no. 1 £ 4 Coy were surrounded by the enemy and with very few exceptions all of the men were killed or taken prisoner.*
*Killed 17*
*Missing 182.'*
*After the attack by the enemy the firing line was reformed in what had hither to been the support trench about 500 yards to the rear of the original trench. The two officers and the remaining OR were put under the command of Lt. Col. Marsden of the 1ˢᵗ Welsh – that Batt being also in occupation of the new firing line.'*

This was the same fighting in which Joseph Booth was killed.

***Jack is remembered on the Menin Gate along with the names of 54,406 other servicemen.***

438

# FRED SAUNDERS

**Fred Saunders** was born in Mobberley in 1897, the son of Charles (a farmer) and Elisabeth of Moss Lane, Mobberley. At 14 he was employed as a cowman at Coppack House Farm, Mobberley.

He enlisted in the army and became Private no. 239127 of the Hereford Regiment but was attached to the 1ˢᵗ Battalion of the Kings (Shropshire Light Infantry).

**Brief history of the Battalion:**

1ˢᵗ Battalion, The King's Shropshire Light Infantry were based at Tipperary with 16ᵗʰ Brigade, 6ᵗʰ Division when war broke out in August 1914. They were mobilised and returned to England, where 6ᵗʰ Division concentrated near Cambridge for training. They proceeded to France on the 10ᵗʰ of September 1914, landing at St Nazaire. They marched to the Aisne to reinforce the hard-pressed BEF. They moved north to Flanders and were in action at Hooge in 1915. In 1916 they were again in action at Battle of Flers-Courcelette on The Somme, and again in The Battle of Morval and The Battle of Le Transloy, in 1917 they were in action at Hill 70 and Cambrai. In 1918 they saw action in the Battle of St Quentin, The Battles of the Lys, The Advance in Flanders, Battles of the Hindenburg Line and The Pursuit to the Selle.

*Thanks to the Wartime Memories Project.*

Fred was killed in action on the 22nd March 1918 whilst attached to the KSLI.

**On that fateful day:**
The war diary shows no entry for this date.

*Fred has no known grave and is remembered on the Arras Memorial along with the names of 34791 other servicemen.*

# ROBERT YARDLEY SIDEBOTTOM

**Robert Yardley Sidebottom** was born in Alderley Edge, Cheshire in 1882, one of three children born to Robert Yardley (a shipping merchant) and Sarah Sidebottom of Firwood, Leycester Road, Knutsford. Robert was a career soldier with the 1st Battalion of the Lancashire Fusiliers. He held the rank of Captain.

At the outbreak of war Robert was with the B.E.F. and went immediately to France.

**Brief history of the Battalion:**
In August 1914 the Regiment was in Dover and was part of 12th Brigade, 4th Division. On the 20 August 1914 they landed at Boulogne and fought with the British Expeditionary force. By 4 November 1915 moved with the Brigade to 36th (Ulster) Division.

Robert was killed in action on the 26th August 1914 – just 22 days after war was declared.

**On that fateful day:**

*'25th/26th.8.14*
*Marched via CAUDRAY-LIGNY to high ground by WAMBAIX STA. arrived there about 4 a.m. & proceeded to site and dig trenches. Heavy tools not available owing to heavy roads. Heavy shells and m.g. fire opened at 6 a.m. Bn. Held pn (position) until about 9 a.m. falling back to pn. above HAUCOURT. Brigade retired late in the afternoon to SELVIGNY thence to VENDHUILLE at night.*
*Casualties.'*

**The published account of the battalion during the war says:**
'The Germans were creeping around the flanks and a retirement was necessary. 'A' and 'D' Companies (the latter now being taken over by Captain R.Y. Sidebottom) withdrew to the cover of a hedge, suffering in doing so. Sidebottom gathered as many men as he could reach with his energetic voice but he fell with very many wounds. Privates Bannister and Hanson tried to remove his body but the enemy were too close, and the former was dangerously wounded.'

*Robert has no known grave and is remembered on the La Ferte-Sous-Jouarre Memorial, France along with the names of 3,739 other servicemen.*

---

***Author's note:***
*I am pleased to say the there is no 'Private Hanson' of the Lancashire Fusiliers listed amongst those killed during the Great War.*

---

# HERBERT SIMCOCK

**Herbert Simcock** was born in Mobberley in 1886, one of nine children born to Joseph (a carter) and Sarah Jane Simcock of Wood Lane, Mobberley. On the death of their father the family moved to Tollend Lane, Hale. Herbert was a grocery assistant.

He enlisted in the ¼th Battalion of the Cheshire Regiment, becoming Private no 4173 later re-numbered to 201530.

**Brief history of the Battalion:**

The 4th Battalion, Cheshire Regiment was a territorial unit of the British Army and was based in Birkenhead with Cheshire Brigade, Welsh Division when war broke out in August 1914. They were at once mobilised and moved to Shrewsbury and Church Stretton but by the end of August were at Northampton. In December 1914 they moved to Cambridge and by March 1915 were at Bedford preparing for service in India. On the 13th of May 1915 the Cheshire Brigade was renamed 159th Brigade, 53rd (Welsh) Division. On the 2nd of July orders arrived to re-equip for service in the Mediterranean and on the 14th they sailed from Devonport to Alexandria and made a landing at Suvla Bay Gallipoli on the 9th of August 1915. They were involved in operations in the Suvla Bay area suffering heavy losses. By the time they were evacuated to Mudros on the 11th of December the Division stood at just 162 officers and 2428 men (pprox.. 15%). From Mudros they went on to Alexandria and to Wardan, where the divisional artillery re-joined in February 1916. They were in action at The Battle of Romani in the Palestine campaign and in 1917 158th Brigade fought at The First Battle of Gaza and the whole Division were in action during The Second Battle of Gaza, The Third Battle of Gaza when they were involved in capture of Beersheba, Tell Khuweilfe, and The Capture of Jerusalem. In December they were in action in The Defence of Jerusalem. In March 1918 they fought at The Battle of Tell'Asur. On the 31st of May 1918 the 4th Cheshires left the Division and sailed for France, joining 102nd Brigade, 34th Division on the 1st of July. They returned to action, at The Battles of the Soissonnais, the Ourcq and the capture of Baigneux Ridge. They took part in the Final Advance in Flanders.

*Thanks to the Wartime Memories Project.*

Herbert died of wounds on the 26th July 1918 and as his service record no longer exists I am unable to discover where and when he received those wounds.

*Herbert is buried in St. Sever Cemetery Extension, Rouen, France along with 8,348 other servicemen. His grave is Q. II. L. 19.*

# HEINRICH HELMUTH SIMON

**Heinrich Helmuth Simon** lived with his wife Edith May Simon at 'Sharston House', Grove Park, Knutsford.

He joined the army, becoming a Major in 'C' Company of 210 Brigade of the Royal Field Artillery.

**Brief history of the Brigade:**
CCX Brigade, Royal Field Artillery served as Divisional Artillery with 42nd (East Lancashire) Division. The East Lancashire Division was a formation of the Territorial Force, when war broke out in August 1914 all units were mobilised at once for war service. They were the first Territorial Division to move overseas, embarking for Egypt on the 9th of September 1914 to defend the Suez Canal from the Turkish forces in Palestine. They were in action in the Turkish attack on the Suez Canal on the 3rd of February 1915. In the first week of May the division embarked from Alexandria, landing at Cape Helles, Gallipoli, where they saw action in the attempts to capture the heights of Krithia and the Battle of Krithia Vineyard which was a diversionary attack for the British Landing at Suvla Bay. The much depleted division were evacuated from Gallipoli in the first week of January 1916, returning to Alexandria via Mudros. They returned to duty on the Suez Canal and were in action in the Battle of Romani in August. In early 1917 they were ordered to the Western Front, departing from Alexandria in February. They went into the front line at Ephey, moved to Havrincourt then were withdrawn to Albert for rest and training during July and August. In September they moved north to Flanders and were in action during the Third Battle of Ypres at Iberian, Borry Farm, Beck House Farm and Sans Souci. At the end of the month they moved to the coast at Nieuport until November when they moved to La Bassee Canal at Givenchy. In 1918 they saw action during The Battle of Bapaume, The First Battle of Arras, The Battle of the Ancre, The Battle of Albert, The Second Battle of Bapaume, The Battle of the Canal du Nord, The pursuit to the Selle and The Battle of the Selle.

*Thanks to the Wartime Memories Project.*

Heinrich (Harry) died of wounds on the 8th September 1917.

445

*Harry is buried in Lijssenthoek Military Cemetery along with 9,877 other servicemen. His grave is XVIII. H. 18.*

*Note:*
*He left over £88,000 pounds in his will.*

# JOHN CHARLES SIMPSON

**John Charles Simpson** was born in High Legh, Cheshire in 1891, one of ten children born to John (a woodman) and Isabella Simpson of Ditchfield Lane, High Legh. On leaving school John became a gardener.

On marrying Jesse he moved to Woodside Cottage, Higher lane Lymm, Cheshire,

He enlisted in the army, becoming Private 235093 of the Royal Army Service Corp before transferring to the Royal Warwickshire Regiment as Private no. 48330.

**Brief history of the Battalion:**

15th (2nd Birmingham Pals) Battalion, The Royal Warwickshire Regiment was raised in Birmingham in September 1914 by the Lord Mayor and a local committee. After training they joined 95th Brigade, 32nd Division on the 26 June 1915. They proceeded to France, landing at Boulogne on the 21st of November 1915. On the 28 December 1915 they transferred to 14th Brigade, 5th Division, one of many units were exchanged to stiffen the inexperienced 32nd Division with regular army troops. On the 14th of January 1916 they transferred to 13th Brigade still with 5th Division In March 1916 5th Division took over a section of front line between St Laurent Blangy and the southern edge of Vimy Ridge, near Arras. They moved south in July to reinforce The Somme and were in action at, High Wood, The Battle of Guillemont, The Battle of Flers-Courcelette, The Battle of Morval and The Battle of Le Transloy. In October they moved to Festubert and remained there until March 1917 when they moved in preparation for the Battles of Arras. On 7 September 1917 the 5th Division moved out of the line for a period of rest before, being sent to Flanders where they were in action during the Third Battle of Ypres. 5th Division was sent to Italy and took up positions in the line along the River Piave in late January 1918. They were recalled to France to assist with the German Advance in late March 1918 and were in action during the Battles of the Lys. On the 14th of August 1918 the 5th Division was withdrawn for two weeks rest. They then moved to The Somme where they were more or less in continuous action over the old battlegrounds until October.

*Thanks to the Wartime Memories Project.*

John was killed in action on the 27th September 1918.

## On that fateful day:
The war diary states:

### 27.9.18 FRONT LINE
*13th Inf. Brigade will take and capture RED OBJECTIVE. Battalion HQ at DEAD MAN'S CORNER.*

*The attack is carried out on a three-Coy front with 'B' Coy on the right, 'A' Coy in the centre and 'C' Coy on the left with 'D' Coy in reserve.*

### 5.20am
*Zero Hour*

*15th R.War R attack at Zero plus 152. Battalion attack and gain objective but is obliged to retire.*

*Casualties:*

*OFFICERS Killed 3 (inc. M.O.) wounded 5 – 1 wounded since died.*

*OTHER RANKS Killed 36 wounded 90 Missing 29 – 2 wounded at duty.*

**John is remembered on the Vis-En-Artois Memorial along with the names of 9,847 other servicemen.**

# DUNCAN SINCLAIR

**Duncan Sinclair** resided with his mother Mrs. E. A. Sinclair at 22, Bexton Road, Knutsford.

Duncan joined the army on the 17th January 1918, becoming Private no. 45527 in the South Lancashire Regiment.

He was discharged as being unfit for war duties on the 24th February 1919. His records no longer exist so we don't know the reason for the discharge.

He died on the 20th May 1920.

*Duncan is buried in Knutsford cemetery,*

# JAMES SKELHORN

**James Skelhorn** was born in Knutsford. On marrying Annie they set up home at 10, Osborne Road Altrincham, Cheshire
He joined the 5th Battalion of the South Wales Borderers in Brecon and became Private no. 29365.

**Brief history of the Battalion:**
5th (Service) Battalion, The South Wales Borderers was raised at Brecon in September 1914 as part of Kitchener's Second New Army and joined 58th Brigade, 19th (Western) Division. They trained at Park House Camp, Tidworth and spent the winter in billets in Basingstoke. On the 10th of January 1915 they converted to be a Pioneer Battalion and moved to billets in Burnham. In March 1915 the moved to Bulford and then in April to Perham Down for final training. They proceeded to France, landing at Le Havre on the 16th of July 1915. 19th (Western) Division concentrated near St Omer and their first action was at Pietre, in a diversionary action supporting the Battle of Loos. In 1916 They were in action during the Battle of the Somme, capturing La Boisselle and being involved in The attacks on High Wood, The Battles of Pozieres Ridge, the Ancre Heights and the Ancre. In 1917 they were in action in The Battle of Messines and the Third Battles of Ypres.

*Thanks to the Wartime Memories Project.*

James was killed in action on the 22nd November 1917.

**On that fateful day:**
The war diary states they had been working under Royal Engineer's instruction for a couple of days:

*22.11.17*
*A Company ROAD IV 5 breaks repaired. ROAD V 3 large shell holes filled in, drainage continued. ROAD VI shell holes repaired, drainage continued. B Company ROAD 0 maintained and drained, 20 GS Wagons metal laid, Road I maintained. Road III drained and metaled, 16 yards corduroy laid, 60 yards track bed levelled. C Company No 1 CAMP MILKYWAY 18 yards roofed. 16 yards covered with tarred felt, 10 lorries unloaded 20 yards of track duckboarded. No 2 CAMP 19 yards roofed, 15 lorries unloaded, 15 yards roof covered, 5 yards duckboarded. D Company DETTINGHEM, POMPEII and RUTLAND CAMPS laying floor for stables.*

The diary makes no mention of any casualties.

*James is remembered on the Thiepval Memorial along with the names of 72,203 other servicemen.*

# FRED &
# GEORGE WILLIAM SLADE
## *(Brothers)*

The brothers **Fred and George William Slade** were born in Knutsford in 1894 and 1885 respectively. They were children of William (an accountant) and Emma who moved to 'Heotsfield', Langley Road, Wealdstone. They were both employed as clerks.

They both enlisted in the 9th City of London Regiment (Queen Victoria Rifles) as Private 5872 and Private no. 5808.

### Brief history of the Battalion:

9th Battalion, The Royal Fusiliers (City of London Regiment) was raised at Hounslow on 21 August 1914 as part of Kitchener's First New Army and joined 36th Brigade, 12th (Eastern) Division. 36th Brigade underwent training at Colchester then final training was undertaken near Aldershot from the 20th of February 1915, with the cavalry, motor machine gun battery, sanitary and veterinary sections joining. The Division proceeded to France between the 29th of May and 1st of June 1915 landing at Boulogne, they concentrated near St Omer and by 6th of June were in the Meteren-Steenwerck area with Divisional HQ being established at Nieppe. They underwent instruction from the more experienced 49th (South Midland) Division and took over a section of the front line at Ploegsteert Wood on the 23rd of June 1915. They were in action in The Battle of Loos from the 30th of September.

Both brothers were killed in action on the 9th September 1915.

**On that fateful day:**
The war diary makes no mention of any casualties for this date – it states:

*9.9.15*
*Working parties of 4 officers and 454 men supplied to R.E. for trench work.*

***Fred is buried in Serre Road Cemetery No. 2 along with 2183 other servicemen. His grave is XV. E. 12.***

# EDWARD PEARCE SMITH

**Edward Pearce Smith** was born in Portland, Dorset in 1869. He moved his wife and five children from Dorset to no. 3, Stanley Road Knutsford. He was a warder.

Despite his age (45 years), he enlisted in the 13th Battalion of the King's (Liverpool Regiment), becoming Private no. 19503. He arrived in France on the 26th September 1915.

**Brief history of the Battalion:**
13th (Service) Battalion, The King's Regiment (Liverpool) was raised at Seaforth in September 1914, part of Kitchener's Third New Army, which assembled in the area around Salisbury. The 13th Kings Liverpool were initially attached as Army Troops to 25th Division. In February 1915 they transferred to 76th Brigade in same Division. They proceeded to France on the 27th of September 1915, landing at Le Havre and concentrating in the area of Nieppe. On the 15th of October 1915 the Battalion transferred with 76th Brigade to 3rd Division then on the 23rd the Battalion transferred to 8th Brigade, still in 3rd Division. On the 4th of April 1916 they transferred to 9th Brigade, 3rd Division. In 1916 they took part in The Actions of the

Bluff and St Eloi Craters then moved to The Somme for The Battle of Albert, The Battle of Bazentin helping to capture Longueval, The Battle of Delville Wood and The Battle of the Ancre.

*Thanks to the Wartime Memories Project.*

Edward was killed in action on the 14th July 1916.

**On that fateful day:**
The written record of Regiment describes and action then went on for several days – see The History of The Kings Regiment (Liverpool) Vol. 2 by Everard Wyrall Pages 280-282 and makes reference to 'a very successful action in capturing Bazentin-le-Grand'.

**The war diary merely states:**

*13.7.16 10.p.m.*
*Left the trenches to take part in the attack on German front line & BAZENTIN-LE-GRAND; attacked at 3.30 a.m. and took the German trench and BAZENTIN-LE-GRAND.*

*14.7.16*
*In captured trench.*
*It makes no mention of any casualties but in the history is says:*

*Casualties*
*Officers 8 killed,*
*9 wounded,*
*1 missing.*
*O.R. 117 killed,*
*243 wounded.*

**Edward is remembered on the Thiepval Memorial along with the names of 72,208 other servicemen who have no known graves.**

# GEORGE ARTHUR SMITH

**George Arthur Smith** was born in Knutsford. He married A.M. Smith and lived in Halifax.

He enlisted in the Scots Rifles before transferring into the 11<sup>th</sup> Battalion of the Manchester Regiment as Private no. 48592, rising to the rank of Acting Sergeant.

**Brief history of the Battalion:**

The Battalion was formed at Chester on 17 September 1914 as part of K3 and came under orders of 75<sup>th</sup> Brigade, 25<sup>th</sup> Division. They moved to Codford St Mary and by November 1914 were in billets in Bournemouth. They then moved to Aldershot in May 1915. On the 26 September 1915 they landed in France.

*Thanks to The Long, Long Trail.*

George was killed in action on the 25<sup>th</sup> April 1917.

**On that fateful day:**

The war diary states:

*'SUNKEN ROAD – MORCHIES-BEAUMETZ*
*25.4.17*

456

*Throughout the day there was intermittent shelling. This continued for several days. When the weather permitted aircraft of both sides were very active.'*

There was no report of casualties.

*George is buried in Duisans British Cemetery along with 3293 other servicemen. His grave is III. H. 22.*

# JOHN HUBERT SOUTHERN

**John Hubert Southern** was born in High Legh, Cheshire in 1897, one of seven children born to William (a woodsman) and Harriet Southern of West Hall Lodge, High Legh. He was a well-built lad, standing nearly 6'. On leaving school he became a chauffeur.

Luckily, his service records still exist so we know that at the outbreak of war he enlisted in the army, becoming Private no. 33126 in the Cheshire Regiment. He embarked for France on the 30th June 1916 but on arrival he was transferred to the 17th Battalion of the Manchester Regiment. The notation on his file relates to Rule A.C.I. 1499 – which are the strict procedures governing the transfer and numbering of soldiers arriving in France.

**Brief history of the Battalion:**
The 17th (2nd City) Battalion, Manchester Regiment was raised in Manchester on the 28th of August 1914 by the Lord Mayor and City. Initially they trained at Heaton Park but moved in April 1915 to Belton Park, where they joined 90th Brigade, 30th Division. They went to Larkhill in September 1915 for final training and proceeded to France on the 6th of November 1915, concentrating near Amiens. In 1916 they were in action during the Battle of the Somme, in which the Division captured Montauban. In 1917 they took part in the pursuit of the German retreat to the Hindenburg Line, the Arras Offensive and The Battle of Pilkem Ridge.

*Thanks to the Wartime Memories Project.*

John was slightly wounded in action on the 20th October 1916 but we don't know how, but we know it was somewhere near Flers, France.

On the 18th July 1917 he was promoted to Lance-Corporal (unpaid). John was killed in action on the 31st July 1917.

**On that fateful day:**
The war diary states:

*'3.50 am – went into action in front of Ypres – 547 OR in the attack. 17th passed through the 16th and consolidated just short of the*

*second objective owing to very heavy machine-gun fire which held up the attack.*
*OR Killed, 34 missing, and 112 wounded.'*

*John has no known grave so is remembered at the Menin Gate Memorial, Ypres, along with the names of 54,406 other servicemen who likewise have no know grave.*

*Note:*
*Three lads with the surname 'Southern' were killed on that day.*

# JAMES SPILSBURY

**James Spilsbury** was born in Knutsford in 1892, one of nine children born to Henry (a general labourer) and Sarah Ann Spilsbury of Half

Way House, Knutsford Road, Mobberley. James took up the trade of Chauffeur.

He enlisted in the 10th Battalion of the Cheshire Regiment as Private no. 35282.

**Brief history of the Battalion:**

The 10th (Service) Battalion, Cheshire Regiment was raised in Chester on the 10th of September 1914 as part of Kitchener's Third New Army and joined 75th Brigade, 25th Division. They trained at Codford St Mary and spent the winter in billets in Bournemouth. They moved to Aldershot for final training in May 1915 and proceeded to France on the 26th of September, the division concentrating in the area of Nieppe. On the 26th of October they transferred to 7th Brigade still with 25th Division. Their first action was in defence of the German attack on Vimy Ridge in May 1916. They then moved to The Somme and joined the Battle just after the main attack, with 75th Brigade making a costly attack near Thiepval on the 3rd of July. The Division was in action at The Battle of Bazentin, The Battle of Pozieres and The Battle of the Ancre Heights. In 1917 they were in action at The Battle of Messines attacking between the Wulverghem-Messines and Wulverghem-Wytschaete roads. In the Third battle of Ypres were in action during The Battle of Pilkem.

*Thanks to the Wartime Memories Project.*

James was killed in action on the 17th February 1917.

**On that fateful day:**
The war diary states:

*17.2.17 MEANEE DAY*
*1 officer and 65 other ranks successfully raided an enemy trench N of FACTORY FARM inflicting heavy casualties – many dugouts*

*were bombed with bomb dumps and trench material destroyed. 10 prisoners were taken – 8 of who were caught in their own machine gun fire and killed in no man's land.*
*OR 28 killed, 62 wounded, 27 missing.*

*James has no known grave and is remembered on the Ploegstreert Memorial, along with the names of 11,386 other servicemen.*

# WILLIAM STREET

**William Street** was born in 1889 to John (a hotel keeper) and Agnes Street of the Mainwaring Arms, Over Peover.

William joined the army, enlisting at Middlewich in the 13th Battalion of the Manchester Regiment as Private no. 5048.

## Brief history of the Battalion:

The 13th (Service) Battalion, Manchester was raised at Ashton-under-Lyne in September 1914 as part of Kitchener's Third New Army, and joined 25th Division as army troops. They moved to Seaford and in October transferred to 66th Brigade, 22nd Division. In November they moved to billets in Eastbourne for the winter, returning to Seaford in March 1915. In May they moved to Aldershot for final training. They proceeded to France in early September, the division concentrating near Flesselles. In October they moved to Marseilles by train and embarked for Salonika on the 27th. 67th Brigade, 9th Borders, 68th Field Ambulance and the Advanced Divisional HQ saw their first action in the second week of December in the Retreat from Serbia. In 1916 the division fought in the Battle of Horseshoe Hill and Battle of Machukovo. In 1917 they were in action during the Battles of Doiran.

*Thanks to the Wartime Memories Project.*

William was killed in action on the 25th April 1917.

## On that fateful day:

### *DORIAN/PIP RIDGE/PETIT COURONNE*

*Pip Ridge attack fell to the 22Div. 8th KSLI and 13th Manchesters. Attack was launched 8.45 am.*

*When the men reached the enemy's wire they met rifle fire all along the line but it did little damage and some advantage was gained.*

*'D' Coy on right met with a party of Bulgars behind a large rock (1 captured- rest escaped)*

*'A' Coy captured and occupied sangers on the KRASTIALI-DONDZELI track and found little opposition. 'B' Coy rushed the objective and found little opposition except 1 prisoner in a dugout.*

*'D' Coy entered and occupied JACKSON'S RAVINE – no opposition.*

*Hostile shelling continued throughout the night.*
*Casualties OR 35 killed, 2 missing, 225 wounded.*

*William is buried in Karasouli Military Cemetery, Greece along with 1,421 other servicemen.*

# ALBERT SUMNER

**Albert Sumner** was born in Knutsford in 1886. He was one of eight children born to Fanny Sumner who by 1911 was a widow living at 6, Garden Road, Knutsford. Albert was a shoemaker.

On marrying Annie he moved to Ollerton, Cheshire. He enlisted in the army in 1915 and was place in the Army Service Corp as a saddler but was discharged after a short while as not becoming an efficient soldier.

Albert enlisted again, this time in the Manchester Regiment, becoming Private no. 38117 but later transferred to the 6th Battalion of the Queens (Royal West Surrey Regiment) as Private no. G/69561.

**Brief history of the Battalion:**

6th Battalion, The Queen's Royal Regiment (West Surrey) was raised at Guildford in August 1914 as part of Kitchener's First New Army and joined 37th Brigade, 12th (Eastern) Division. They trained at Purfleet with final training being undertaken near Aldershot from the 20th of February 1915, with the cavalry, motor machine gun battery, sanitary and veterinary sections joining the Division. They proceeded to France between the 29th of May and 1st of June 1915 landing at Boulogne, they concentrated near St Omer and by 6th of June were in the Meteren-Steenwerck area with Divisional HQ being established at Nieppe. They underwent instruction from the more experienced 48th (South Midland) Division and took over a section of the front line at Ploegsteert Wood on the 23rd of June 1915. They were in action in The Battle of Loos from the 30th of September, taking over the sector from Gun Trench to Hulluch Quarries consolidating the position, under heavy artillery fire. On the 8th they repelled a heavy German infantry attack and on the 13th took part in the Action of the Hohenzollern Redoubt, capturing Gun Trench and the south western face of the Hulluch Quarries. During this period at Loos, 117 officers and 3237 men of the Division were killed or wounded. By the 21st they moved to Fouquieres-les-Bethune for a short rest then returned to the front line at the Hohenzollern Redoubt until the 15th of November, when they went into reserve at Lillers. On the 9th of December, 9th Royal Fusiliers assisted in a round-up of spies and other suspicious characters in the streets of Bethune. On the 10th the Division took over the front line north of La Bassee canal at Givenchy. On the 19ᵗʰ of January they began a period of training in Open Warfare at Busnes, then moved back into the front line at Loos on the 12ᵗʰ of February 1916. In June they moved to Flesselles and carried out a training exercise. They moved to Baizieux on the 30ᵗʰ June and went into the reserve at Hencourt and Millencourt by mid-morning on the 1ˢᵗ of July. They relieved the 8ᵗʰ Division at Ovillers-la-Boisselle that night and attacked at 3.15 the following morning with mixed success. On the 7ᵗʰ they attacked again and despite suffering heavy casualties in the area of Mash Valley, they succeeded in capturing and holding the first and second lines close to Ovillers. They were withdrawn to Contay on the 9ᵗʰ July. They were in action in The Battle of Pozieres on the 3ʳᵈ of August with a successful attack capturing 4ᵗʰ Avenue Trench and were engaged in heavy fighting until they were withdrawn on the 9ᵗʰ. They moved north and in 1917 were in action at Arras in The First Battle of the Scarpe, The Battle of Arleux and The Third Battle of the Scarpe. They remained in the Arras sector until the 30ᵗʰ of October when they moved to Hesdin for the Cambrai offensive in which the Division suffered heavy losses. In March 1918 they moved by motor lorry from Busnes to Albert and were in action in The Battle of Bapaume and spent the spring engaged in heavy fighting a the enemy advanced across the old Somme battlefields. On the 1ˢᵗ of July 1918, they attacked Bouzincourt. But were repelled by the enemy. They were relieved on the 10ᵗʰ and moved to the area south of Amiens. They were in action in The Battle of Amiens and were engaged in heavy fighting from the 22ⁿᵈ pushing the enemy back and capturing Meaulte, Mametz, Carnoy, Hardecourt and Faviere Wood within a week. In September they were in action in a successful attack on Nurlu and pursued the enemy back to Sorel Wood. They were in action during The battles of the Hindenburg Line, including The Battle of Epehy and The Battle of the St Quentin canal. In October they fought in The Final Advance in Artois reaching the Scheldt Canal by the 27ᵗʰ. They were withdrawn for rest on the 30ᵗʰ and after the Armistice moved to the area east of Douai and were engaged in battlefield salvage and sports until demobilisation began.

*Thanks to the Wartime Memories Project.*

Albert was killed in action on the 27th August 1918.

**On that fateful day:**
The war diary states:

***27.8.18 In the line near MEAULTE***
*The Bde moved up and advanced through the 36th Biigade at 4.55am. The Bn was in Brigade support but eventually held the front line in conjunction with the 6th West Kents.*
*Casualties OR 2 killed* (including Albert) *14 wounded.*

***Albert is buried in Danzig Alley British Cemetery, Mametz along with 2,053 other servicemen, His grave is IX. W. 3.***

# ALFRED TAYLOR

**Alfred Taylor** was born in Knutsford in 1892, one of four children born to Alfred (a stoker at the gas works) and Elisabeth M. Taylor of 10, Stanley Road, Knutsford.

He initially joined the Middlesex Regiment but was soon transferred into the Lancashire Fusiliers.

Following his death his sister Ada wrote to her friend stating that he had only been at the front for ten weeks, when he received a wound from which he never recovered 'despite everything being done to relieve his suffering'.

# HENRY TAYLOR

**Henry Taylor** was born in Knutsford to John and Ellen Taylor, who moved to Rush Green, Lymm, Cheshire.

He enlisted in the 10th Battalion of the Cheshire Regiment, becoming private no. 24744.

**Brief history of the Battalion:**

The 10th (Service) Battalion, Cheshire Regiment was raised in Chester on the 10th of September 1914 as part of Kitchener's Third New Army and joined 75th Brigade, 25th Division. They trained at Codford St Mary and spent the winter in billets in Bournemouth. They moved to Aldershot for final training in May 1915 and proceeded to France on the 26th of September, the division concentrating in the area of Nieppe. On the 26th of October they transferred to 7th Brigade still with 25th Division. Their first action was in defence of the German attack on Vimy Ridge in May 1916.

*Thanks to the Wartime Memories Project.*

Henry was killed in action on the 21st May 1916.

**On that fateful day:**

The war diary states:

*'21.5.16*

*The CT suffered and some damage caused by shell fire and minenwerfer. At 3.45 an intense bombardment by all CT and supports. The fire was particularly heavy to the left of our sector. The bombardment continued with unabated violence for 4 hours and at the end of that time most of our trenches had been levelled and a very large proportion of our men had been killed or wounded.*

*At 7.45 the enemy attacked and took our outpost with little resistance as there was nobody left to oppose them.*

*A counter attack was delivered at 2am which was successful in retaking the line.*

*33 OK killed.'*

This is the same action in which John Eyres was killed.

*Henry is buried in Ecoivres Military cemetery, along with 1500 other servicemen. His grave is I. O. 3.*

# THOMAS TAYLOR

**Thomas Taylor** was born in High Legh. He married Alexandrina and together they lived at 53, Longfield Road, Harrowgate, Darlington.

He enlisted in the 21$^{st}$ Battalion of the King's Royal Rifles, becoming Riflemen no.12556.

**Brief history of the Battalion:**
21st (Yeoman Rifles) Battalion, The King's Royal Rifle Corps was raised in September 1915 from volunteers from the farming communities of Yorkshire, Durham and Northumberland by the Northern Command. They trained at Duncombe Park, Helmsley, moving to Aldershot to join 124th Brigade, 41st Division for final training. They proceeded to France in the first week of May 1916, the division concentrating between Hazebrouck and Bailleul. In 1916 they were in action at The Battle of Flers-Courcelette and The Battle of the Transloy Ridges on the Somme.

*Thanks to the Wartime Memories Project.*

Thomas was killed in action on the 17th September 1916.

**On that fateful day:**
The war diary states:

*'16th/17th.9.16 DELVILLE WOOD*
*The Battn paraded at 11.00 at the QUARRY DUMP to move to the SWITCH TRENCH where they remained about an hour. Then they received orders to move to FLARE ALLEY and remained in support until the following evening, when they were relieved and returned to POMIERES.'*

***Thomas is remembered on the Thiepval Memorial, along with the names of 72,208 other servicemen.***

# WILFRED TAYLOR

**Wilfred Taylor** was born in Padgate, Warrington in 1898, the son of James (a farm labourer) and Mary Emily Taylor of Free Green Cottage, Higher Peover, Cheshire.

On enlisting in the army Wilfred became Guardsman no. 26832 of no. 2 Company of the 3rd Battalion of the Grenadier Guards.

**Brief history of the Battalion:**

The 3rd Battalion of the Grenadier Guards was formed in August 1914 and was stationed at in Wellington Barracks, London District. They then moved overseas 27 July 1915, landing at Le Havre. On the 19 August 1915 they came under command of 2nd Guards Brigade, Guards Division.

Wilfred died of wounds on the 8th September 1917. I have been unable to discover where and when he sustained those wounds.

***Wilfred is buried in Dozinghem Military Cemetery along with 3240 other servicemen. His grave is VI. A. 8.***

# SIDNEY THOMAS

**Sidney Thomas** was born in 1892, the son of Lydia Thomas of 34, Mobberley Road, Knutsford. On leaving school he became a thatcher.

He was a regular soldier, enlisting in the 5th Battalion of the Cheshire Yeomanry in 1908 as Private no. 819.

He enlisted in the Army in 1914, becoming Private no. 1771 of the 1/5th Battalion of the Cheshire Regiment.

**Brief history of the Battalion:**
The 1/5th (Earl of Chester's) Battalion, Cheshire Regiment was a Territorial unit based in in Chester with Cheshire Brigade, Welsh Division, when war was declared in August 1914. They were immediately mobilised and moved to Shrewsbury and Church Stretton, by the end of August they moved to Northampton and then in December to Cambridge for final preparations. They proceeded to France on the 15th of February 1915, landing at at Le Havre to join 14th Brigade, 5th Division. They were in action in The Battle of Mons and the subsequent retreat, The Battle of Le Cateau, The Battle of the Marne, The Battle of the Aisne, The Battles of La Bassee and Messines and The First Battle of Ypres. In 1915 they were in action at The Second Battle of Ypres and the Capture of Hill 60.

Sidney died of wounds on the 29th April 1915.

**On that fateful day:**
I have been unable to discover where and when he received his wounds.

*Sidney is buried in Spoilbank Cemetery, Belgium along with 520 other servicemen. His grave is I. F. 7.*

*Note:*
*His Medals Were Never Collected.*

# GEORGE THORNBER

**George Thornber** was born in Denton, Lancashire. A native of Cross Town, Knutsford. He lived with his mother and step-father James (a general labourer). His mother was Ellen Smith later moved to 3, Trinity Terrace, Roft Road, Oswestry.

He enlisted in the 1/5th Battalion of the Cheshire Regiment, becoming Private no. 803.

He arrived in France on the 15th February 1915.


**Brief history of the Battalion:**

The 1/5th (Earl of Chester's) Battalion, Cheshire Regiment was a Territorial unit based in in Chester with Cheshire Brigade, Welsh Division, when war was declared in August 1914. They were immediately mobilised and moved to Shrewsbury and Church Stretton, by the end of August they moved to Northampton and then in December to Cambridge for final preparations. They proceeded to France on the 15th of February 1915, landing at at Le Havre to join 14th Brigade, 5th Division. They were in action in The Battle of Mons and the subsequent retreat, The Battle of Le Cateau, The Battle of the Marne, The Battle of the Aisne, The Battles of La Bassee and Messines and The First Battle of Ypres. In 1915 they were in action at The Second Battle of Ypres and the Capture of Hill 60. In autumn 1915, many units were exchanged with units from the newly arrived volunteer 32nd Division, to stiffen the inexperienced Division with regular army troops.

*Thanks to the Wartime Memories Project.*

George was killed in action on the 18ᵗʰ October 1915.

**On that fateful day:**
There is no entry in the war diary for this date.

*George is buried in Suzanne Communal Cemetery extension, Somme, along with 387 other servicemen. His grave is C. 1.*

# GEORGE TICKLE

**George Tickle** was born in Lower Peover, Cheshire in 1899, one of thirteen children born to Henry (a farm labourer) and Mary Tickle of Fox Covert, Lower Peover.

He joined the 18th Battalion of the Welsh Regiment as Private no. 61275.

**Brief history of the Battalion:**
18th (2nd Glamorgan Battalion, The Welsh Regiment was raised at Cardiff in January 1915 as a Bantam Battalion. They moved to Porthcawl and joined 43rd Division. In July they moved to Prees Heath, transferring to 119th Brigade, 40th Division. They moved to Aldershot in September. The Division proceeded to France in the first week of June 1916 and concentrated near Lillers. They went into the front line near Loos and were later in action in The Battle of the Ancre on the Somme. In 1917 they saw action during The German retreat to the Hindenburg Line, The capture of Fifteen Ravine, Villers Plouich, Beaucamp and La Vacquerie and The Cambrai Operations, including the capture of Bourlon Wood in November. In 1918 they fought in The Battle of St Quentin and The Battle of Bapaume on the Somme then the Battle of Estaires and The Battle of Hazebrouck in Flanders, suffering heavy losses.

George was killed in action on the 13th April 1918.

**On that fateful day:**
The war diary states:

*9th – 13th April 1918*
*At 4.20am the enemy barraged our front line and attacked in force. Battalion fought in rear-guard action until the 13th*
*During the early morning considerable shelling took place. A Division of the ANZAC Corp having taken up a position in front of us (4th Australian Division) during the night, instructions were received to withdraw the troops to PRADELLES and this was completed by 2.30pm. The combined troops of the Brigade then marched to LE BRIGARDE – had a meal and marched to STAPLE and lay there the night.*

The diary makes no mention of any casualties for the day.

*George has no known grave and is remembered on the Ploegstreet memorial along with the names of 11,386 other servicemen.*

# FRED TIMMIS

**Fred Timmis** was born in Leigh, Lancashire but came to live in Knutsford, where he enlisted.

He became Private no. 27653 of the 10th Battalion, Cheshire Regiment.

**Brief history of the Battalion:**

The 10th (Service) Battalion, Cheshire Regiment was raised in Chester on the 10th of September 1914 as part of Kitchener's Third New Army and joined 75th Brigade, 25th Division. They trained at Codford St Mary and spent the winter in billets in Bournemouth. They moved to Aldershot for final training in May 1915 and proceeded to France on the 26th of September, the division concentrating in the area of Nieppe. On the 26th of October they transferred to 7th Brigade still with 25th Division. Their first action was in defence of the German attack on Vimy Ridge in May 1916. They then moved to The Somme and joined the Battle just after the main attack, with 75th Brigade making a costly attack near Thiepval on the 3rd of July. The Division was in action at The Battle of Bazentin, The Battle of Pozieres and The Battle of the Ancre Heights. In 1917 they were in action at The Battle of Messines attacking between the Wulverghem-Messines and Wulverghem-Wytschaete roads. In the Third battle of Ypres were in action during The Battle of Pilkem. In 1918 they were in action on The Somme, in the Battles of the Lys suffering heavy lossed. On the 21st of June 1918 the battalion was reduced to cadre strength with many troops transferring to the 9th Cheshires.

*Thanks to the Wartime Memories Project.*

Fred was killed in action on the 17th April 1918.

**On that fateful day:**
The war diary states:

*'17.4.18 Support Line – WOLFACE*
*During the day the position was heavily shelled by guns of all calibre and with heavy bombardment with gas shells'*

*Fred is remembered on the Tyne Cot Memorial, Belgium along with the names of 34,952 other servicemen who have no known graves.*

# WILLIAM RUSSELL TONGE

**William Russell Tonge** was the son of Henry Dacre (a merchant) and Alma Tonge. He later resided at Alwarden Hill Knutsford.

He enlisted as a 2/Lieutenant in the 17th Battalion of the Manchester Regiment.

**Brief history of the Battalion:**

The 17th (2nd City) Battalion, Manchester Regiment was raised in Manchester on the 28th of August 1914 by the Lord Mayor and City. Initially they trained at Heaton Park but moved in April 1915 to

Belton Park, where they joined 90th Brigade, 30th Division. They to Larkhill in September 1915 for final training and proceeded to France on the 6th of November 1915. Concentrating near Amiens. In 1916 they were in action during the Battle of the Somme, in which the Division captured Montauban.

*Thanks to the Wartime Memories Project.*

William was killed in action on the 13th January 1916.

**On that fateful day:**
The war diary states:

*'SUZANNE*
*2/Lieut Tonge was killed in the trenches – being picked off by a sniper in a little used part of the fire trench of the right section. The mud was so bad that it was impossible to move him and he was buried in the trench'.*

**William is remembered on the Thiepval Memorial along with the names of 72,208 other servicemen who have no known graves.**

# FRANCIS ALLABY TUNSTALL
## *(Brother of Henry)*

**Francis Allaby Tunstall** was born in 1882 in High Legh, the son of Henry (a postmaster) and Mary Tunstall of The Post Office, High Legh. Francis emigrated to Canada.

On the outbreak of was he enlisted in the 27th Battalion of the Canadian Infantry and became Private no. 875341.

**Brief history of the Battalion:**
Please see Appendix Seven.

Francis was killed in action on the 3rd May 1917.

**On that fateful day:**
The war diary states:

*Trenches.*
*Battalion ready for assault. Zero hour now 3.45 am. 1st Canadian Batt. On right took FRESNOY – joining with this Batt at XXXX. 31st Canadian Batt on left was held up by wire and enemy fire. During the night they dug connecting trench with us at XXXX. Batt was hampered by darkness and wire. With heavy casualties the objectives were reached and consolidated to left by bombing parties. Casualties – Killed OFF 3 OR 34, Died of wounds OFF 2 OR 6, Wounded OFF7 OR 179, Missing OR 30.*

We can only assume that Francis was one of the 'missing OR' for he has no known grave.

*Francis is remembered on the Vimy Memorial along with the names of 11,169 others of his countrymen.*

# WILLIAM HENRY TUNSTALL
*(Brother of Francis)*

**William Henry Tunstall** was born in High Legh, Cheshire in 1880, the son of Henry (postmaster/farmer) and Mary Tunstall of High Legh. He became a solicitors clerk.

He enlisted in the 16th (City of Westminster) Battalion of the London Rifles as Private no. 7307 later re-numbered to 553666.

**Brief history of the Battalion:**

1/16th (County of London) Battalion (Queen's Westminster Rifles), The London Regiment were a territorial unit with Headquarters at 58 Buckingham Gate when war broke out in August 1914. They were part of the 4th London Brigade, 2nd London Division. They were mobilised and moved to the Hemel Hempstead area, being billeted in Leverstock Green in the late summer and early autumn of 1914, where they are commemorated with a stained glass window in the local church. They preceded to France on the 3rd of November 1914, landing at Le Havre to join 18th Brigade, 6th Division. On the 10th of February 1916 they transferred to the newly reformed 169th Brigade, 56th (London) Division which concentrated in the Hallencourt area. In 1916 they were in action on The Somme taking part in the diversionary attack at Gommecourt on the 1st of July. Also The Battle of Ginchy, The Battle of Flers-Courcelette, The Battle of Morval in which the Division captured Combles and The Battle of the Transloy Ridges. In 1917 they were in action during The German retreat to the Hindenburg Line and the Battles of Arras in April, then The Battle of Langemarck in August, then the Cambrai Operations in November.

*Thanks to the Wartime Memories Project.*

William died of wounds on the 8th April 1917. I have been unable to discover where and when he received his wounds.

*William is buried in Warlincourt Halte British Cemetery, Saulty, France along with 1,297 other servicemen. His grave is VI. J. 5.*

# JOHN VENABLES

**John Venables** was born in 1894, the son of Thomas and Mary Venables of 4, Heathfield Square, Knutsford.

He attested on the 2nd September 1914 and joining first a cavalry unit before being transferred to the Duke of Wellington (West Riding) Regiment as Private no. 16554.

He was posted on the 28th April 1915 with the 8th Battalion.

**Brief history of the Battalion:**

The 8th Battalion was raised at Halifax in August 1914 as part of Kitchener's First New Army and joined 34th Brigade in 11th (Northern) Division. Moved to Belton Park (Grantham) on the 18th of January 1915 they transferred to 32nd Brigade still in 11th (Northern) Division. They moved to Witley in April 1915 for final training and in July sailed from Liverpool for Gallipoli, via Mudros. They landed near Lala Baba at Suvla Bay on the 6th and 7th of August. On the 19th and 20th of December 1915 the Division was withdrawn from Gallipoli, moving to Imbros then to Egypt at the end of January. They concentrated at Sidi Bishr and took over a section of the Suez Canal defences on the 19th of February. On the 17th of June 1916 the Division was ordered to France to reinforce Third Army on The Somme. They departed from Alexandria on with the last units leaving on the 3rd of July. By the 27th July, they were in the front line on the Somme and took part in the capture of the Wundt-Werk, The Battle of Flers-Courcelette and The Battle of Thiepval. In 1917 they were in action in Operations on the Ancre then moved north to Flanders for The Battle of Messines, The Battle of the Langemarck, The Battle of Polygon Wood, The Battle of Broodseinde and The Battle of Poelcapelle. On the 13th of February 1918 the battalion was disbanded in France at the reorganisation of the Army.

*Thanks to the Wartime Memories Project.*

John survived the war but succumbed to influenza. He died on the 27th May 1919.

His service records still survive and it appears that his family believed he was entitles to receive the Military Medal – but it appears he never received it.

*John is buried in Knutsford Cemetery.*

# HARRY VERNON
*(Brother of Percy Vernon)*

**Harry Vernon** was born in 1892 in Knutsford, one of four children born to John (a market gardener) and Mary Vernon of 116, King Street, Knutsford. He became a coachman.

He enlisted at Liverpool in the Royal Field Artillery as Gunner 24421 and was initially posted to no. 62 Battery which on reorganisation on the 30th August 1916 became no. 64 Battery. He went to France on the 1st June 1915.

On the 22nd March 1915 he was promoted to Corporal.

**Brief history of the Battery:**

LXIV Brigade, Royal Field Artillery, served with 12th (Eastern) Division. 12th (Eastern) Division was formed in August 1914 as part of Kitchener's First New Army. The Division concentrated in late August with 35th Brigade and artillery near Shorncliffe, 36th Brigade at Colchester, 37th Brigade at Purfleet, Engineers and RAMC at Hounslow, ASC initially were at Aldershot then moved to Lord's Cricket Ground. Final training was undertaken near Aldershot from the 20th of February 1915, with the cavalry, motor machine gun battery, sanitary and veterinary sections joining. They proceeded to France between the 29th of May and 1st of June 1915 landing at Boulogne, they concentrated near St Omer and by 6th of June were in the Meteren-Steenwerck area with Divisional HQ being established at Nieppe. They underwent instruction from the more experienced 48th (South Midland) Division and took over a section of the front line at Ploegsteert Wood on the 23rd of June 1915. They were in action in The Battle of Loos from the 30th of September, taking over the sector from Gun Trench to Hulluch Quarries consolidating the position, under heavy artillery fire. On the 8th they repelled a heavy German infantry attack and on the 13th took part in the Action of the Hohenzollern Redoubt, capturing Gun Trench and the south western face of the Hulluch Quarries. During this period at Loos, 117 officers and 3237 men of the Division were killed or wounded. By the 21st they moved to Fouquieres-les-Bethune for a short rest then returned to the front line at the Hohenzollern Redoubt until the 15th of November, when they went into reserve at Lillers. On the 9th of December, 9th Royal Fusiliers assisted in a round-up of spies and other suspicious characters in the streets of Bethune. On the 10th the Division took over the front line north of La Bassee canal at Givenchy. On the 19th of January they began a period of training in Open Warfare at Busnes, then moved back into the front line at Loos on the 12th of February 1916. In June they moved to Flesselles and carried out a training exercise. They moved to Baizieux on the 30th June and went into the reserve at Hencourt and Millencourt by mid-morning on the 1st of July. They relieved the 8th Division at Ovillers-la-Boisselle that night and attacked at 3.15 the following morning with mixed success. On the 7th they attacked again and despite suffering heavy casualties in the area of Mash Valley, they succeeded in capturing and holding the first and second lines close to Ovillers. They were withdrawn to Contay on the 9th July. They were in action in The Battle of Pozieres on the 3rd of August with a successful attack capturing 4th Avenue Trench and were engaged in heavy fighting until they were withdrawn on the 9th. They moved north and in 1917 were in action at Arras in The First Battle of the Scarpe, The Battle of Arleux and The Third Battle of the Scarpe.

*Thanks to the Wartime Memories Project.*

Harry was killed in action on the 3rd June 1917.

**On that fateful day:**
I have been unable to locate the war diary.

*Harry is buried in Bunyan Cemetery, Tilloy-Les-Mofflains, France, together with 54 other servicemen.*

# PERCY VERNON
*(Brother of Harry Vernon)*

**Percy Vernon** was born in 1896 in Knutsford, one of four children born to John (a market gardener) and Mary Vernon of 116, King Street, Knutsford. He became a cabinet maker.

Percy attested in Knutsford on the 28th December 1914 and was posted to the 70th Field Company of the Royal Engineers as a carpenter. His service no. being 59693.

**Brief history of the Company:**

70th Field Company, The Royal Engineers served with 12th (Eastern) Division. 12th (Eastern) Division was formed in August 1914 as part of Kitchener's First New Army. The Divisional Engineers trained at Hounslow and final training was undertaken near Aldershot from the 20th of February 1915. They proceeded to France between the 29th of May and 1st of June 1915 landing at Boulogne, they concentrated near St Omer and by 6th of June were in the Meteren-Steenwerck area with Divisional HQ being established at Nieppe. They underwent instruction from the more experienced 48th (South Midland) Division and took over a section of the front line at Ploegsteert Wood on the 23rd of June 1915. They were in action in The Battle of Loos from the 30th of September, taking over the sector from Gun Trench to Hulluch Quarries consolidating the position, under heavy artillery fire. On the 8th they repelled a heavy German infantry attack and on the 13th took part in the Action of the

Hohenzollern Redoubt, capturing Gun Trench and the south western face of the Hulluch Quarries. During this period at Loos, 117 officers and 3237 men of the Division were killed or wounded.

Percy was wounded on the 18th October 1915 and died on the 20th.

*Percy is buried in Lillers Communal Cemetery, France, together with 894 other servicemen. His grave is IV. D. 7.*

# CHARLES VICKERS

**Charles Vickers** was born in Tabley, Cheshire in 1894, one of eleven children born to George (a labourer) and Ellen Vickers of Tabley Brook, Tabley. Chares was a farm labourer.

He enlisted in the 8th Battalion of the South Lancashire Regiment (Prince of Wales Volunteers) and became Private no. 15307 having formally been in the Cheshire Regiment as Private no. 15612.

Charles never got the opportunity to go abroad as he died from complications following an operation for appendicitis in Portsmouth hospital on the 15th March 1915.

*Charles is buried in Over Tabley (St Pauls) Churchyard.*

# WILLIAM WARD

**William Ward** was born in Mobberley. His Father William was a farm labourer of Town Lane, Mobberley. He too went on to be a farm labourer.

He enlisted in the 8ᵗʰ Battalion of the Cheshire Regiment, becoming Private no.33528

**Brief history of the Battalion:**

The 8ᵗʰ (Service) Battalion, Cheshire Regiment was raised in Chester on the 12ᵗʰ of August 1914 as part of Kitchener's First New Army and joined 40ᵗʰ Brigade, 13ᵗʰ (Western) Division which assembled on Salisbury Plain. 40ᵗʰ Brigade moved to Chiseldon and Cirencester in September 1914. Near the end of February the Division concentrated at Blackdown in Hampshire. They moved to the Mediterranean from the 13ᵗʰ of June 1915 landing at Alexandria then moving to Mudros, by the 4ᵗʰ of July to prepare for a landing at Gallipoli. The infantry landed on Cape Helles between the 6ᵗʰ and 16ᵗʰ of July to relieve 29ᵗʰ Division. They returned to Mudros at the end of the month, and the entire Division landed at ANZAC Cove between the 3ʳᵈ and 5ᵗʰ of August. They were in action in The Battle of Sari Bair, The Battle of Russell's Top and The Battle of Hill 60, at ANZAC. Soon afterwards they transferred from ANZAC to Suvla Bay. They were evacuated from Suvla on the 19ᵗʰ and 20ᵗʰ of December 1915, and after a week's rest they moved to the Helles bridgehead. They were in action during the last Turkish attacks at Helles on the 7ᵗʰ of January 1916 and were evacuated from Helles on the 8ᵗʰ and 9ᵗʰ. The Division concentrated at Port Said, holding forward posts in the Suez Canal defences. On the 12ᵗʰ of February 1916 they moved to Mesopotamia, to join the force being assembled near Sheikh Sa'ad for the relief of the besieged garrison at Kut al Amara. They joined the Tigris Corps on the 27ᵗʰ of March and were in action in the unsuccessful attempts to relieve Kut. They were in action in The Battle of Kut al Amara, The capture of the Hai Salient, the capture of Dahra Bend and The passage of the Diyala, in the pursuit of the enemy towards Baghdad. Units of the Division were the first troops to enter Baghdad, when it fell on the 11 March 1917. The Division then joined "Marshall's Column" and pushed north across Iraq, fighting at Delli 'Abbas, Duqma, Nahr Kalis, crossing the 'Adhaim on the 18 April and fighting at Shatt al 'Adhaim. Later in the year they were in action in the Second and Third Actions of Jabal Hamrin and fought at Tuz Khurmatli the following April. By the 28th of May 1918, Divisional HQ had moved to Dawalib and remained there until the end of the war, enduring extreme summer temperatures.

*Thanks to the Wartime Memories Project.*

William died on the 2nd January 1918 and as his service records no longer exist it must be assumed that he died from disease which was rampant during that campaign.

*William is remembered at the Baghdad (North Gate) Cemetery memorial along with another 4,160 servicemen.*

# COLIN WEBB

**Colin Webb** was born in 1890 and lived with his grand-parents George (A farm labourer) and Elizabeth in Broad Oak Lane, Mobberley, Cheshire.

He was a career soldier, enlisting in the army in 1908, becoming Private no. 9033 of the 2nd Battalion of the Cheshire Regiment.

**Brief history of the Battalion:**
The 2nd Battalion, Cheshire Regiment was a regular unit of the British Army and was in Jubbulpore, India when war broke out in August 1914. They returned to England, landing at Devonport on the 24th of December 1914. They joined 84th Brigade, 28th Division, at Winchester and proceeded to France, embarking at Southampton and landing at Le Havre on the 17th of January 1915. 28th Division concentrated in the area between Bailleul and Hazebrouck. They saw action in the Second Battle of Ypres, where casualties were high and The Battle of Loos. In October 1915 were ordered to Egypt and sailed from Marseilles for Alexandria, then on to Salonika in January 1916. They took part in the occupation of Mazirko and the capture of Barakli Jum'a in October 1916.

*Thanks to the Wartime Memories Project.*

On the 21st February 1916 he was promoted to Lance Corporal.

He was slightly wounded in the eye on the 10th May 1915.
He was transferred to the 8th Cheshires on his arrival in Mesopotamia.

**Brief history of the Battalion:**
On the 12th of February 1916 the 8th Battalion moved to Mesopotamia, to join the force being assembled near Sheikh Sa'ad for the relief of the besieged garrison at Kut al Amara. They joined the Tigris Corps on the 27th of March and were in action in the unsuccessful attempts to relieve Kut. They were in action in The Battle of Kut al Amara, The capture of the Hai Salient, the capture of Dahra Bend and The passage of the Diyala, in the pursuit of the enemy towards Baghdad.

*Thanks to the Wartime Memories Project.*

Colin died of disease on the 27th May 1916.
His medals were sent to his mother, Mary Agnes Ward at Alexandra Park, London.

---

*Note:*
*Like Gallipoli, conditions in Mesopotamia defy description. Extremes of temperature (120 degrees F was common); arid desert and regular flooding; flies, mosquitoes and other vermin: all led to appalling levels of sickness and death through disease. Under these incredible conditions, units fell short of officers and men, and all too often the reinforcements were half-trained and ill-equipped. Medical arrangements were quite shocking, with wounded men spending up to two weeks on boats before reaching any kind of hospital. These factors, plus of course the unexpectedly determined Turkish resistance, contributed to high casualty rates.*

---

*11012 killed*
*3985 died of wounds*
*12678 died of sickness*
*13492 missing and prisoners (9000 at Kut)*
*51836 wounded*

**Data -** *"Statistics of the Military Effort of the British Empire" ( London HMSO, 1920).*

*Colin is buried in Amara War Cemetery, Iraq, together with another 4621 other servicemen. He is buried in Grave XV. J. 3.*

# JAMES HENRY WHITE

**James Henry White** was born in Lymm, Cheshire, one of five children born to John Campbell (a joiner) and Anne White of Higher Lane, Lymm.

He enlisted in Knutsford for the 1st Battalion of the Scots Guards, becoming Guardsman no. 13704.

He arrived in France on the 6th October 1915.

**Brief history of the Battalion:**
1st Battalion, The Scots Guards were based in Aldershot with the 1st (Guards) Brigade, 1st Division when war broke out in August 1914. They proceeded to France landing at Le Havre on the 14th, being amongst the first troops of the British Expeditionary Force. They fought in The Battle of Mons and the retreat from Mons, The Battle of the Marne, The Battle of the Aisne, the First Battle of Ypres and the Winter Operations of 1914-15. In 1915 they were in action during The Battle of Aubers. On the 25th of August 1915 they transferred to 2nd Guards Brigade, Guards Division and were in action in The Battle of Loos. In 1916 they fought on The Somme in The Battle of Flers-Courcelette and The Battle of Morval, capturing Lesboeufs.

*Thanks to the Wartime Memories Project.*

James was killed in action on the 5th April 1916.

**On that fateful day:**
The Battalion war diary for that date states:

**'*5.4.16 YPRES***
*In trenches. Bombardment continues. Enemy retaliation on our left front during afternoon. Coy relieved in afternoon. Fine. C.S.M. Clarke wounded.'*

There is no mention of any other casualties that day.

*James is buried in Potijze Chateau Wood Cemetery, Belgium along with over 850 other servicemen. His plot is at B.18.*

# ERNEST WHITTAKER

Ernest Whittaker was born in Tabley, Cheshire, the son of Joseph (a cowman) of Pownell Green Cottages, Over Tabley.

He enlisted in the Cheshire Regiment as private 76704 before transferring to the 10th battalion of the Kings (Shropshire Light Infantry) becoming Private no. 30090.

**Brief history of the Battalion:**

10th (Shropshire & Cheshire Yeomanry) Battalion was formed at Cairo on 2<sup>nd</sup> March 1917 from the dismounted troopers of the Shropshire Yeomanry and the Cheshire Yeomanry. It served in Palestine in the 231<sup>st</sup> Brigade of the 74<sup>th</sup> "Broken Spur" Division.

It took part in the second and third battles of Gaza, July-November 1917 and then in the operations for the capture of Jerusalem (December 1917) and in the capture of Jericho (February 1918). In the attack on Birj-el-Lisaneh, near Tel Asur, on March 10<sup>th</sup> 1918, Pte. Harold Whitfield won the only VC to a Shropshire regiment for the Great War.

In May 1918, the 10<sup>th</sup> went to France, serving on the Lys in August and then at Epehy and captured the notorious " Quadrilateral" in November.

Having captured Tournai – where the 53<sup>rd</sup> had been in action in 1794 – it ended the war near Ath in Belgium and was disbanded in Shrewsbury in June 1919.

Ernest was killed in action on the 12<sup>th</sup> October 1918 – just 29 days before the armistice was signed.

**On that fateful day**:
The war diary states that the Battalion were advancing between Herlies and Faches. There was no action reported that day – shelling was reported and several OR were lost to it. It would appear that Ernest was one of them.

*Ernest is buried in Aubers Ridge British Cemetery along with over 700 other servicemen. His grave is VI. B. 11.*

# GEORGE WHITTAKER

**Photograph courtesy of *The Knutsford Guardian***

**George Whittaker** was born in 1888 to John and Mary Whittaker of Parkside, Nether Tabley, Cheshire. He was an assistant Elementary school teacher in Manchester.

He enlisted in late 1914 and his call-up came early in 1915. He joined the 6ᵗʰ Battalion of the Manchester Regiment becoming Private 1680 and was dispatched with them to The Dardanelles campaign, arriving on the 5ᵗʰ May 1915.

George was a great letter writer and the photographs he sent home from Egypt had copious notes inscribed on the rear, giving every detail of the image overleaf – however, despite numerous lines of enquiry, I have been unable to trace these.

**Brief history of the Battalion:**
The 1/6ᵗʰ Battalion, Manchester were a Territorial unit, when war broke out in August 1914 they were based in Stretford Road, Hulme as part of the Manchester Brigade, East Lancashire Division. They were mobilized and moved to Rochdale to prepare for service overseas. They

proceeded to Egypt arriving at Alexandria on the 25th of September to defend the Suez Canal from the Turkish forces in Palestine. They were in action in the Turkish attack on the Suez Canal on the 3rd of February 1915. In the first week of May the division embarked from Alexandria, landing at Cape Helles, Gallipoli, where they saw action in the attempts to capture the heights of Krithia and the Battle of Krithia Vineyard which was a diversionary attack for the British Landing at Suvla Bay.

*Thanks to the Wartime Memories Project.*

George was killed in action on the 5th June 1916.

*The 6th Manchesters just before the attack of the 4th June 1915*

**On that fateful day:**
Here is a report from one member of the Manchester regiment about the attack in which George was killed:

*At noon, the leading platoons of Manchesters ("A" Company and half each of "B" & "D") left the protection of their trenches and charged across the 200 yards of No Man's Land in good order. They were hit by devastating rifle and machine gun fire. Within 5 minutes, they were in the Turkish front line and were engaged in fierce hand-to-hand fighting. As they secured the trench, the other half of the 6th Manchesters ("C" Company and the other platoons of "B" & "D") overlapped them to take the Turkish support trench. The attack of the*

*5th, 7th and 8th Manchesters had also gone well. However, units on either side of the Manchester Brigade had been less successful. The Turks were now on three sides of the Brigade and, by mid-afternoon, it was becoming impossible to hold the position. An order for withdrawal back to the original Turkish front line was ordered at 6.30pm. 770 men of the 6th Manchesters had gone into action. By nightfall, when the roll was called, only 160 were fit enough to answer. 48 men had been killed. Tom and Alexander Milne are believed to have been members of "C" Company. It had been virtually wiped out but, as far as is known, the two friends had come through unscathed. The Battalion would be in the firing line for three more days before it was relieved and would suffer another 100 deaths.*

This is how the newspaper reported his death:

*June 4 – Private George Whittaker 26, son of Mr and Mrs John Whittaker, Parkside Tabley. He took part with the 1/6 Manchester on the 4th June in a charge and was not afterwards heard of.*

*His death was not notified until Jan 1916 when it was discovered that his body had been buried by the 1/5 Batt. Kings Own Scottish Borderers.*

**George is remembered on the Helles Memorial, Turkey, along with the names
of 20,885 other servicemen.**

# WILLIAM WHISTON

**William Whiston** was born in Knutsford in 1900, the son of Arthur (a paper maker) and Sarah of Coronation Square, Knutsford.

He joined the 3ʳᵈ Battalion of the Cheshire Regiment, claiming he was a 19 year old warehouseman but did not serve.

He died of illness on the 20ᵗʰ August 1915.

*William is buried in Knutsford Cemetery.*

# JAMES WILDING

**James Wilding** was born in Knutsford in 1894, one of fourteen children born to Emma (a widow) of 116, Mobberley Road, Knutsford. On marrying Florence May Done, James moved to 17, Princes Street, Knutsford. He was a nursery gardener.

They had one child.

James enlisted in the army on the 7th April 1916 at Knutsford and became Private no. 4620 (later re-numbered to 49653) of the 13th Battalion of the Cheshire Regiment.

He received a gunshot wound to his neck on the 21st October 1916.

**Brief history of the Battalion:**

The 13th (Service) Battalion, Cheshire Regiment was raised at Port Sunlight on 1 September 1914 by Gershom Stewart, MP. They moved to Chester and joined 74th Brigade, 25th Division in Kitchener's Third

New Army. The Division assembled in the area around Salisbury for training and the 13th Cheshires spent the winter in billets in Bournemouth. The division moved to Aldershot in May 1915 for final training. They proceeded to France on the 25th of September 1915 and concentrated in the area of Nieppe. Their first action was in defence of the German attack on Vimy Ridge in May 1916. They then moved to The Somme and joined the Battle just after the main attack, with 75th Brigade making a costly attack near Thiepval on the 3rd of July. The Division was in action at The Battle of Bazentin, The Battle of Pozieres and The Battle of the Ancre Heights. In 1917 they were in action at The Battle of Messines attacking between the Wulverghem-Messines and Wulverghem-Wytschaete roads. In the Third battle of Ypres were in action during The Battle of Pilkem.

*Thanks to the Wartime Memories Project.*

On the 23rd April 1917 James was certified as 'Bomber 1st Class'. He was killed in action on the 14th June 1917.

**On that fateful day:**
The war diary has no entry for this date.

*James is buried in La Plus farm Cemetery, Belgium, along with 336 other servicemen. His grave is III. A. 8.*

> *Note:*
> *Florence received a pension of 18s 9p for herself and her child.*

# WILLIAM BENJAMIN WILKINSON

**William Ben Wilkinson** was born in Toft, Knutsford in 1877, the son of William and Elisabeth (both farmers) of Moss Farm, Toft. He was also employed on the farm.

On the death of his parents he emigrated to Canada.

At the outbreak of war he enlisted in the army, becoming Private 426743 of the 28th Battalion of the Canadian Infantry.

**Brief history of the Battalion:**
The 28th (North West) Battalion was recruited in 1914, the men coming mostly from the Manitoba/Saskatchewan areas of Canada. The came to Britain in June 1915 and joined the 6th Brigade, 2nd Division of the Canadian Corp. They arrived in France in September.

In 1916 they took a full and active part in the Battle of the Somme. William died on the 2$^{nd}$ October 1916.

**On that fateful day:**
The war diaries for the 28$^{th}$ are freely available and on the 2$^{nd}$ October they were resting – I have been unable to locate exactly where and when William died, other than to say it was during the battle of the Somme.

*William is buried in Regina Trench Cemetery, Grandcourt, France along with 2.279 other servicemen.*

# ERNEST WILLIAMS

**Ernest Williams** was born in Harphurhey, Manchester in 1897, one of two children of Edward (a publican) and Annie Williams of The Rose and Crown, Knutsford, they later moved to 38, Cranford Avenue.

He enlisted in the 1/6th Battalion of the Manchester Regiment as Private no. 2062.

He went with his Battalion to Gallipoli, arriving on the 5th May 1915.

**Brief history of the Battalion:**

The 1/6th Battalion, Manchester were a Territorial unit, when war broke out in August 1914 they were based in Stretford Road, Hulme as part of the Manchester Brigade, East Lancashire Division. They were mobilized and moved to Rochdale to prepare for service overseas. They proceeded to Egypt arriving at Alexandria on the 25th of September to defend the Suez Canal from the Turkish forces in Palestine. They were in action in the Turkish attack on the Suez Canal on the 3rd of February 1915. In the first week of May the division embarked from Alexandria, landing at Cape Helles, Gallipoli, where they saw action in the attempts to capture the heights of Krithia and the Battle of Krithia Vineyard which was a diversionary attack for the British Landing at Suvla Bay. The much depleted division were evacuated from Gallipoli in the first week of January 1916, returning to Alexandria via Mudros. They returned to duty on the Suez Canal and were in action in the Battle of Romani in August.

Ernest was killed in action on the 31st May 1915, having received a gunshot wound to the abdomen.

As he was laid to rest A. C. Brooke-Taylor read the service.

**On that fateful day:**

The war diary gives no account of any action on this day.

*Ernest is remembered on the Hellas Memorial, Turkey along with the names of 20,885 other servicemen. He also has a small memorial in Knutsford Cemetery.*

*Note:*
*His medals were never claimed and returned under rule 1743 of the Kings Regulations 1912 for "medals unclaimed after 10 years will be returned and broken up".*

# HAROLD WILSON

**Harold Wilson** was born at Grange-over-Sands in1893, one of five children born to Fred (a taxi driver) and Margaret Wilson of 2, Hayton Street, Knutsford. Harold was employed as a junior clerk.

He attested at Liverpool on the 4<sup>th</sup> September 1914 and arrived in France on the 7<sup>th</sup> November 1915 as private no. 16756 of the 18<sup>th</sup> (Pals) Battalion of the Kings (Liverpool Regiment) – he later transferred to the 12<sup>th</sup> Battalion.

**Brief History of the Battalion:**

12<sup>th</sup> (Service) Battalion, The King's Regiment (Liverpool) was raised at Seaforth in September 1914 as part of Kitchener's Second New Army, and joined 20<sup>th</sup> (Light) Division as Army Troops. After training close to home with little equipment, they moved to Aldershot. In January 1915 the 12<sup>th</sup> Kings Liverpool joined 61<sup>st</sup> Brigade, still with 20<sup>th</sup> (Light) Division. In February 1915 they Division moved to Guildford, then to Salisbury Plain in April for final training and preceded to France on the 27<sup>th</sup> of July 1915, landing at Boulogne, the division concentrating in the Saint-Omer area. They moved to the Fleurbaix area for trench familiarisation. In 1916 they were in action at The Battle of Mount Sorrel, in which the Division, along with the Canadians, recaptured the heights. They were in action on the Somme in The Battle of Delville Wood, The Battle of Guillemont, The Battle of Flers-Courcelette, The Battle of Morval and The Battle of Le Transloy. In 1917 they were in action during The German retreat to the Hindenburg Line, The Battle of Langemarck, The Battle of the Menin Road Ridge, The Battle of Polygon Wood and The Cambrai Operations.

*Thanks to the Wartime Memories Project.*

Harold achieved the rank of Sergeant in 1916.
He was killed in action on the 20<sup>th</sup> November 1917.

**On that fateful day:**

The war diary has no entry for this date, and the only reference to the 12<sup>th</sup> battalion on the 20<sup>th</sup> November 1917 is in the History of the Kings Regiment (Liverpool) Vol 2 by Everard Wyrall:

'Battle narrative of operations on the 20th – The behaviour of all ranks, under exceptionally trying circumstances was magnificent.'

*Harold has no known grave and is remembered on the Cambrai Memorial along with the names of 7,057 other servicemen.*

# WALTER NEWTON WILSON

**Walter Newton Wilson** was born in Marthall in 1882, the son of Samuel (a farmer) and Emma Wilson of Marthall Burn, Little Marford, Cheshire. Walter was a joiner/builder.

He enlisted in the army and became Sapper no.67173 of the 147 (Army Troop Company) of the Royal Engineers.

**Brief history of the Company:**
In 1914, the General Headquarters of the BEF in France and Flanders incorporated a GHQ Signals Company, two Corps Signals Companies (one each for I and II Corps), and specialist units for railways and printing. GHQ always maintained certain engineering units, including the Special Companies RE whose job was gas warfare, Meteorological, Special Works Park (camouflage) and other specialists.

As the army grew in size, the number of Corps increased and were organised into Armies. At Army level, several different types of Engineers units developed, and Corps were left with only one Company-sized unit, in motor and cable sections. Each of the five Armies on the Western Front contained the following, with the establishment varying between Armies and over time.

Advanced RE Parks (responsible for stores and dumps of goods and equipment)

Pontoon Parks (looking after bridging equipment)

Electrical and Mechanical Companies (responsible for machinery, including underground boring)

Army Workshops (for repairs and maintenance of equipment)

Anti-Aircraft Sections (searchlight operations)

**Army Troops Companies** (established similar to Field Companies, but for behind-the-lines bridging and water work)

Transportation Works Companies (maintaining vehicles)

Forestry Companies

*Thanks to the Long, Long Trail.*

Walter died of wounds on the 23rd September 1917. Unfortunately I have been unable to trace where and when he received his wounds.

*Walter is buried in Mendinghem Military Cemetery, Greece along with 2,443 other servicemen. His grave is VII. D. 8.*

# PERCY RALPH WINSER

**Percy Ralph Winser** was born in Bebbington in 1896, one of three children born to Percy Winser (a soap Manufacturer) and Any Winser, who originally lived in Bebbington but moved to Heath House, 5, Gaskell Avenue, Knutsford.

Percy was educated at Bedales Public School in Hampshire.

His service records no longer exist but we know that enlisted in the army in 1915, becoming a Second Lieutenant in the 149th Battery of the Royal Horse Artillery.

**Brief history of the Battery:**
The CXLIX Brigade, Royal Field Artillery served as divisional artillery with 30th Division. 30th Division was formed in April 1915 from units of Kitchener's 5th New Army and concentrated near Grantham. In the autumn they moved to Larkhill, Salisbury and proceeded to France in November, sailing to Le Havre and Boulogne and concentrating near Amiens. In 1916 they were in action during the Battle of the Somme, in which the Division captured Montauban. In 1917 they took part in the pursuit of the German retreat to the Hindenburg Line, the Arras Offensive and The Battle of Pilkem Ridge.

*Thanks to the Wartime Memories Project.*

Percy was killed in action on the 23rd April 1917.

**On that fateful day:**
I have been unable to locate the war diary.

*Percy is buried in Henin Communal Cemetery, France together with 193 other servicemen. His grave is II. E. 21.*

# ALBERT EDWARD WRIGHT

**Albert Edwards Wright** lived at 89, Mobberley Road, Cross Town, Knutsford with his wife Dorothy.

He joined the Royal Army Service Corp and became Driver/093219.

He died at home on the 30th December 1920.

# GODFREY SANDY WUNSCH

**Godfrey Sandy Wunsch** was born in Knutsford in 1890, one of five children born to Edward (a cotton Merchant) and Mary Wunsch of Brooke House, Brooke Street, Knutsford.

514

Godfrey emigrated to Canada.
On the outbreak of the war he enlisted in the 11th (Vancouver) Battalion of the Canadian Infantry, becoming Private no. 21105.
He was promoted to the rank of Sergeant Armourer.
He was killed in training whilst in Britain on the 19th January 1915.

*Godfrey is buried in Bulford Cemetery, Wiltshire along with 74 other servicemen. His grave is I. I. 6.*

# JOHN YARWOOD

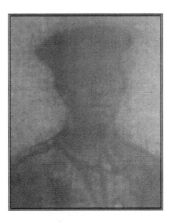

**John Yarwood** was born in Knutsford in 1891, one of four children born to Henry (a gardener) and Margaret Ann (a housekeeper) of 47 Mobberley Road, Knutsford.

On leaving school, John took up employment as a nurseryman. His service record no longer exist but we know he joined the 9th Battalion of the West Yorkshire Regiment (Prince of Wales Own) in 1915, becoming Private no. 10522.

He sailed for the Balkans on the 11th July 1915.

**Brief history of the Battalion:**
The 9th (Service) Battalion, West Yorkshire Regiment (Prince of Wales's Own), was a Kitchener Battalion, raised at York on the 25th of August 1914, as part of 32nd Brigade, 11th (Northern) Division. After initial training they moved to Grantham in Lincolnshire, and then on the 4th of April 1915 they moved to Frensham for final training. On the 3rd of July 1915 they sailed from Liverpool to Mudros. Their first action was the landing at Suvla Bay, Gallipoli on the 6th of August 1915.

*Thanks to the Wartime Memories Project.*

John died of wounds in hospital in Cairo, Egypt on the 10th August 1915.

Unfortunately, as his records no longer exist, it has proved impossible to discover when and where (other than at Gallipoli) that John received his wounds.

*John is buried in Cairo War Memorial Cemetery, Egypt along with 2,306 other servicemen. His Grave is D. 97.*

# APPENDIX ONE

## General procedure when a man was wounded.

The speed at which a wounded man could receive attention depended on many factors, including –
• The location he was in at the time he received his wound.
• Were they in action or not.
• The sheer number of casualties.

## Location:

If a man received his would whilst in a trench or in the rear areas it was likely that aid would be there fairly quickly, for all units, while in the trenches were generally provided with a medical officer, and also trained stretcher-bearers who had some first aid knowledge. The wounded could then be taken to a 'bearer post' where men who were more highly skilled could treat the wound. It was then easier to get the man to the field ambulance and away to hospital.

However, if the man was wounded outside the trench, in no man's land, in and attack or one of the numerous other exercises they undertook, mostly at night, i.e. trench raid, wiring party, digging new' saps' etc.

then this was a different story. It might be his mates might bring him in, or he could get back under his own steam – but in an attack, with thousands of men falling (59000 killed wounded or missing on day one of the Somme offensive) – he could have a long wait for help. Most units had eight stretcher-bearers attached to it – so they were pretty hard pressed to get the wounded in. man lay out there sometime for days, awaiting rescue, and many died during that wait, their bodies getting covered with earth from other shell blasts and becoming lost.

## Action:
The bravery of the stretcher-bearers was outstanding, and lots of them were the so-called cowardly' conscientious objectors' who went over the top time and time again to recover the wounded, even in the ferocious of shell-fire.

It was hazardous work and many were lost. There are also many pictures of German prisoners of war assisting in the carrying of the wounded and visa-versa.

## The sheer number:
The number of casualties in an attack counted in the hundreds if not thousands and the effort in just locating them over the whole front of an attack must ave been almost impossible. Then getting them 'home',

with the ground all churned up, and as we know at Passchendaele, the mud was almost impassable, and the famous picture of the seven men carrying one stretcher, makes it clear what these lads had to go through.

On top of that they had to try and keep the stretcher steady so as not to cause the wounded man any more pain than was necessary – incredible work they did.

*That iconic picture*

There is a story of one man; shot in the chest lying in no man's land for eleven days before being found by a stretcher party.

Once back in their own lines the wounded would be moved along the evacuation trench to the field ambulance – but don't forget – they could still be under fire, even here.

**Field Ambulance:**
Don't think of this as a high speed vehicle, screaming off to hospital, claxons blaring – this was a mobile medical unit of which each British division had three. This gave the wounded soldier some better care and treatment and some of the wounded were treated there and returned to duty – the more serious cases were moved on along the chain.

**Dressing Station:**
These were situated wherever they could find, cellars, bombed out building, in fact anywhere that afforded the staff some protection

from shelling. These were usually staffed by members of the Royal Army Medical Corp.

Once treated, the casualty would be moved to the Casualty Clearing Station, which was situated some way behind the lines.

**Casualty Clearing Station:**

The casualty clearing station (CCS) was usually a large tented area set up out of the enemy's artillery range, for the treatment of the casualties too wounded to be immediately returned to duty. This was not a place for long-stay casualties. It was generally set up close to lines of communication such as roads or railways. From here it was a trip to the base hospital.

The Casualty Clearing Stations were to facilitate movement of casualties from the battlefield on to the hospitals. The general rule was one CCS per Division but they were under Army Corps rather than under Divisional control. To date, 72 have been traced.

A CCS was a very large unit, and could hold a minimum of 50 beds and 150 stretchers in order to treat a minimum of two hundred sick and wounded at any one time. In normal circumstances the team would be seven Medical Officers, one Quartermaster and seventy-seven other ranks, there would also be a Dentist, a Pathologist, seven QAIMNS and other non-medical personnel attached. In times of stress this number could be increased and a specialised 'Surgical Team' could be brought forward. Because they were so large they needed up to about half a mile square of real estate. Each CCS would carry its own marquees and wooden huts so as to create medical and surgical wards, kitchens, Sanitation, Dispensary, Operating Theatres, Medical stores, surgical stores, Incineration plant, Ablutions and Mortuary, as well as sleeping accommodation for the Nurses, Officers and Soldiers of the unit. Sanitation was dug, and a water supply assured.

They were usually situated about 20 kilometres behind the front lines; roughly mid-way between the front line and the Base Area, and about 500 yards from a main railway line or waterway system.

Transportation to a CCS could have been via horse-drawn or motor ambulances. This was the first line of surgery and the furthest forward of nursing staff but treatment could still only be limited.

*Wounded soldiers in hospital wore a distinctive uniform of bright blue to identify themselves as such.*

Casualty Clearing stations were usually grouped in twos or threes and would have worked in relay, that is, one would be closed and treating casualties for evacuation by train or ambulance to the Base Area, whilst the other would be empty and ready to receive new casualties. When this became full it would close, but the first would by now be empty and ready to receive new casualties again. A third would only be treating the sick, but would evacuate to receive battle casualties in an emergency. The CCS's collected the casualties from the MDS's by sending forward the Motor Ambulance Convoys [MAC's] that were attached to them. The ambulances of the MAC's were Army Service Corps vehicles [ASC] and each had an ASC driver and an RAMC attendant. In exceptional circumstances a Field Ambulance would be attached to assist. There were six mobile X-Ray units serving in the British Expeditionary

Force during the Great War and these were sent to assist the CCS's during the great battles. The Rontgen Tube had been in use during the South African War of 1898-1902 and complete trailer X-Ray equipment was attached to every CCS from very early in the Great War.

The holding capacity was about four weeks in order for men to be returned to their units or be transferred by Ambulance Trains or Inland Water Transport to a hospital. The seriousness of many wounds challenged the facilities of the Casualty Clearing Stations and as a result their positions are marked today by large military cemeteries.

**Base Hospitals:**

A General Hospital was located on or near railway lines to facilitate movement of casualties from the Casualty Clearing Stations on to the Ports. The Great Hotels and other large building such as casinos were requisitioned but other hospitals were hutted and constructed on open ground. Many of the general hospitals were Voluntarily Hospitals supplied by the British Red Cross and St. John Combined Organisation and by the titled ladies of Great Britain, and some became Convalescent Depots.

*Nurse Dora Lancashire of Heaton Mersey Red Cross Hospital – with two of 'her boys', (She will be one of the subjects of my next book).*

In the Base Areas such as Etaples, Boulogne, Rouen, Havre, Paris, Plage, General Hospitals operated as normal civilian hospitals do, having all the departments and paraphernalia. Bacteriological and X-ray units would be attached, and pathological research on the field conditions found was undertaken.

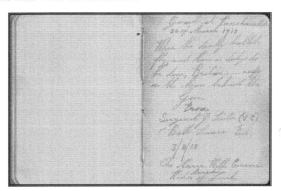

*Extract from Nurse Dora Lancashire's autograph book – signed by Joseph Lister V.C.*

The general hospitals in the Base Areas had complete X-Ray departments and operated as separate sections within the hospital's complex. Also working to support the hospitals Mobile Hygiene and Bacteriological Laboratories. There was one Hygiene and two Bacteriological Laboratories allocated to each Army.

The holding capacity was such that a patient could remain until fit to be returned to his unit or sent across the Channel via Hospital Ships to the UK for very specialist work, or discharge from the forces. Once admitted there was a good chance of survival, the Official History states that whilst 36,879 men died on hospital, 169,842 returned to duty after treatment. Some of the General Hospitals were still handling the treatment of held patients until well into 1919, and others went forward into Germany to care for the British Forces holding the Rhine.

*Thanks to the Royal Army Medical Corp for the information, (and of course the great work they do).*

# APPENDIX TWO

# The make-up of a Division.

## The 31st Division in 1914-1918

### The history of 31st Division

On 10 December the War Office authorised the formation of the Fifth New Army. Like the other Kitchener Armies, it comprised six Divisions, in this case numbered 37 to 42. What eventually became 31st Division was originally numbered 38th. In April 1915, the original Fourth New Army was broken up and its units converted for training and draft-finding purposes. When this took place the Fifth New Army became Fourth New Army and its Divisions were renumbered to 30th – 35th: thus what we remember as 31st Division was born.

 The Division was largely comprised of locally raised units often known as "Pals". The units from Accrington, Leeds, Bradford, Barnsley and Hull are among the best known of all 1914-raised infantry, simply because of the amount of research and publicity they have received, particularly since the 1980s. It was a predominantly Northern Division, with most units originating in Lancashire or Yorkshire – hence the use of the red and white roses in the Divisional symbol.

On 16 December 1914, two Companies of the 18th (Service) Bn (1st County), the Durham Light Infantry became the first troops of the New Armies to come under enemy fire, when they were manning the trenches of the Tyne and Tees defences which were shelled by the German ships Derfflinger, Von Der Tann and Blucher. After in most cases commencing training near home, the units were moved

to concentrate at South Camp at Ripon in April and May 1915. There were severe shortages of arms, ammunition and much equipment. It was not until September that the Division moved for final training and firing practice at Fovant on Salisbury Plain.

In late November 1915 the Division received a warning order to prepare to sail for France. Advance parties began to depart. But on 2 December final orders were received that the Division would go to Egypt, accompanied by the artillery of 32$^{nd}$ Division. Its own artillery would join 32$^{nd}$ Division in France. The advanced parties were recalled and the Division sailed from 7 December, with Divisional HQ being established at Port Said on Christmas Eve. The last units arrived in Egypt on 23 January 1916.

### 1916
The Division took over the No 3 Sector of the Suez Canal defences and Divisional HQ moved to Kantara on 23 January. The stay in Egypt was short, and between 1-6 March the Division sailed to Marseilles for service on the Western Front. The 31$^{st}$ Division subsequently remained in France and Flanders and took part in these actions:
The Battle of Albert* including the attack on Serre
The Battle of the Ancre*
* the battles marked * are phases of the Battles of the Somme 1916

### 1917
Operations on the Ancre
The Third Battle of the Scarpe**
The Capture of Oppy Wood**
** the battles marked ** are phases of the Arras Offensive 1917

### 1918
The Battle of St Quentin^
The Battle of Bapaume^

The First Battle of Arras^

^ *the battles marked ^ are phases of the First Battles of the Somme*

## 1918
The Battle of Estaires^^
The Battle of Hazebrouck^^
The Defence of Nieppe Forest^^
The attack at La Becque^^
^^ *the battles marked ^^ are phases of the Battles of the Lys*
The capture of Vieux Berquin+
+ *the battles marked + are phases of the Advance in Flanders*
The Battle of Ypres++
The action of Tieghem++
++ *the battles marked ++ are phases of the Final Advance in Flanders*

The Division's advance across Flanders continued on 9 November when units forced a crossing of the River Scheldt. At the time when the Armistice came into effect, 11am on 11 November, the advanced units had reached Everbecque and the River Dender.

The Division moved back to the Arques-Blendecques are and here men began to be demobilised. The Division ceased to exist on 20 May 1919.

The Great War had cost 31st Division a total of 30091 men killed, wounded or missing.

## The order of battle of the 31st Division

### 92nd Brigade
*On 16 April 1918 it was decided that due to the heavy casualties recently sustained, the 92nd and 93rd Brigades would be temporarily amalgamated and called the 92nd Composite Brigade. It was broken up two days later and the 92nd and 93rd Brigades were reconstituted soon after.*

| | |
|---|---|
| 10<sup>th</sup> Bn, the East Yorkshire Regiment | (Hull Commercials) |
| 11<sup>th</sup> Bn, the East Yorkshire Regiment | (Hull Tradesmen) |
| 12<sup>th</sup> Bn, the East Yorkshire Regiment | left February 1918 (Hull Sportsmen) |
| 13<sup>th</sup> Bn, the East Yorkshire Regiment | left February 1918 (Hull t'Others) |
| 92<sup>nd</sup> Machine Gun Company | joined 20 May 1916, moved to 31st Bn MGC 21 February 1918 |
| 92<sup>nd</sup> Trench Mortar Battery | joined by 11 April 1916 |
| 11<sup>th</sup> Bn, the East Lancashire Regiment | joined February 1918 (Accrington Pals) |

**93<sup>rd</sup> Brigade**

| | |
|---|---|
| 15<sup>th</sup> Bn, the West Yorkshire Regiment | (1st Leeds Pals) |
| 16<sup>th</sup> Bn, the West Yorkshire Regiment | left February 1918 (1st Bradford Pals) |
| 18<sup>th</sup> Bn, the West Yorkshire Regiment | left February 1918 (2nd Bradford Pals) |
| 18<sup>th</sup> Bn, the Durham Light Infantry | (Durham Pals) |
| 93<sup>rd</sup> Machine Gun Company | joined 20 May 1916, moved to 31st Bn MGC 21 February 1918 |

93rd Trench Mortar Battery                                  joined by 12 April 1916

13th Bn, the York & Lancaster Regiment   joined February 1918
                                                            (1st Barnsley pals)

---

## 94th Brigade

*The Brigade was broken up between 11 and 16 February 1918. It was reformed on 30 May 1918, principally from units that had been reduced down to training cadres. It was fully reconstituted on 21 June 1918 by the addition of units from the 74th Division, and designated 94th (Yeomanry) Brigade.*

11th Bn, the East Lancashire Regiment      left February 1918
                                                            (Accrington Pals)

12th Bn, the York & Lancaster Regiment   disbanded February
                                                            1918 (Sheffield City
                                                            Battalion)

13th Bn, the York & Lancaster Regiment   (1st Barnsley Pals)

14th Bn, the York & Lancaster Regiment   disbanded February
                                                            1918 (2nd Barnsley Pals)

94th Machine Gun Company                    joined 21 May 1916,
                                                            moved to 31st Bn MGC
                                                            21 February 1918

94th Trench Mortar Battery                     joined by 11 April 1916

2nd Bn, the Royal Munster Fusiliers         joined as cadre May
                                                            1918, left June 1918

2nd Bn, the Loyal North Lancashire
Regiment                                              joined and left June 1918

| | |
|---|---|
| 12th Bn, the Norfolk Regiment | joined June 1918 (Norfolk Yeomanry) |
| 12th Bn, the Royal Scots Fusiliers | joined June 1918 (Ayr & Lanark Yeomanry) |
| 24th Bn, the Royal Welsh Fusiliers | joined June 1918 (Denbighshire Yeomanry) |

### *4th (Guards) Brigade*

*Brigade joined from Guards Division on 8 february 1918, left for GHQ Reserve on 20 May 1918*

4th Bn, the Grenadier Guards

3rd Bn, the Coldstream Guards

2nd Bn, the Irish Guards

4th Guards Trench Mortar Battery

### *Divisional Troops*

| | |
|---|---|
| 12th Bn, the King's Own Yorkshire Light Infantry | joined as Divisional Pioneer Battalion May 1915 |
| 243rd Machine Gun Company | joined 18 July 1917, moved to 31st Bn MGC 21 February 1918 |
| 31st Battalion MGC | formed 21 February 1918 |

## *Divisional Mounted Troops*

B Sqn, the Lancashire Hussars          left 9 May 1916

31st Divisional Cyclist Company,      left 9 May 1916
Army Cyclist Corps

---

## *Divisional Artillery*

*The original Divisional Artillery joined the 32ⁿᵈ Division between 30 December 1915 and 3 January 1916*

CLV Brigade, RFA

CLXI Brigade, RFA

CLXIV (Howitzer) Brigade, RFA

CLXVIII Brigade, RFA

31ˢᵗ Divisional Ammunition Column RFA

*The original artillery of the 32nd Division moved to France to join the 31ˢᵗ Division on 8 December 1915*

---

## **CLXV Brigade, RFA (James' Battery)**

CLXIX Brigade, RFA          broken up 24 January 1917

CLXX Brigade, RFA

CLXXI (Howitzer) Brigade, RFA      broken up 27 August 1916

31ˢᵗ Divisional Ammunition

Column RFA

| | |
|---|---|
| V.31 Heavy Trench Mortar Battery, RFA | formed by 4 June 1916, broken up 5 February 1918 |
| X.31, Y.31 and Z.31 Medium | formed 31 March 1916; |
| Mortar Batteries, RFA | by 15 February 1918, Z broken up and batteries reorganised to have 6 x 6-inch weapons each |

---

**Royal Engineers**
210th (Leeds) Field Company

211th (Leeds) Field Company

223rd (Leeds) Field Company

31st Divisional Signals Company

---

**Royal Army Medical Corps**
93rd Field Ambulance

94th Field Ambulance

95th Field Ambulance
71st Sanitary Section                    left to join XIII Corps 4-11 March 1917

## Other Divisional Troops

31$^{st}$ Divisional Train ASC — originally 217, 218, 219 and 220 Coys, but this Train remained in Egypt in March 1916, joining 52$^{nd}$ (Lowland) Division. 221, 222, 223 and 279 Companies joined from 32$^{nd}$ Division in France

41$^{st}$ Mobile Veterinary Section AVC

228$^{th}$ Divisional Employment Company — joined June 1917

31$^{st}$ Divisional Motor Ambulance Workshop — left for 52$^{nd}$ (Lowland) Division 21 April 1916

# APPENDIX THREE

## Field Punishment:

Field Punishment was introduced in 1881 following the abolition of flogging, and was a common punishment during World War I. A commanding officer could award field punishment for up to 28 days, while a court martial could award it for up to 90 days, either as Field Punishment Number One or Field Punishment Number Two.

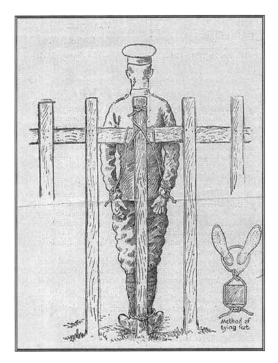

*An example of Field Punishment No. 1*

Field Punishment Number One, often abbreviated to "F.P. No. 1" or even just "No. 1", consisted of the convicted man being placed in fetters and handcuffs or similar restraints and attached to a fixed object, such as a gun wheel or a post, for up to two hours per day. During the early part of World War I, the punishment was often applied with the arms stretched out and the legs tied together, giving rise to the nickname "crucifixion". This was applied for up to three days out of four, up to 21 days total. It was usually applied in field punishment camps set up for this purpose a few miles behind the front line, but when the unit was on the move it would be carried out by the unit itself. It has been alleged that this punishment was sometimes applied within range of enemy fire. During World War I Field Punishment Number One was issued by the British Army on 60210 occasions.

The way in which soldiers had to endure this punishment varied in 'cruelty', depending on the commanding officer and so, in an effort to standardize the punishment all commanders received the following government directive for the implementation of Field Punishment No. 1.

### 12<sup>th</sup> *January 1917*


*Sir,*

*I am commanded by the Army Council to inform you that they have had under consideration the question of the method of carrying out Field Punishment No. 1, with special reference to paragraphs 2 (b) and 2 (c) of the Rules for Field Punishment (Manual of Military Law, page 721), and they have decided that, with a view to standardizing the method in accordance with which a soldier may be attached to a fixed object, the following instructions will, in future, be strictly adhered to:-*

*With reference to paragraph 2 (b), the soldier must be attached so as to be standing firmly on his feet, which if tied, must not be more than twelve inches apart, and it must be possible for him to move each foot at least three inches. If he is tied round the body there must be no restriction of his breathing. If his arms or wrists are tied, there must be six inches of play between them and the fixed object. His arms must hang either by the side of his body or behind his back.*

*With reference to paragraph 2 I, irons should be used when available, but straps or ropes may be used in lieu of them when necessary. Any straps or ropes used for this purpose must be of sufficient width that they inflict no bodily harm, and leave no permanent mark on the offender.*

It is said that some soldiers were tied in such a position as to face the enemy, invariably out of range, but this was not always the case.

When not suffering the 'punishment', the soldier was on normal duties.

# APPENDIX FOUR

## The influenza pandemic:

In three waves, the Spanish flu spread quickly, killing an estimated 50 million to 100 million people around the world. The 1918 flu pandemic (January 1918 – December 1920) was an unusually deadly influenza pandemic which infected 500 million people across the world, including remote Pacific islands and the Arctic, and killed 50 to 100 million of them—1 to 3 percent of the world's population at the time—making it one of the deadliest natural disasters in human history. To maintain morale, wartime censors minimized early reports of illness and mortality in Germany, Britain, France, and the United States; but papers were free to report the epidemic's effects in neutral Spain (such as the grave illness of King Alfonso XIII), creating a false impression of Spain as especially hard hit—thus the pandemic's nickname Spanish flu.

*Picture of an emergency camp set up as a result of the influenza pandemic.*

Most influenza outbreaks disproportionately kill juvenile, elderly, or already weakened patients; in contrast the 1918 pandemic killed predominantly previously healthy young adults. Modern research, using virus taken from the bodies of frozen victims, has concluded that the virus kills through a cytokine storm (overreaction of the body's immune system). The strong immune reactions of young adults ravaged the body, whereas the weaker immune systems of children and middle-aged adults resulted in fewer deaths among those groups.

**Some facts:**

The pandemic is estimated to have infected up to one billion people worldwide – that is half of the world's population at that time.

The virus killed more people than any other single outbreak of disease, surpassing even the Black Death of the Middle Ages.

Although it probably originated in the Far East, it was dubbed Spanish Flu because the press in Spain, not being involved in the Great War, so not being liable for censorship, was the first to report extensively on its impact.

The virus caused three waves of disease, the second of these, between September and December 1918, resulted in the heaviest loss of life.

Arguments still abound about whether the pandemic had any part in ending the war, as soldiers were too sick to fight. At that late stage of the war more men on both sides died of flu than were killed by weapons.

Most people who were infected with the virus recovered within a week to ten days following bed-rest but some died within 24 hours of infection.

# APPENDIX FIVE

In August 1914, the 2$^{nd}$ Ox and Bucks arrived on the Western Front as part of the 5$^{th}$ Infantry Brigade, 2$^{nd}$ Division – one of the first divisions of the British Expeditionary Force (BEF) to arrive in France. The battalion took part in the first British battle of the war, at Mons, where the British defeated the German forces that they had encountered on 23 August. The battalion subsequently took part in the 220 mile retreat, in exceptionally hot weather, that began the following day, not stopping until just on the outskirts of Paris, then halting the German advance at the First Battle of the Marne (5–9 September). The 2$^{nd}$ Ox and Bucks later took part in all the subsidiary battles of the First Battle of Ypres (19 October – 22 November) that saw the heart ripped out of the old Regular Army, with 54,000 casualties being sustained. On 11 November the Germans made another attempt to capture Ypres, sending—on the orders of the German Kaiser—the élite Prussian Guard against the British forces. The 2$^{nd}$ Battalion counter-attacked them at Nonne Bosschen wood, preventing their advance and then routing them; almost one hundred years after the 52$^{nd}$ had defeated Napoleon's Imperial Guard at Waterloo. First Ypres was the last major battle of 1914. The 2$^{nd}$ Ox and Bucks sustained 632 casualties during the first five months of the war and by 1915 it was a very different battalion from that which had arrived on the Western Front at the start of the war.

In 1915 trench warfare commenced with both sides developing impregnable defences leading to high casualties in return for minimal gains. At the Battle of Festubert (9–16 May) – which was launched in support of the French attack south of Vimy Ridge – the 2$^{nd}$ Ox and Bucks were part of the second wave of the 5$^{th}$ Brigade attack and, during the course of the battle, suffered just under 400 casualties: the largest number the regiment had sustained in a single battle since the Siege of Badajoz (1812) over 100 years earlier. The Battle of Festubert was the first British night action of the war. The 2nd Ox and Bucks were involved in heavy fighting at Richebourg l'Avoue on 15–16 May. The 2nd Ox and Bucks and other battalions of the regiment also saw action at Loos (25 September – 8 October): 2nd Ox and Bucks took part in the subsidiary attack at Givenchy with 263 casualties on 25 September. The 2nd Battalion took part in the subsequent attack against the Hohenzollern Redoubt (13–19 October). Following the battle of Loos few pre-1914 2nd Ox and Bucks officers remained, they had either become casualties or promoted to take up positions in other battalions.

In January 1916, the 2nd Ox and Bucks were at Cottes St.Hilaire; the 2nd Division was at that time taking its turn in the corps reserve. The Battalion later moved to Bethune and then returned to the Festubert trenches. The 1/4th Ox and Bucks took part in the First Day of the Somme on 1 July 1916, in which the British Army suffered over 60,000 casualties – the largest number sustained in a day by the British Army. The battalions of the Ox and Bucks on the Western Front saw extensive service during the Battle of the Somme (1 July – 18 November), suffering heavily, including at Mametz Wood, Pozières and at Ancre, the last major subsidiary battle. On 28 July the 2nd Ox and Bucks moved to front-line trenches near Waterlot farm and sustained heavy casualties at the battle there on 30 July. The 2nd Ox and Bucks fought on the Somme battlefield at Delville Wood, Guillemont and on 13 November in the battle of Beaumont Hamel: a large attack on the Redan Ridge in the battle of the Ancre. The 2nd Ox and Bucks sustained many casualties during the battle of Beaumont Hamel, including Captain RB Kite who within the previous 12 months, had been awarded the Military Cross and twice mentioned in despatches.

The New Year of 1917 brought with it a period of severe weather conditions on the Somme plain which led to an unofficial truce between the two sides. In March 1917, the Germans began the withdrawal to the Hindenburg Line (14 March – 5 April) and at the end of March the 2nd Ox and Bucks moved from the Somme to the back areas of

Arras. The $2^{nd}$ Ox and Bucks and other battalions of the regiment saw much involvement in the Arras Offensive (9 April – 16 May), including at the Battles of Scarpe and Arleux. The $2^{nd}$ Ox and Bucks took part in the battle of Arras from 11 April and had a leading role in the battle of Arleux on 28–29 April: during the battle the battalion protected the right flank of the Canadian $1^{st}$ Division which was critical to the capture of the village of Arleux and sustained more than 200 casualties. In the summer of 1917, the $2^{nd}$ Ox and Bucks held the line at Bailleulemont, near Arras. The battalions of the Ox and Bucks saw further service in many of the subsidiary battles during the Battle of Passchendaele (also known as Third Ypres) that took place between 31 July-6 November. Some of the battles that the Ox and Bucks took part in included Menin Road and Polygon Wood in September and early October. The $2^{nd}$ Ox and Bucks and the $6^{th}$ (Service) Battalion, Ox and Bucks also took part in the Battle of Cambrai (20 November-3 December) that saw the first large-scale use of tanks by the British and was the last major battle of the year.

In January 1918, the $2^{nd}$ Ox and Bucks marched to Beaulencourt, later that month they moved to Havrincourt Wood and then on 9 February to Metz-en-Couture. The $2^{nd}$ Ox and Bucks were at Vallulart Camp, Ytres when on 21 March 1918 the Germans launched the last-gasp Spring Offensive (Operation Michael). The $2^{nd}$ Ox and Bucks and other battalions of the regiment sustained heavy casualties as part of the defence of the Somme during the Battle of St. Quentin (21–23 March), the First Battle of Bapaume (24–25 March) and in subsequent battles that saw the Germans achieve significant gains. After that offensive lost its momentum, the Germans launched Operation Georgette in April which the Ox and Bucks defended against in the Battle of the Lys and subsequent actions. By August the German offensives had failed and the Allies had launched a counter-attack. In August the $2^{nd}$ Ox and Bucks took part in the Battle of Albert (1918) (21–23 August) and the Second Battle of Bapaume (31 August – 3 September) while the $2/4^{th}$ Ox and Bucks and the $2/1^{st}$ Buckinghamshires took part in the advance into Flanders, with both offensives seeing the Allies advance to the Hindenburg Line by early September. The 2$^{nd}$ Ox and Bucks took part in the offensive against it that saw the Allies break through the defences, taking part in the Battle of Havrincourt (12 September), Battle of the Canal du Nord (27 September – 1 October) and the Second Battle of Cambrai (8–9 October). The Regiment then took part in the last actions of the war, taking part in the Battle of the Selle and the Battle of Valenciennes. The 2$^{nd}$ Ox and Bucks final battle of the war was the Battle of the Selle (17–25 October).

The 2$^{nd}$ Ox and Bucks, commanded by Lieutenant Colonel Richard Crosse from June 1916, following its leading role in the final British offensive, crossed the German frontier at Malmedy on 9 December 1918. The 2$^{nd}$ Ox and Bucks, as part of the army of occupation, were stationed in Zons, near Cologne. The war had ended on 11 November 1918 with the signing of the Armistice between the Allies and Germany. At the end of the war there were only 66 2$^{nd}$ Ox and Bucks of all ranks still serving with the battalion from those that had left Aldershot for the Western Front on 13 August 1914: of these 39 served throughout the war. 15,878 members of the regiment lost their lives during the First World War.

# APPENDIX SIX
# 'Bantam Battalions'

*Recruiting poster for 'Bantams'.*

### What is a 'Bantam'?

A **bantam**, in British army usage, was a soldier of below the British Army's minimum regulation height of 160 cm.

During the First World War, the British Army raised battalions in which the normal minimum height requirement for recruits was reduced from 5 ft 3in (160 cm) to 5 ft (152 cm). This enabled otherwise healthy young men to enlist.

Bantam units were drawn from industrial and coal mining areas where short stature was no sign of weakness. The name derives from the former town of Bantam in Indonesia, from which a breed of small domestic fowl is thought to have originated. Bantamweight was a weight category in boxing that had originated in the 1880s and produced many notable boxers.

The first bantam battalions were recruited in Birkenhead, Cheshire, after Alfred Bigland, MP, heard of a group of miners who, rejected from every recruiting office, had made their way to the town. One of the miners, rejected on account of his size, offered to fight any man there as proof of his suitability as a soldier, and six men were eventually called upon to remove him. Bantam applicants were men used to physical hard work, and Bigland was so incensed at what he saw as the needless rejection of spirited healthy men, he petitioned the War Office for permission to establish an undersized fighting unit.

When the permission was granted, news spread across the country and men previously denied the chance to fight made their way to Birkenhead, 3,000 successful recruits being accepted for service into two new "Bantam battalions" in November 1914. The requirement for their height was between 4 ft 10in (147 cm) and 5 ft 3in (160 cm). Chest size was one inch (2.5 cm) more than the army standard.

The men became local heroes, with the local newspaper, The Birkenhead News, honouring the men of the 1st and 2nd Birkenhead Battalions of the Cheshire's with enamel badges – "BBB" – Bigland's Birkenhead Bantams. Soon renamed the 15th and 16th Battalions, Cheshire Regiment, they undertook grueling training and served in some of the most hard fought battles of the war, such as the Battle of Arras in 1917. Eventually two whole divisions, the 35th and the 40th, were formed from 'Bantam' men, who were virtually annihilated during the Battle of Bourlon. Heavy casualties, transfers to specialized Army tunneling companies and tank regiments, the introduction of conscription, and replacements by taller men, eventually led to Bantam units becoming indistinguishable from other British divisions

# APPENDIX SEVEN

## The Canadian Infantry.

The **27th City of Winnipeg Battalion** was the first independent battalion to be raised in Manitoba in the First World War. Officially it was not given a name and fell among the many nameless Canadian battalions raised to conform with the new numbering system introduced by Col. Sam Hughes, Canada's defense minister in 1914.

The battalion was raised as part of a response to the demand for fresh reinforcements early in 1915, as Canada struggled overseas with its single division. It became part of the 2nd Division, 6th Infantry Brigade along with its sister 28th Battalion, 29th, and 31st Calgary Battalions. A common private of the 27th Battalion during the First World War could expect to earn between $1.00 and $1.10 a day, or around $30 a month.

The 27th Battalion, with the 2nd Division, arrived in France in September, 1915, and met up with the 1st Division by mid-month. Together these two divisions formed the Canadian Corps and were led by General Alderson. The Canadian Corps, including the 27th, would not participate in any major offensive for almost a full year, when the Battalion would receive its 'baptism of fire' at the Battle of St. Eloi, 5 kilometres from Ypres.

It was reported the officers of the 27th had not slept for over 100 hours, this was most apparent with the Commander, I.R. Snider, a veteran of the North-West Rebellion of 1885 and the South African War, of the 27th Battalion who, during the battle of St. Eloi, stayed awake for 6 straight days trying to relieve the strain 'on his beloved boys'. After the battle he broke down and cried, he was removed from command 'being diagnosed with shell shock'. The Battle of St. Eloi had claimed 40 of his men's lives and wounded another 189.

The Somme Valley became the new objective of the Canadian Corps. When the Canadians arrived in the Somme Valley the British had been fighting for 3 months and they had traded 250 000 men for 8 kilometres German trenches. On the opening day of the Somme offensive alone, July 1, 1916, 20 000 British, Canadian and Commonwealth soldiers died and another 40 000 were wounded; it was the single heaviest day of casualties in history.

One of the most notable battles of Somme the 27th Battalion participated in was the Battle of Courcelette on September 15, 1916. This battle marked the first time in history tanks were used in warfare. However, all 6 tanks that used that day were knocked out; they were incredibly unreliable. The Canadians suffered around 7000 casualties during the battle which lasted until the 22nd of September. Despite all this the Canadians, more specifically the 27th, were successful as they were at the Battle of Thiepval Ridge, September 26, 1916; in fact the Canadians did not lose a single battle in the First World War.

Battalions wanted to ensure they received the glory and credit for their captures. One way of doing this was marking the prisoners with the battalion's insignia or the unit's designation. For example, at the Battle of Courcelette some of the men of the 27th had brought some green paint forward and marked the 250 prisoners they took with a rectangle and a circle above it as they sent back to the rear.

It was no surprise that Germans would rank the Canadian 1st and 2nd divisions among the top 8 deadliest and most dangerous divisions. The 2nd Division came overseas following the 1st Division and consequently had big expectations riding on them. At the Second Battle of Ypres in the spring of 1915, only arriving on the battlefield a week before with little experience in warfare, the 1st Canadian Division was the only Division that held its ground against the German's gas attack. Neither the British nor the French could hold their ground and had to fall back. It was largely due to the stubbornness of the Canadians that the Allies were able to repulse the attack.

# APPENDIX EIGHT

## Losses in Russia after World War One ended.

In the spring of 1918 the main Russian Government, neutral towards Germany and Austria, was surrounded by various hostile regional Governments on the fringes of the former Russian Empire. Its Western front was open, and German troops had been transferred in very large numbers to France. Finland, independent since December, 1917, was torn by the struggle between "White" and "Red", and strong German forces entered the country and secured, in May, 1918, the ascendency of the "White" Government. The North Russian ports, through which the Allies had assisted Russia with supplies and munitions, were now open to German occupation. The Black Sea, the Caucasus and the Caspian Sea were as yet beyond the reach of Allied forces, and the Russian half of the barrier between the Central Powers and India had failed. Lastly, there had emerged from the late Russian armies the two Czechoslovak Divisions, formed of ex-Austrian prisoners, which were known to be making for Archangel or Vladivostok in order to join the Allies. All these facts suggested intervention; it took the form of landings in the North and Military and Naval Missions, armaments and stores in the South and East. The Northern expedition lasted from 1918 to 1919, and was a separate military operation. The intervention in the South was linked with the advance of detachments from the Allied armies in Greece and Mesopotamia, and it lasted from 1919 to 1920. In April, 1918, a force of 150 Royal Marines landed at Murmansk, off which a British battleship had for some time been stationed. By the end of May 500 British Marines and sailors, 300 French soldiers, 1,400 Serbian soldiers and 500 Finnish "Red Guards" (the Finnish Legion) were holding the Kola Peninsula and Kandalaksha. The danger at present lay in Finland, and the Murman force, gradually strengthened, occupied the line of the Murmansk railway as far South as Soroka by the end of June. These operations were begun with the consent of the main Russian Government. On the 1$^{st}$-2$^{nd}$ August, 1918, another Allied force occupied Archangel. It advanced in August and September Westward to Onega and South and South-East, along the Vologda railway and the Dvina, to Yemtsa and beyond Bereznik (Semenovka). Behind these two forces were the friendly local Soviets, but already both had become engaged in hostilities with the Russian Bolshevik troops. On the 18$^{th}$ September Admiral Kolchak announced the formation of an anti-Bolshevik Government and "assumed power" over all the Russias, basing himself on Siberia and the South. By October, 1918, nearly 20,000 British, French, American, Italian, Polish and Russian troops were on the Archangel front, and nearly 15,000 British, French, Italian, Serbian and Russian on the Murmansk front. The danger from Finland disappeared in December, with the withdrawal of the German troops and the establishment of a friendly Coalition Government; the hope of junction with the Czechs was disappointed. The winter was spent in repelling determined Bolshevik attacks on the Archangel force and in advancing the forward positions of the Murmansk force beyond Segeja. With the early spring of 1919 news arrived of considerable successes won by Admiral Kolchak in the East and by General Denikin, the "White Russian" commander in the South; but in March and April the Allied Governments decided on an early evacuation of North Russia. War against the Bolshevik Government had not been one of their objects. The two North Russian forces were to be strengthened, disengaged by local offensives, and withdrawn; the friendly Governments were to be helped to establish themselves, if possible, on a firm military basis; and the Siberian army of Admiral Kolchak might perhaps be linked, before the Allied soldiers left, with the troops of the Archangel Soviet. General Lord Rawlinson was sent to co-ordinate the operations. Only the first of these aims could be realized. The Murmansk force reached Lake Onega by the 18$^{th}$ May and fought small actions on or near the lake through the summer; it captured Lijma on the 14$^{th}$-16$^{th}$ September, and within another month it had successfully evacuated Murmansk. The Archangel force, fighting on a wider front and more severely attacked, won the Battle of Troitsa on the 10th August, and evacuated Archangel without further difficulty on the 27th September. The friendly Governments held out for some months, but the Bolsheviks entered Archangel on the 20th February, 1920. On the Finnish border fighting between Soviet forces and Finnish troops or Karelian insurgents continued at intervals until the end of 1921. Kolchak's Siberian forces were decisively defeated in the summer of 1919. Denikin, after a successful summer campaign which reached as far as Kiev in September, was driven back throughout the winter of 1919-20 until his last position, at Novorossisk, was lost in March. In November, 1920, General Wrangel, who still held the Crimea, was forced out of Sevastopol, and organized resistance to the Russian Soviet Government ended.

# APPENDIX NINE

## As I see Life,

Life can do most things to us. It can
make or break us, It can scatter
our golden dreams of Happiness
like gusts that whip up lifes sand
It can offer us sweet temptations
that we fail to resist, It can
bestow on us the utter loneliness
caused by anothers Twist. But Life
cannot Break our Sphrit's if we seek to
do what's right. for tears of Sorrow will
never Rust on Spears of Faith that stay
Bright, To blow out a Hope lit in
some-ones Soul is to leave them in lifes
Dark with no means of Control. Oh
how carefull we should be with all those
we meet, We dont send them Drifting
down Life's Empty Street. So let us be
Carefull in stating our Views, we dont
cause a heart its High faith in us to
loose Driving on a life to Sadness of
Sorrow. When all that was needed were
Kind Words for the Sorrow.

# APPENDIX TEN

APPENDIX G.                                                          4.

## 1st BATTALION NORTHUMBERLAND FUSILIERS.

### ACCOUNT OF ACTION  21 - 24th AUGUST  1918.

1.            At 11.45 p.m. on the night of the 20th AUGUST
1918 the battalion left its bivouacs at HANNESCAMPS and
moved into assembly positions reconnoitred in the afternoon,
just behind the front line system of trenches between
AYETTE and ABLAINZEVILLE.

2.            ZERO hour was fixed for 4.55 a.m. on the 21st at
which hour the battalion advanced immediately in rear of
the 1st BERKS REGT. 2nd DIVISION, who were to take the
1st objective.  On the RIGHT of the battalion was the
"ANSON" Bn. R.N.D. and on the LEFT was the 13th Bn.
THE KINGS' (Liverpool) Regt.

3.            The battalion dispositions were as follows :-
RIGHT FRONT "W" COY.  LEFT FRONT "Z" COY.  RIGHT SUPPORT
"Y" COY.  LEFT SUPPORT "X" COY.  "Z" and "W" Companies
had definite objectives on the Railway between ACHIET-LE-
GRAND and COURCELLES.

            "Y" Company was to be prepared to form a
defensive flank on the RIGHT and "X" Company was in
Battalion reserve.

4.            The morning was very foggy and at times it was
impossible to see more than 20 yards, so that the whole
march to the objective had to be done by compass bearing.

5.            It was impossible for one company to take its
direction from another but each company marching
independently crossed the BLUE LINE with the limits of the
line allotted to the battalion.

6.            Owing to the fog the mopping up of the 2nd
DIVISION was somewhat incomplete and several casualties
occurred as a result of this before the BLUE LINE was
reached, and some 80 prisoners and several M.Gs. taken.

7.            After passing this line very little opposition
was met but heavy Machine Gun fire was continuous from the
RIGHT flank.  150 prisoners and some machine guns were
taken near the dugouts in A.20.a.  The M.C. crews were
killed also at DOROTHY trench 60 more prisoners and 8
machine guns were taken.

8.            Shortly after leaving DOROTHY trench the RIGHT
flank of the advance was held up by M.G. fire from
positions in A.27.b. & c.  No tanks were with this company
and no trace of the 63rd DIVISION could be found.  The O.C.
this company took up a position under bank S.E. of DOROTHY
trench and in trench at A.27 central, which was captured
together with one Field Gun.

9.            Meanwhile on the LEFT one company reached the
railway about A.22 d.1.4. at 8.15 a.m. where opposition
was encountered from the LEFT.

            The O.C. company therefore moved to the LEFT
astride the railway and about 100 of the enemy with
8 M.Gs. and 1 T.M. surrendered.

10.            The SCOTS FUSILIERS then came up and this part
of the objective was handed over to them.

11.

11.    The NORTHUMBERLAND FUSILIER Company then moved SOUTH astride the railway until touch was established with another company of the battalion which had reached the railway about 28 Central.

12.    Together the companies pushed SOUTH astride the railway until they were held up by the high ground about the crossing at A.28.a.9.1.

13.    Here Major TOWER Comdg. 4th ROYAL FUSILIERS with about 1 company of his battalion and one tank came up, and an attack was organized against the M.G. position, which were holding up the progress towards the SOUTH. 2 Field Guns were captured at A.28.a.8.8.

14.    The mist was then beginning to lift and heavy M.G. fire was coming from many positions down the line and from the Valley WEST of the line, causing heavy casualties.

15.    Two attempts to secure the RIGHT of the objective failed and finally a position was taken up switching from the Railway about A.28.a.1.9. to A.28.c.7.5. which was occupied by a Company of the 2nd SUFFOLK REGT. The latter Company withdrew at night fall.

16.    On the morning of the 22nd the enemy attacked the Railway between A.28.b.0.5. and A.28.c.8.3. and endeavoured to envelope the RIGHT flank. He succeeded in capturing a post at A.27.b.4.0. but was driven off elsewhere. This post was recaptured at 9.0 p.m. under cover of a barrage put up by 1 Stokes Mortar, 3 officers, 56 other ranks and 3 M.Gs. were captured. A small counter-attack made in the morning by the RIGHT front company resulted in the capture of 13 prisoners and one M.G.

17.    On the morning of the 23rd orders were received to advance in conjunction with the second Division to the GREEN LINE and the leading companies went over at 11.0 a.m, having only ¼ hour's notice to start. A few casualties occurred while approaching the railway, but on reaching the other side the enemy surrendered freely and 250 were sent back by these companies.

18.    The GREEN LINE was occupied by the Battalion and other troops passed through. In the evening the Battalion was ordered to concentrate in a position of readiness. The SUNKEN ROAD IM was used for this purpose, on the morning of the 24th owing to shell fire 2 companies and Headquarters moved behind the bank running at RIGHT ANGLES to the SUNKEN ROAD.

19.    At 3.0 p.m. the battalion received orders to withdraw to F.17. The Battalion moved back at 4.0 p.m.

---

The dispositions on the Railway objectives quoted in the above account differ in one important instance from those reported during the action, namely that the RIGHT FLANK of the battalion's leading company reached some 800 yards from where it was reported to rest. This would appear to be an impossible mistake to have made,

and

and I must accept full responsibilities as I visited the
position on the morning of 21st and never thought to
question the dispositions as shown by the Company Commander.
Some doubt was thrown on the situation on the morning of
the 22nd and I sent an officer down to the Company H.Q.
with a compass, and, together with the Company Commander,
the position was verified as the position originally stated.

It was not until I saw the positions after the
advance on 23rd that I realized how inaccurately they had
been reported.

                    W.N. HERBERT    Lieut.Colonel,
          Commanding 1st Battalion, Northumberland Fusiliers.

26th August, 1918.

# APPENDIX ELEVEN

8th (Service) Battalion NORTHUMBERLAND FUSILIERS.

Report on Operations for Week ending
30th September 1916.

On the night of the 25/26th September 1916, the
Battalion relieved the 5th York and Lancaster Regiment in
the trenches. R.33 b.5.9., R.27 d.9.1., R.28 c.2.1.
The Relief was complete by 3.30 a.m. on the 26th September
and presented no special difficulties, and only one
casualty. The congestion in the Trenches was considerable
and the fact that Packs were being worn made it difficult
for anyone to pass up or down.
The night was exceptionally quiet, with a little
shelling and rifle fire.
A Rum issue was made to the Troops half an hour before
the Assault.
The Battalion Head Quarters was at POZIERES CEMETERY,
where also was the 1st Echelon of Reserve Officer. The
2nd Echelon was at CRUCIFIX CORNER.
At Zero hour, 12.35 p.m., the Troops left the Trenches
and almost immediately the enemy's Barrage started on the
front line, also considerable Machine Gun Fire from the
MOUQUET FARM and the ZOLLERN REDOUBT.
An inspection of the ground on the next day showed that
many men were killed within 40 yards of our front line and
some were hit whilst getting out of the Trenches.
What now happened is somewhat obscure. There is no
doubt that the men pressed on most gallantly and reached
approximately the centre of the ZOLLERN REDOUBT, at
R. 27 b. 4.6. The number of flags found in the vicinity
proves this. By that time, all the Officers with one
exception, had fallen. Lieut. R.G.McDONALD, the only
Officer left, found himself with one man at about 200 yds
east of R.27 b. 4.6. He at once started collecting all
the men in his neighbourhood and digging himself in
By night fall he had about 59 men, wounded and unwounded,
under his command. The Platoon of Letter "X" Company,
which had orders to keep in touch with the 1st Canadian
Division, proceeded in single file up the sunken road,
which runs due north from R. 28. c. 3.3. The Platoon
Officer and Sergeant soon fell and only five men were left.
These under No.16954 Corporal T. AITCHESON, formed a
Bombing Post at about R.28.a.3.2. and were in touch with
the Canadians on their right. Several men actually joined
the Canadians in the fighting and two letters have been
received from officers of the 10th Canadian Infantry
commending their services. Meanwhile the Commanding
Officer at POZIERES CEMETERY waited anxiously for messages,
but none were received, although Lieut. R.G.McDONALD sent
a message which failed to arrive. At 2.30 p.m. he
decided to move his Head Quarters to the ZOLLERN REDOUBT,
which he understood had been taken. Owing however, to
heavy Machine Gun Fire from that direction he was obliged
to return, after having tried for three hours to get there.
Later at 11 p.m., he sent Lieut. F.G.BUCKLEY and Lieut.
J.N.ARMSTRONG to reconnoitre the ZOLLERN REDOUBT, with
orders to see if they could find anything of the
whereabouts of the Battalion. Lieut. F.G.BUCKLEY returned
at 5 a.m. on the 27th Sept. reporting that he could find
no trace of the Battalion and that the enemy were in

occupation of part of the ZOLLERN REDOUBT, which statement
was confirmed by Lieut. J.N.ARMSTRONG.
At 3.30 a.m. on the 27th September, the 2nd Echelon
of Reserve Officers and men joined Battalion Head Quarters
at POZIERES CEMETERY.
At 6 a.m. the Commanding **Officer** and Signalling Officer,
under instructions from the 34th Brigade, proceeded to
STUFF REDOUBT via CHALK PIT and Midway Line. At R.26 b.9.4
the C.O. observed two Machine Guns at R. 27. a. 5. 9., was
fired on and had two casualties. He reported from there
by pigeon and thought it inadvisable to proceed any further
by that route.
Meanwhile the 2nd in Command, with Lieut. F.G.BUCKLEY,
was sent to ZOLLERN REDOUBT, with orders to collect what
men they could find there and reorganise the Battalion
further back. They found the Redoubt had been vacated
by the enemy during the night and from R.27. b. 1. 7. could
plainly see the enemy in STUFF REDOUBT and were fired at by
Machine Guns from that point., which was reported to the
34th Brigade. In various Shell Holes a few men were
found and these were sent back to Battalion Head Quarters
The Commanding Officer later also proceeded to the Redoubt
and collected a few men.
During the day and night of the 27th September, about
170 men who had taken part in the assault were reassembled
at Battalion Head Quarters. These included men used for
Carrying Parties, who were unarmed.
In the afternoon of the 27th September, the Battalion
came under the Orders of the 32nd Brigade and was used as
Working and Carrying Parties to the front line continuously.
On the morning of the 28th September, the Commanding
Officer was wounded by a shell.
On the 29th September the Battalion moved back to
OVILLERS CORNER, leaving for ACHEUX the next morning.
The casualties were as follows:-

        19 Officers and 430 Other Ranks. (approximate).


        (Signed)   A. H. JAMES.

                                            Major.
1st October 1916.  Commanding 8th (S) Battn. North'd Fusiliers

# APPENDIX TWELVE

## The Times Monday 18th February 1918

### TWO AIR RAIDS.

### WEEK-END ATTACKS ON LONDON.

### ENEMY MACHINE DOWN.

### SUNDAY'S RAID.
The following communiqué was issued by the Field-Marshal Commanding-in-Chief, Home Forces, at 11.40 last night:-
Hostile aeroplanes came in over the Thames Estuary shortly after 10 p.m. and proceeded towards London. Some bombs have been dropped in the capital. The raid is still in progress

### SATURDAY'S RAID.
The following communiqués have been issued by the Field Marshal Commanding-in-Chief, Home Forces:-

### SATURDAY MIDNIGHT.
Hostile aircraft crossed the Kent coast of the Thames Estuary shortly before 10 this evening, and proceeded towards London. The raid is still in progress.
So far only one bomb is reported as having been dropped in London.

### SUNDAY. 10.45 A.M.
About half-a-dozen enemy aeroplanes made the mouth of the Thames about 9.45 last night and carried out an attack against London.
All were turned back save one machine. which penetrated into the capital along the line of the river and dropped a single bomb

in the South-West district about 10 p.m. This bomb demolished a house and buried an invalided officer, his wife, and two children. Several other bombs were dropped by the raider in the eastern outskirts on its way in, but no serious casualties or damage are reported.

An attack which was delivered against Dover about 10.45 p.m. was driven off, some bombs being dropped in open country.

Several of our pilots engaged the enemy. One of them fought an action over the Kent coast, and shortly afterwards a large enemy machine was seen from the shore to crash into the sea. Police reports of casualties and damage have not yet been received, but are apparently light.

*GERMAN official report, Feb. 17:-*
Our airmen last night attacked with bombs London, Dover, and Dunkirk, as well as the fighting forces on the North Coast of France. -Admiralty, per Wireless Press.

**BOMBS NEAR DOVER.**

**RAIDER AFLAME SEEN TO FALL INTO SEA.**

**(FROM OUR CORRESPONDENT.)**
*DOVER, FEB. 17.*
Enemy aircraft were in this district last night, and 14 bombs are reported to have been dropped, practically all falling on open ground. Some of these bombs were dropped evidently without any idea of direction, the machine being in difficulties and the pilot having to drop all his load with the utmost speed in order to lighten the craft. which had been under heavy gunfire, to enable her to rise to a greater height. All the bombs fell in a small field. The engine of the machine which dropped the bombs had been heard very distinctly for some little time previously, and as the sound stopped almost immediately

people in the distinctly are strongly of opinion that the machine fell into the Channel. A great many people also state that one of the enemy was struck by gunfire while passing over the cliffs, as seen to catch fire, and descend rapidly in the Channel. There was loud cheering at this spectacle. from several eye-witnesses who saw the affair from various points, I learn that two searchlights from different angles picked up the aeroplane and held it, whilst it was heavily shelled, with the result stated. The guns were served splendidly on each occasion.

The raid occurred between 10 o'clock and half-past. The night was beautifully clear.

## MIDNIGHT COMBAT.

## FIGHTING WATCHED BY COAST-TOWN RESIDENTS.

## (FROM OUR CORRESPONDENT)
*A COAST TOWN, Feb. 17.*

A raider just before midnight on Saturday came from inland and tried to get out. The guns, however. put up an effective barrage, which turned the Gotha to the westward. The moon was now very low: hence the searchlights were most effective. They succeeded in picking the enemy machine up, and try as it might it could not escape the rays. it was seen as clear as in day time. Then followed a quarter of an hour full of excitement. People flocked out of their houses and watched the combat. Shells were fired at the Gotha from all directions. Cries of "Got him ! " were sent up time after time. The machine twisted and turned and dived. Shells burst simultaneously round the machine, but it kept on its way. Suddenly a well-aimed shot burst under it. Immediately the machine dropped out of the rays, and people cheered as it went out of sight down towards the sea. Onlookers were convinced that it was hit, and the guns stopped. Three minutes later firing was heard out at sea.

## The Times Tuesday February 19th 1918

## ANOTHER RAID ON LONDON

## FAILURE OF ATTACK

The following communiqués were issued by the Field-Marshal Commanding-in-Chief, Home Forces, yesterday

### LAST NIGHT'S RAID.
*MIDNIGHT.*
Hostile aircraft crossed the coast of Essex shortly after 9 o'clock to-night, and proceeded towards London. None of the raiders penetrated the defences, and so far no damage or casualties have been reported.

### SUNDAY 'S RAID.
Last night's air raid appears to have been carried out by six or seven enemy aeroplanes, of which only one penetrated into London.
The first raider passed the Isle of Thanet about 9.45 p.m., and proceeded up the Thames Estuary into London, crossing the capital from south-east to north-west. Bombs were dropped in various districts between 10.40 and 10.55 p.m. The remaining raiders, which attempted to reach London from the north-east across Essex, or from the east along the line of the River Thames, were all turned back. The casualties caused by last night's aeroplane raid were:-
KILLED. - 13 men. 3 women - total, 16.
INJURED. - 27 men, 10 women - total, 37.

### SATURDAY'S RAID.
The total casualties caused by the aeroplane raid on Saturday night were:-
KILLED.- 3 men, 5 women, 3 children - total. 11.
INJURED.- 1 man, 3 children - total, 4.

## GERMAN REPORT: "ONE AEROPLANE."

Yesterday afternoon's (German communiqué (which will be found elsewhere), after describing other air activity, said that "one aeroplane attacked London."

## LONDON'S IMPROVED DEFENCES.

London was again raided by hostile aircraft last night. The moon was in the first quarter, high up in the sky ; it was very cold, and there was a slight ground mist. but no wind. The weather conditions, as on Saturday and Sunday, were, in fact, all in the enemy's favour, and he appears to have taken full advantage of them but it is only necessary to compare the present series of raids with those which have occurred in similar weather conditions in the past to realize the greater efficiency of our present defensive system. Experience has apparently endowed our airmen with a skill, rapidity, and precision which render enemy attempts on London more hazardous than they were. Last night showed the increasing difficulty which the enemy is experiencing in penetrating our defences.

Between the maroon warnings and the first sound of gunfire the public had plenty of time to take shelter, which they did quickly and in an orderly way, as people now thoroughly accustomed to such work. Indeed, they appear to do so nowadays in the most unconcerned way possible. It may. however, be pointed out that there appears to be a certain dearth of shelters in the West-end, especially for playgoers coming out of the theatres some time after the warning has been issued. These people find the usual places of refuge, such as the tubes, already crowded, and it might be well to permit them to remain inside the theatres after the close of the performances.

## REPELLED BY COAST GUNS.
## (FROM OUR CORRESPONDENT.)

### *SOUTH-EAST COAST, Feb. 18*

The anti-aircraft batteries on the South-East Kent coast heavily engaged enemy aeroplanes last night for varying periods at about 10 o'clock and again later on their return. The Invaders were to all appearances attempting to cross the coast on the first occasion, but so vigorously were they shelled that they turned tail and went back across the Channel. They made several attempts to get in at various points, but found the gunners in full readiness for them at each place. The guns at the coast batteries were again heavily pounding away at enemy aeroplanes that then seemed to be coming from an inward direction on their way home. The enemy machines were flying very widely separated, and the guns along a frontage of some miles were firing. There is a report that one machine was brought down. No bombs appear to have been dropped in this district on either occasion.

## WORK OF A SINGLE RAIDER.

Owing to the present system of defence only one raider penetrated into the London area on Sunday night. This raider must have carried a very considerable number of bombs. The system of giving raid warnings by maroons is generally recognized to be quite successful. The preliminary warning on Sunday was received in good time, and with little or no delay the maroons were tired at a large number of places all over London, two being fired in each locality at intervals of 30 seconds. All the bombs were dropped in London within half an hour. The most serious damage occurred where a hotel was hit and several people were killed and injured. It seems desirable to draw attention once again to the foolhardiness of people coming outside of buildings during a raid to I watch its progress. If this had not been done by two or three servants at the hotel in question they would probably be alive to-day. There vas a good deal of debris all around and many windows on the other side of the street were broken. Not far away from this hotel a bomb dropped in a mews and killed a horse.

In one district six or eight bombs appear to have been dropped. A bomb was dropped only a few yards away from a London County school, where a number of people were sheltering. It exploded in the roadway, which was badly damaged, and a man was killed. Not far away a bomb dropped near another building where a considerable number of people were sheltering, but it buried itself in a heap of scrap iron and no damage was done. A bomb struck the back of a house occupied by a clergyman and his family, but the inmates escaped uninjured, although they were badly shaken. Another bomb dropped in a road abutting on a small park and made fairly big crater. At another spot a bomb dropped in a road.

## HOW TO SUMMON AID.

It is found that where bombs from enemy aircraft are dropped on houses or in streets, causing casualties, owing to the conditions which prevail at the time of an air raid there may be some delay in reporting what has happened to the local police. The Commissioner thinks it desirable, therefore to invite the occupiers of damaged premises or of neighbouring houses, or any other person who has first knowledge of the happening, to acquaint the police at once by the nearest telephone, the caller giving the call "Police," and specifying the exact locality. This will enable the police to give immediate help by the dispatch of surgeons, nurses, first aid workers, ambulances, and constabulary, either from the Reserve at Headquarters or from the nearest police-station. The Controller of the London Telephone Service will give priority to such messages as fat as practicable.

# ACKNOWLEDGEMENTS

Tina Large and the Manchester Airport Community Trust Fund.

Chris Baker and the Long, Long Trail

The Wartime Memories Project

Numerous military museums in the UK, Canada and Australia